# TWENTIETH CENTURY VIEWS

The aim of this series is to present the best
in contemporary critical opinion on major
authors, providing a twentieth century perspective on their changing status in an era
of profound revaluation.

Maynard Mack, *Series Editor*
Yale University

## OTHER VOLUMES IN THIS SERIES

CAMUS, edited by Germaine Brée

T. S. ELIOT, edited by Hugh Kenner

ROBERT FROST, edited by James M. Cox

WHITMAN, edited by Roy Harvey Pearce

SINCLAIR LEWIS, edited by Mark Schorer

STENDHAL, edited by Victor Brombert

HEMINGWAY, edited by Robert P. Weeks

THOREAU, edited by Sherman Paul

PROUST, edited by René Girard

# FIELDING

## A COLLECTION OF CRITICAL ESSAYS

Edited by

*Ronald Paulson*

Prentice-Hall, Inc., *Englewood Cliffs, N. J.*

1962

© 1962

BY PRENTICE-HALL, INC.

ENGLEWOOD CLIFFS, N. J.

LIBRARY OF CONGRESS CATALOG NO.: 62-13653

Printed in the United States of America

31449-C

# Table of Contents

INTRODUCTION—*Ronald Paulson*                                            1

FIELDING'S IRONY: ITS METHOD AND EFFECTS—
*A. R. Humphreys*                                                        12

FIELDING'S EARLY AESTHETIC AND TECHNIQUE—
*Winfield H. Rogers*                                                     25

SHAMELA—*Ian Watt*                                                       45

JOSEPH ANDREWS AND PAMELA—*Maynard Mack*                                 52

COMIC RESOLUTION IN FIELDING'S *JOSEPH ANDREWS*—
*Mark Spilka*                                                            59

JONATHAN WILD—*Aurélien Digeon*                                          69

NOTES FOR A PREFACE TO FIELDING'S *TOM JONES*—
*André Gide*                                                             81

TOM JONES—*Arnold Kettle*                                                84

FIELDING'S "SEXUAL ETHIC" IN *TOM JONES*—
*John Middleton Murry*                                                   89

TOM JONES AND CLARISSA—*Ian Watt*                                        98

TOM JONES—*William Empson*                                              123

FIELDING'S *AMELIA*: AN INTERPRETATION—*George Sherburn*                146

FIELDING AND "CONSERVATION OF CHARACTER"—
*John S. Coolidge*                                                      158

Table of Contents

Chronology of Important Dates            177

Notes on the Editor and Contributors     179

Bibliography                             181

# Introduction

## by Ronald Paulson

### I

To speak of a twentieth century view of Fielding we must distinguish at the outset between readers and scholar-critics. Readers have never deviated from enjoyment of Fielding's novels. The critics are another matter. To the nineteenth century critic Fielding was interesting but immoral, at best lacking "high seriousness." The effect of twentieth century Fielding criticism has been to prove him moral—even perhaps at the expense of a certain interest. Wilbur Cross, in his definitive biography, supplanted the romantic fiction of a dissipated rake with the truer picture of an average, kindly, not always exciting gentleman; and the next step was to replace the influence of Shaftesbury (and Deism) on Fielding with that of the Latitudinarian divines, who preached a Christian version of benevolence. James A. Work's essay, "Henry Fielding, Christian Censor," demonstrating the Christian content of Fielding's thought, has led to a number of reinterpretations along religious lines.[1]

Instead of looking to the escapades of Tom Jones or Billy Booth, we turn today to the periodicals, the essays, the legal tracts and reports, and the discursive parts of the novels for Fielding's attitudes and ideas. In these we see his public mask, a pose that apparently corresponds to the lawyer, the Bow Street magistrate and social reformer, the conscientious citizen whom Cross and Work describe. Fielding *is* one of the most civic-minded of English writers, a living example of the Augustan ideal of the public man. But the public is only one aspect of Fielding, the one through which he expresses his intentions and his positive scheme of values, which he transforms into art elsewhere. Submerged in the public image is the Fielding who creates Lady Booby and Slipslop, Trulliber and Blifil, Adams and Jones. Although it has been an important corrective, the Christianizing of Fielding stresses an aspect of his work that is neither the most characteristic nor (I am sure readers of Fielding will agree) the most interesting one.

[1] Unless otherwise noted, all critical works referred to in this Introduction are cited in the Bibliography at the end of the book.

For the pertinent question about Fielding remains: given his pious intention, does he meet the moral problems of our experience maturely and seriously in his fictions? F. R. Leavis' refusal to admit *Tom Jones* into "the great tradition" of the English novel is typical of the negative answer.[2] Presented with all the evidence of Fielding's "intense moral preoccupation," Leavis would still dismiss him as a rhetorician, without depth of insight. Most of the essays in this volume take, in one way or another, a different view from this. John Middleton Murry's position, for example, is that Fielding shows a profound insight into the ethics of love; William Empson's is that the theme of *Tom Jones*, far from being conventional, contains a "secret doctrine." A yet more radical response is to hold that Fielding is not, despite appearances, religiously committed and so not stereotyped in his responses. André Gide is among those who question his Christian orthodoxy: Fielding, he notices, is very hard on sins of reason and hypocrisy, very tolerant of sins of sense and passion. Aurélien Digeon and Arnold Kettle also, in their different ways, detect a strain of anarchism under Fielding's appearance of religion. By ignoring his expressed intentions one might also show deep veins of existentialism, great fissures of Richardsonian inconsistency—his public mask saying one thing, his daemon saying another. But these are isolated tendencies in Fielding which, with respect to any of his novels as a whole, lead nowhere.

A truer (if more prosaic) answer is that the subject matter of Fielding's best work is not the medicine of Christian morality but the disease for which it may be prescribed. So long as he dramatizes the Evil, or the Evil preying on the Good, with an implicit judgment of both, Fielding writes in his most effective mode, which is satire. To be sure, one usually reads that, at his best, he "rose above" satire to the comic[3]—and Parson Adams' terrific vigor as he trots ahead of the coach does belong to the comic: "Mrs. Slipslop desired the coachman to overtake him, which he attempted, but in vain; for the faster he drove, the faster ran the parson, often crying out, 'Ay, ay, catch me if you can' . . ." (Bk. II, chap. vii). Certainly Fielding, more than any of his English predecessors except Chaucer, uses comedy as a vehicle; but as a vehicle for satire. Even the episode just mentioned is satiric in that it nicely balances the forgetful but untrammeled spirits of the good-natured parson and the stuffy pseudo-gentility of the lady's maid within the coach (in which she has sequestered Joseph).

Although we think of Fielding as a contemporary of Richardson and Johnson, as a writer of the 1740's and 1750's, he began his career by consciously and ostentatiously joining the tradition of the Augustan satirists, Pope and Swift. He began to write just two years after the appearance of

---

[2] *The Great Tradition* (London: Chatto & Windus, Ltd. 1948), pp. 3-4.
[3] Cf. the essays of Erwin and Dyson on comedy and satire in Fielding's works. Maynard Mack (*"Joseph Andrews* and *Pamela"*) uses *comedy* in a larger-than-generic sense which would include both comedy and satire.

*Gulliver's Travels* and at almost exactly the time when Pope's *Dunciad* and Gay's *Beggar's Opera* seized the imagination of literary London. Fielding drew upon these works as he did upon Homer and Virgil, and carried on the same war against dullness, making his association with the great Augustans unmistakable by the pseudonymn Scriblerus Secundus. Twenty-five years later he was still fighting a "paper war" with dullness in the *Covent-Garden Journal*.

The "rehearsal" plays, the farces, and *Jonathan Wild* are Fielding's best-known satires in the Augustan manner; in these he shows a larger-than-life symbol of man's perversity attempting to engross, amoeba-like, all that comes within reach. But there is another strain of Fielding's satire, perhaps deriving from his interest in the moral philosophers and Latitudinarian divines, in which the central figure is a good-natured man running a gauntlet of selfish, lustful, or malicious types. Though this form derives from the picaresque of the Spaniards, Fielding's hero gains moral as well as prudential knowledge from his ordeals. To this extent, Fielding's fictional form is analagous to that of his essays and periodicals, where the public mask (the self-conscious narrator of the novels) guides the reader (often "you") through a maze of good and bad examples, defining a positive and detailed code of proper conduct. Much of the time (as in *Joseph Andrews*) Fielding keeps his reader's attention focused on the Trullibers and Tow-wouses, whose unamiable qualities are exposed by contact with the good man. But in two ways the emphasis tends to shift from the Evil to the Good; either Fielding becomes so sympathetic with his good-natured man's plight that he substitutes this character's suffering for the vigorous wrongdoing of his persecutors, or he gives us too detailed a picture of the Good. At his best, in *Tom Jones*, he maintains a balance between the evil and good forces which suggests to the reader that not the violently symbolic world of the Augustan satirists but the *whole* world is being presented. At his worst, he allows the two forces to separate, in *Amelia*, into the pitiful, tear-stained goodness of the Booth family and the diabolic, almost motiveless evil of the noble Lord, Mrs. Ellison, and Amelia's sister Betty.

## II

Those modern critics who have not given their attention to defining Fielding's "intense moral preoccupation" have sought to determine more exactly what is Fielding's characteristic form. Is it novel, epic, mock-epic, satire, or a medley of these? An answer to this question has always been contingent upon the current position of his rival and contrary, Samuel Richardson.

Most recent revaluations of Fielding's work indicate that the old Richardson-Fielding contrast has now come full circle—from the belief that Richardson was sentimental and moral and Fielding was realistic and immoral to its exact opposite. With Richardson's morality gone, he appears to many in the age of anxiety to be a profound searcher of the darker areas of human nature, as well as an impressive innovator in fictional form. Fielding, because he looks healthy or pious, or perhaps simply because he is more successful in doing what he sets out to do, strikes them as less interesting, both as a psychologist and novelist. Furthermore, most recent studies typically assume that the novel, the true "novel," is realistic in the particular way that Richardson's novels are. Such a view naturally entails the conclusion that Fielding is truly successful only as he reaches toward the Richardsonian novel. To see this logic illustrated, one may consider Ian Watt's treatment of the two men in a recent distinguished book.[4] Watt strives to be eminently fair, giving Richardson the palm for "realism of presentation" and Fielding for "realism of assessment"; but since he defines the "novel" in terms of Richardsonian "realism," he cannot escape the implication that Richardson leads forward to the mature novel of our day, Fielding backward to the forms of the neoclassical satirists.

Watt finds the crux of the matter to be mimetic: he asks what Fielding or Richardson is trying to imitate. Fielding inherited from the Augustan satirists the sophisticated devices of irony, the ironic persona, the analogical situation, and the high and low burlesque—the rhetoric of literary imitation, parody, and allusion. Winfield H. Rogers' essay, "Fielding's Early Aesthetic and Technique," describes these techniques of "multidimensional" satire in the plays; Digeon shows their effect in *Jonathan Wild* and Watt in *Shamela*. The imitation of literary models is antithetical to the imitation of "nature," and it is true that the "novel" as we know it appears to rely heavily on the latter. To many critics it has seemed of first importance to show the various ways in which Fielding merges these two kinds of imitation, and to discover the distinctive reality he attains. While Watt approaches the problem of realism from the direction of Richardson, Maynard Mack approaches from the direction of Fielding, giving a more sympathetic interpretation. He has avoided the problem of the novelist *manqué* by contrasting Fielding's comic world with Richardson's tragic world, showing that we cannot expect the same sort of vision from both and that each is equally valid. Watt, however, has hinted that Fielding may have gone halfway to meet the demands of Richardsonian realism, and John S. Coolidge shows the effect of stylization, of type characters and universals, mixed with "realistic" characters and locales in *Amelia*.

The truth of the matter, of course, is that Fielding wrote something uniquely his own: a species of novel in which irony plays much of the role that Richardson assigns to psychological detail. When Fielding came

⁴ Behind Watt's argument are the studies of Erich Auerbach (*Mimesis* [Princeton: Princeton University Press, 1953]) and of José Ortega y Gasset (e.g., "The Nature of the Novel," *Hudson Review*, X [1957], 11-42).

to write *Joseph Andrews,* his intention was to correct the unhealthy tendencies of the Richardsonian novel in the same spirit in which he had corrected the excesses of the pantomimes and operas. In his preface he claims that his presentation of reality is a better, a truer, one than Richardson's, maintaining that to present true reality the novelist must correct his personal bias with reference to the larger view of tradition, developing the novel's affinities with the classic genres—as opposed to the rootless, tentative, "original" form of the Richardsonian novel. He must have a detached, a comic attitude toward the world in order to portray it accurately. The ironic pose itself implies such a contrast between a limited and conventional view and a more inclusive one.

Fielding's ironic inclusiveness is very different from Richardson's gathering of a great mass of minutiae and particulars within a small space; but it is nevertheless inclusiveness of a crucial kind. If Richardson's realism is one of plenitude, Fielding's is one of opposites and larger reference; if Richardson achieves verisimilitude by an oppressive intimacy, Fielding does the same by polarizing his views of people, his kinds of people, and their experiences and motives. The analogues he introduces in *Joseph Andrews* have the effect of suggesting both the complexity and the interrelations of life; ironic similes connect Slipslop and a tiger, Adams and Colley Cibber, Lady Booby and Cupid, Joseph and the Biblical Joseph. We might distinguish between reality as a placing of something in a proper, a true relationship to everything else in the world (Fielding's type); and reality as an exposition of the authenticity of something (Richardson's type).

Irony, though inclusive in that it acknowledges both the wrong and the right, is rigorously *ex*clusive in its cleavage to the latter. Yet in Fielding's use of irony we may detect the same tolerance we have noted in his Latitudinarian view of man. In an essay on this subject, A. R. Humphreys distinguishes Fielding's ironic practice from that of his model, Swift. Fielding's irony implies a more general audience, a somewhat lower common denominator than Swift admitted, less rigor, less subtlety, and a less violent distinction between the wrong and right. In fact, Humphreys substantiates Cross's image of the good-natured gentleman in the most useful way—by reference to the style of the novels. But the evolution of irony in this direction was inevitable, and Fielding was simply the experimentalist who most fully exploited the gains of the preceding quarter century, assisting in the transformation of irony from a rhetorical device to a vehicle of psychological, cognitive, and even metaphysical meaning.[5]

[5] The following conclusions, based on data presented by Norman Knox's *The Word Irony and Its Context, 1500-1755* (Durham: Duke University Press, 1961), are substantially those in my review of Knox in *JEGP,* LXI (January, 1962). If Humphreys and I differ, particularly on the consistency of Fielding's ironic pose, it is probably because he deals primarily with early works.

As a rhetorical device, irony influences an audience in order to convey a moral, presenting the reader with the discrepancy between what he is and what he ought to be. As a psychological device, it presents the discrepancy between what a character thinks he is and what he is. And as a metaphysical device, it presents the discrepancy between the apparent and the real *for the purpose of establishing the real* (as opposed to the rhetorical purpose of proving a point). Historically, the transition appears in the development from local or incidental irony to a sustained point of view, and from irony operative on an idea to that operative on a character.

The Augustan sense of decorum, which included consistency, must have played an important part in curtailing the use of irony as a local effect. Consistency leads to a greater sense of probability; and extended over many pages, irony appears to be less a device for persuasion than a point of view brought to bear on reality. A further convention of Augustan decorum insisted that the proper ironic pose is one of mock-gravity. The pose of the incidental ironist was characteristically accompanied by the curled lip; Shaftesbury and the Augustans in general associated this with controversial irony, preferring for higher flights the grave irony of Cervantes and Swift, which in practice was usually the high burlesque or mock-heroic—a form of blame by praise which relies heavily on a pose of fairness. This mask produces the impression so necessary to Fielding's conception of the novel, of neutrality and authority, even sympathy, as opposed to the satirist's disreputable, prejudiced, limited vision.

But if the ironic pose, when consistently applied to experience, may earn the reader's confidence and belief, it may also create a kind of psychological verisimilitude when applied to a character. From Swift onward there is a relentlessly humanizing tendency in irony. Simple concession (accepting the opponent's point of view), fallacious argument, and high burlesque (both mad extensions of the enemy's own logic) are all moving in the direction of a dramatic imitation of the enemy—allowing him to speak for himself, or take himself at his own evaluation—and so toward the presentation of character rather than abstract idea. Strange things happen when irony is applied consistently and evenly to a character. In *Joseph Andrews* Lady Booby's mock-heroic utterances ("Whither doth this violent passion hurry us! What meanness do we submit to from its impulse!") not only set her lust in perspective but demonstrate her self-delusion, revealing the unhappy, misguided woman who sees her petty affair as a great Didoesque love.[6] Again Mrs. Slipslop "at last gave up Joseph and his cause, and with a triumph over her passion highly commendable" went off to get drunk. The author's ironic praise is obvious; but what it says in its context is that *she felt* that she had triumphed and should be commended. The mock-heroic of *Jonathan*

---

[6] Mack has pointed out this effect, p. 56 below.

*Wild* works in the same way, except that the self-delusion is now mixed with aspiration to a false ideal, "greatness." Whether from the character's own lips or from those of the commentator, the irony tends to become an expression of the character's psychology.

The great model for this function of irony is *Don Quixote.* Cervantes's irony lies in his accepting the premise of chivalry, that the world is full of giants and forlorn maidens, while playing it out against real wind-mills and country wenches. But when the irony is embodied in an old scarecrow of a man who thinks he is a knight errant, the two parts of the irony become his illusion and his real situation. Cervantes, more-over, goes beyond irony as a way of revealing a character's mind to irony as an expression of reality—from the impression that Quixote is mad to the impression that his illusion contains some truth. At length the worlds of knight-errantry and of inns and windmills are no longer mutually exclusive, and the reader concludes that *both* parts of the irony contain elements of truth.

Now we have taken Fielding's mock sympathy for the lecherous Lady Booby as both denigration and an expression of her thoughts about her-self; but there is also a third effect, which William Empson character-izes when he says that Fielding "seems to leave room for the ideas he laughs at." [7] In some sense Lady Booby really is, as she claims, heroically battling her passions. While this is a very slight impression indeed as concerns Lady Booby, Empson finds what he calls "double irony" to be a controlling principle in *Tom Jones.* We might call this "both/and" irony, which gives some credence to both "the contrary" and "what one means," or to the praise and the blame. When Fielding says that Black George, who has just stolen Tom's money, really does love Tom, he is saying a number of different things: that Black George has persuaded himself by rationalization that he loves Tom, but also that there is a sense in which Black George really does love him, even if, at the mo-ment, he loves money more.

Empson has here offered the best answer to those critics who wish Fielding to be a Richardsonian novelist. While single irony implies the author's grasp of all circumstances and eventualities, with the proper subordination of the false to the true, double irony suggests a greater tolerance, a delicate poise, or mere uncertainty. The effect is close to the unsubordinated copia of Richardsonian realism, and so a movement that contains "realism of presentation" as well as "realism of assess-ment."

Fielding was not impervious to the success of other kinds of realism than his own. The general impression given by *Tom Jones* is very different from that of *Joseph Andrews*. We recognize the Richardsonian signs at once: more facts, more information about everything, more extenuating circumstances recorded, and more different motives and atti-

[7] *Some Versions of Pastoral* (New York: Macmillan Co., 1935), p. 197.

tudes to choose from, all creating a general plenitude. The irony helps to generate this impression; instead of a single statement (such as the one about Lady Booby) Fielding ordinarily gives us two or more statements, some very plausible. Here are Mrs. Wilkins's reasons for obeying Allworthy: "Such was [1] the discernment of Mrs. Wilkins, and such [2] the respect she bore her master, [3] under whom she enjoyed a most excellent place, that her scruples gave way to his peremptory commands. . . ." Or we are told why Tom avoids a fight with Blifil: ". . . for besides that [1] Tommy Jones was an inoffensive lad amidst all his roguery, and [2] really loved Blifil, [3] Mr. Thwackum being always the second of the latter, would have been sufficient to deter him." Substantiating the apparent multiplicity of motives is the author's pose of ignorance: "I know not for what reason" Jenny jumps up when Mrs. Partridge enters the room where she and Partridge are studying Latin. Wherever we turn we encounter the word *perhaps,* or phrases such as *a matter not so easy to determine.* All of this is the counterpart of the doubt, confusion, and lack of subordination that characterize the non-ironic Richardsonian realism.

It is easy enough to take "Black George really loved Tom" as an ambiguity, but in the cases where Fielding lists multiple possibilities and says, "Take them all," one detects the pose of the Socratic ironist. In the examples concerning Wilkins and Tom above, (1) and (2) are commendable motives, but (3) is prudential, and it has the effect of exposing the other two as rationalizations. All of the author's alternatives simply point to the ironic recognition that Wilkins obeys out of fear for her position and that Tom is shy of the birch. Again the author's ignorance is surely a mock-ignorance when he meditates on the motive of Allworthy's friend for recommending Thwackum as a tutor: "doubtless" because of Thwackum's qualifications of learning and religion, "though indeed" the friend was M.P. for a borough controlled by Thwackum's family.

The author is revealing a discrepancy between words (or rationalizations) and deeds that is not unlike the exposure of Square behind Molly Seagrim's arras. He asks his reader to pass judgment on Wilkins, Tom, and the friend of Allworthy. But the very recording of multiple motives and qualifying clauses invites the reader to embrace them in his assessment. And acceptance of the invitation is made easy in many instances by the fact that the truth, or a missing portion of truth, is not revealed until hundreds of pages later. The basic unit in *Joseph Andrews* is the word contradicted by action or by the revelation of motive. Now this same contradiction takes place in *Tom Jones,* eventually. But the latter, unlike *Joseph Andrews,* deals in suspense and surprise, with facts and actions long unknown to the reader. And so the emphasis falls not on the contradiction but on the speaker's speculations of the moment—which, though solidified later, nevertheless give to the novel an air of complexity and doubtfulness which is not swept away by the denouement. When we see Bridget Allworthy showing generosity and kindness to little Tommy Jones (deviating from the pattern of the Wilkins-like harpy we believe her to be), we feel that here is a real person, not a type. And when we eventually discover the "truth," this impression is not wiped away. Her prudence, like Wilkins's, is made to appear no longer a ruling passion but only one aspect of a multifaceted personality.

This is Fielding's technique for suggesting the complexity of reality, and the mitigating forces that make the "mixed" character in whom he is most interested, without succumbing to what he considered the chaos that accompanied Richardson's method. His irony remains essentially rhetorical and psychological. As A. D. McKillop has put it, in Fielding's novels the discrepancy between appearance and reality "is not treated as an ultimate metaphysical problem, as in *Don Quixote*. Fielding is not trying to present or to pluck out the heart of a mystery; he is continuously corroborating a position which he has made clear from the first. . . ." [8] But it is important to notice how far Fielding has gone beyond the self-imposed limits of the satirist. As a satirist he is overwhelmingly interested in actions, and his aim is to distinguish the good from the evil; but, as he learns how misleading not only words but even actions and consequences can be, he finds it increasingly difficult to judge them except in terms of motives. In short, he rejects the satirist's simple but commonsensical acceptance of effect as the chief criterion of virtue in favor of the Shaftesburyian belief that an action can be neither good nor evil in itself, but only as its motive is charitable or self-seeking. This belief may involve him in philosophical problems that are over his head, but it sets him to searching into people's characters and trying to understand them as individuals. Through the ironic complexity of *Tom Jones* he seems to say that motive is so difficult to assign that only much later, by surprise, by accident, can we see behavior as good or evil.

He acknowledges and unfolds the infinite complexity of the world, but he employs a method which enables him to do this without precluding assessment. The situation of Fielding's fiction is very close to experiential reality: we are always passing judgment or having to make an attempt at doing so, and yet we are (or should be) aware of how little we actually have to base our judgments on. At the bottom of this epistemology is the concern with tolerance and charity that informs all of Fielding's work from the novels down to the essays and poems. In this sense, his character, thought, and style are all one.

What happens to this amalgam of artifice and realism after Fielding? Leavis sees J. B. Priestley and the rowdier aspects of Dickens as the only Fielding tradition. The more general view is that Fielding is inimitable and so sterile. But this is to ignore the species of novel in which an

[8] "Some Recent Views on *Tom Jones*," p. 19.

author consciously sets the real conduct of everyday against the large
abstractions of moral values, classical literature, or myth. The tradition
of this, the ironic novel, includes not only the range from Austen to
Thackeray, but in our own time the experimental novels of Joyce and
Gide. Though the author of *Ulysses* does not speak in the first person, he
presents the two kinds of realism we saw in *Tom Jones*, catalogues of
trivialities set off against the absolute of the *Odyssey*. The result is an
intensification of the ordinary. Fielding's bequest to the English novel is
tireless experimentation and a form which tests conduct against a pre-
ordained standard; but even more important, by combining the veri-
similar with a larger frame of reference, he shows later English novelists
one way to poeticize experience without sentimentalizing it.


                                        III

    In outlining a few aspects of our contemporary view of Fielding, I
have indicated the general direction of the essays in this volume. My
criteria of selection have been first the quality of the essay, second its
importance as an expression of a distinctive point of view toward Fielding's fiction. The only restriction I have imposed is that it must be
concerned primarily with Fielding's literary works, not with the man, his
life or ideas in isolation. Thus I have had to exclude Work's important
essay on Fielding's Christian thought as too abstract; Murry and Empson
both largely substantiate Work's view with specific reference to *Tom
Jones*.
    The arrangement of the essays is quite simple. Since the object of
this book is to bring to the reader's attention contemporary attitudes
toward Fielding's art, I have grouped the essays around each of
the major works (and in one case around the plays as a whole).
Humphreys' general study of Fielding's ironic style will, I hope, offset
the views of this introduction and offer a way into the more particular
studies that follow.
    The essays on the three great novels appear in pairs or in clusters,
one view balanced by another. Mack discusses the tradition and basic
assumptions about man that underlie *Joseph Andrews*, while Mark
Spilka gives us a close analysis of the climactic scenes in the Booby household. One places the novel in a large generic context, the other examines
its comic mechanism. Two complementary comic theories emerge, one
drawing attention to the reader's detachment from, the other to his
involvement with, the comic scene. On *Tom Jones* we have Gide's rigorist
Protestant dissection of Fielding's pretension to religion, Kettle's Marxist
reading, Murry's post-D. H. Lawrence exposition, Watt's mimetic-generic
analysis, and Empson's—it can only be called his Empsonian—approach.
    George Sherburn's essay on *Amelia* is typical of contemporary criticism
in that it tries to rehabilitate an unappreciated work: it seeks to under-

stand the author's intention and add up the credit rather than the debit side of the ledger. Like so many of these essays, it begins with the conviction that Fielding's work is somehow valuable and attempts to catch and formulate what makes it so. Coolidge's essay, on the other hand, is directly in the mimetic-generic line of Watt's essay, showing how Fielding falls between the two stools of realism and stylization, particularity and universality. In general, each novel attracts the two basic approaches of generic criticism and exegesis—both attempts to place it in a larger context and to establish exactly what it means.

# Fielding's Irony:
# Its Method and Effects

## by A. R. Humphreys

Practical criticism, as applied to the novel, is still in the stage of experiment. The critic who is dealing with modern novelists of a highly developed sensibility, has no difficulty in proving the delicacy of their perceptions through the analysis of representative passages of their prose, by looking for degrees of subtlety and precision not very different from those expected in poetry. But criticism of most of the eighteenth and nineteenth century novelists still proceeds in terms of character, plot, and *mise-en-scène*, the established counters of critical discussion. It is still somewhat of an adventure to explore a novelist's qualities of mind through the local alertness of his writing.

Fielding's work, satirical and serious, gives, as Sir Leslie Stephen said, "quite a peculiar impression of solidity and reality." It does so for various reasons, mainly perhaps through the vigorous humor of its character-drawing and its sturdy forthrightness of style, but more generally and fundamentally because in its habits of thought and its social attitudes it is organically related to its century. His irony, far from being radically disturbing like that of Swift, is, in intention, corrective and orthodox; it undermines deviations from a healthy, sensible, social morality; it prunes society of perversions. Unlike the irony of Gibbon or Samuel Butler II, it does not unsettle traditional ethics and Christian orthodoxy—it is the irony of integration rather than disintegration.

This suggests, perhaps, a certain philosophical simplicity about Fielding's irony, and it is true that in comparison with many of the other great ironists he appears to launch his attacks in no very subtle manner. His strategy is frontal and conceived in daylight; the ambiguities between what is said and what is intended are clear on the surface, and do not attempt to spring surprises and betrayals. Swift, Gibbon, Butler, and Shaw imply, perhaps, a certain good-humored contempt for the reader, and invite him to realize his own stupidity by engaging his assent to

"Fielding's Irony: Its Method and Effects." From *The Review of English Studies*, XVIII (1942), 183-196. Reprinted by permission of the author and the Clarendon Press.

propositions embodying his current prejudices, which then prove themselves to be preposterous. Fielding wishes merely to stand on a sensible, neighborly, decent ethic, and (at least up to the time of *Amelia*) is unconcerned with any fundamental ills. His work has the characteristic virtues and drawbacks inherent in so organic a relationship to its century. Many types of experience are alien to it, many of its judgments little more than contemporary prejudices. On the other hand, the native assurance typical of its age, the sense of knowing just where one is and of grounding oneself on the sturdy principles of common sense, aware of a vigorous social order and a reasonable, if limited, religious orthodoxy —these advantages are obvious on every page. Similar perspicacities and blind spots are widely shared by Fielding's generation. In particular, his irony reinforces the scorn for "theory" and subtle ratiocination so typical of his empirical and practical age. Johnson, we remember, "refuted" Berkeley by kicking his foot against a stone. It was the sort of proof Fielding himself liked, and any deviations from common sense, whether prompted by sincere Christian zeal or by hypocrisy, are chastened by the most forthright, unsubtle, ironic devices. Parson Adams, after reproaching Joseph for the strength of his worldly attachment to Fanny, bursts into lamentations when his son is reported drowned; the philosopher of stoic virtue, Square, is found cowering in Molly Seagrim's bedroom.

Such orthodox irony, in support of so sensible a frame of mind, might be supposed to have lost interest after the passage of two centuries and the transition from a foursquare world to a disintegrating one. Yet it has not done so. Folly, one supposes, being perennial, can never be too much chastised, and common sense, being infrequent, can never be too much reinforced. That being so, the technique of this irony which has for two centuries poured scorn on hypocrisy deserves some attention. At first one is puzzled to account for its effectiveness—or rather, for the fact that despite its crudity of outline it appears so mature. Fielding's practice with the drama—one remembers the slapdash success of *Pasquin*, *The Author's Farce*, and *Tom Thumb*—might give his satire decisiveness and energy, but the reasons why it has had so long a success involve an examination of his whole outlook and temper of mind.

One may assume, perhaps, that the severest exercise of the ironist's art is not to give the game away. In that respect, irony differs from sarcasm. The most outrageous things are to be said with a straight face, with unbroken seriousness of demeanor: the poise is so consistently maintained that the reader is forced to realize the real inner meaning the more keenly by discovering it for himself. If intelligent, he succeeds; if stupid, he is taken in—the ironist's great triumph. But Fielding's art is not severe in this fashion. He is not writing for a very experienced audience, but for the eighteenth century's "common reader," and he is not trying to score off that reader but to reinforce his native tendency toward good sense. *Jonathan Wild* could not suffer the fate of Butler's *Fair Haven*, which some reputable reviews took to be serious. Behind the vigorous sparring is the fighter who stands firmly on a sensible orthodoxy. In comparison with Swift, his irony is less intellectual, more muscular, less subtly integrated, more vehement, proceeding less from a profound inner organization of mind, more from the zeal of the practical reformer. Although the first of the following passages does not represent Swift at his best, tailing off as it does from irony into open sarcasm, it affords a close enough parallel to the second to stimulate one into drawing some comparisons.

(a) I had the curiosity to enquire, in a particular manner, by what methods great numbers had procured to themselves high titles of honour and prodigious estates; . . . perjury, oppression, subornation, fraud, pandarism and the like infirmities were among the most excuseable arts they had to mention, and for these I gave, as it was reasonable, due allowance. But when some confessed they owed their greatness and wealth to vice, others to the betraying their country or their prince; some to poisoning, more to the perverting of justice in order to destroy the innocent; I hope I may be pardoned, if these discoveries inclined me a little to abate of that profound veneration which I am naturally apt to pay to persons of high rank, who ought to be treated with the utmost respect due to their sublime dignity by us, their inferiors.

*(Gulliver's Travels*: "Laputa," chap. viii)

(b) He was none of those half-bred fellows who are ashamed to see their friends when they have plundered and betrayed them; from which base and pitiful temper many monstrous cruelties have been transacted by men, who have sometimes carried their modesty so far as to the murder or utter ruin of those against whom their consciences have suggested to them that they have committed some small trespass, either by debauching a friend's wife or daughter, belying or betraying the friend himself, or some other such trifling instance. In our hero there was nothing not truly great; he could, without the least abashment, drink a bottle with the man who knew he had, the moment before, picked his pocket; and when he had stripped him of everything he had, never desired to do him any further mischief; for he carried good nature to that wonderful and uncommon height, that he never did a single injury to man or woman, by which he himself did not expect to reap some advantage.

*(Jonathan Wild:* chap. xi)

The qualities of feeling are somewhat different. Swift's "grave verisimilitude" is different from the ready exaggeration, the macabre caricature, of Fielding. Swift tends relentlessly and unremittingly in one calculated direction; Fielding leaps from posture to posture. Swift has the inner and outer consistency of unruffled logic; Fielding the brilliant manifold brandishings of cut-and-parry debate—one never detects him in the same stance two sentences running. "Half-bred" suggests supercilious scorn for those not brazened in rascality, whether in Wild's or Walpole's circles (where bad manners would arouse more disgust than bad morals); the forcefulness of "plundered and betrayed" proceeds from another criterion—that of the outraged moralist; "base and pitiful temper" shifts again—to Wild's diabolic scorn for the promptings of shame; "monstrous cruelties" might be Wild hypocritically deprecating superfluous villainy, or it might be the outraged moralist stating a fact; "carried their modesty" is pure sarcasm; "murder or utter ruin" is again the moralist stating a fact; "consciences" is a sneer; "small trespass . . . debauching a friend's wife or daughter . . . trifling instance" is angry sarcasm; "nothing not truly great" is ironic (and, implies Fielding, a statement of fact, the pun in "great" reminding us of the Court-Crime equation); "without the least abashment" is ironic praise; "never desired to do him any further mischief" is ironic praise by the standards of normal morality, but real praise in comparison with the vindictiveness of less "magnanimous" criminals; "good nature" is sarcasm; "wonderful and uncommon height" is both sarcasm and, Fielding implies, an actual statement of fact; while "expect to reap some advantage" is again ironic praise by the standards of normal morality, but real praise in comparison with Wild's meaner fellows. The interplay of different tones throughout is so alive that almost any phrase seems to shift its ground the more one looks at it.

When Swift groups "perjury, oppression, subornation, fraud, pandarism and the like infirmities," the effect is very different. The even litheness of tone prevents the cool ingenious understatement from being too insistent. The abstract terms *conceal* the contrast between mere infirmities and the crimes mentioned. Perjury, oppression, and the rest are "infirmities" because they are commonly treated as venial offences, but even more, Swift implies, because they are essential frailties of human nature. One would be surprised by their absence, not by their presence. The common view holds them as mere trifles. Fielding, specifying debauchery of a friend's wife or daughter, by this very coarseness makes its discrepancy from a "small trespass" broad and obvious. By implication, therefore, only those taking the diabolic point of view could condone it. Beyond the momentary sardonic belittlement, there is the strongest hint that normal morals would condemn such an act. Throughout *Jonathan Wild*, the praise or condoning of treachery is too blunt to persuade us that it is more than a pose: the reader automatically supplies the corrective of practical decency, as Fielding intended he should. The very tone and technique of the irony anchor him to orthodoxy, and because of this firmness, this central stability, he can allow himself to indulge apparently cynical or immoral points of view on the clear understanding, implied in his relationship to his reader, that it is all make-believe. The differences between Swift and Fielding in the implications of their irony define the different views they hold about human nature. Both envisage as a standard of comparison a sane moral order from which deviations can be judged; but by the perfect suavity of his tone Swift engages the reader to see it only as an abstract superhuman idea, practiced only in the fictional world of Brobdingnag or the Houyhnhnms (the King of Brobdingnag's Olympian dismissal of humanity as "the most pernicious race of little odious vermin that Nature ever suffered to crawl upon the surface of the earth" is characteristic), and supplanted in practice by an orthodoxy based on observed behavior and therefore essentially selfish and immoral. Fielding limits his denunciations to cases, admittedly numerous, of hypocrisy and ill-nature, which are always recognized as deviations from a healthy social conscience existing in the here and now, embodied not only in shadows like Heartfree and Mr. Allworthy, but in creatures of flesh and blood like Adams, Tom Jones, Sophia, and Amelia.

Fielding's irony, then, in comparison with Swift's, represents the social stability of its age, and instead of undermining reinforces orthodox morality. Consistently with this, it lacks philosophical and verbal complexity. This does not mean that it is a waste of time to attend to its small details, even though the reward is not so startling as it can be in the case of Swift, but simply that such "ambiguities" as there are are soon exhausted. The reader must be awake to what Fielding is saying, since, whatever his practice as a playwright, he was extremely careful as a novelist. But the close significance is that of perfect aptness to define and delimit the subject rather than, as with Swift, Gibbon, and Samuel Butler, to refer it through wide ranges of implication to a large context of moral scepticism. There is in Fielding's irony a superb felicitousness of detail—Miss Laetitia Snap, for instance, "often confessed to her female confidantes, if she could ever have listened to the thought of living with any one man, Mr. Bagshot was he," where the whole effect depends on the intrusive "one"—but in most cases of innuendo or double-entendre (Fielding's favourite types of ambiguity) the possible meanings are sharply limited and soon exhausted. The typical double-entendre or pun is marked by its flatly clear and separable components—as, for example, in *Jonathan Wild*, "that final exaltation which . . . is the most proper and becoming end of all great men"—representing the matter-of-fact definition of central eighteenth-century prose with its concern for plain meanings.

Fielding's irony illuminates the whole temper of his mind. It has been a commonplace of criticism to dub him a realist, and his subject matter justifies the label; but he shares the real strength of eighteenth-century realism in the imposition on his material of a firm and controlled pattern. The very stiltedness of style in which the more impassioned speeches are written is a mark of this (largely instinctive) formalization. The formal elaboration of speech, though to eighteenth century taste it engaged the reader's emotions more strongly than it can do today, maintained a certain distance and decorum. Tom Jones' addresses to Sophia, for example, are rooted in the good sense which *The Spectator* had made such an integral part of the century's social behavior. The most familiar difference between Richardson and Fielding is that the former, by every device in his power, invites the reader to indulge in strained and excessively stimulated states of feeling, while the latter, the master of the comic, preserves his own status, and that of the reader, as an observer. The rhythmical assurance, the grip over movement, the cogency and unobtrusive symmetry of the sentence, are indices of Fielding's real temper, though at present I can only refer to them in passing as the most potent means of implying the artist's self-control and self-possession.

In the sphere of irony, this quality of disciplined formalization shows itself in the elaborate preparation of simple deductions, the scrupulous proof of the obvious, the frankly prepared bathos. It also has close affinities with the deliberate pattern which, for the purposes of comedy, is imposed on characters' behavior. (This will be considered later—a type of formalization designed to sharpen outlines and to reduce the complex spontaneity of an individual's behavior to the clearly apprehensible definiteness beloved of the cartoonist.) The most complete fund of Fielding's ironic mannerisms is to be found in *Jonathan Wild*, and most of the evidence will be taken from that book, though it differs from the other novels only in the degree to which it bases itself on irony.

The life of this enterprising character, at once thief-taker and receiver of stolen goods, exercised a particular fascination over the imaginations of the 1720's and 1730's. Digeon[1] lists a number of ballads, broadsides, and pamphlets which followed on his execution in 1725, and ten years later that collection of criminal biographies called *Lives of the Most Remarkable Criminals* begins its account by observing that there was no precedent for the alacrity with which romantic stories were fathered upon him in his life, and legendary accounts written of him after his death. Not only did these accounts gratify the normal human relish for the nefarious, but they saw in Wild's career something symbolic of the era of systematic corruption which has remained the standard charge against Walpole. Even the pot-boilers anticipated Fielding's "thief-statesman" equation. "We need make no apology for collecting these materials and offering them to the public," says one of them,

> for here they will meet with a system of politics unknown to Machiavel; they will see deeper stratagems and plots form'd by a fellow without Learning or Education than are to be met with in the conduct of the wisest Statesman.

It goes on precisely in Fielding's vein to explain how Wild "show'd early signs of a forward genius," and by a cunning forgery "laid the founda-

[1] *The Novels of Fielding* (New York: E. P. Dutton & Co., 1925), pp. 97-99.

tions of all his future greatness." Wild had become an ironic popular legend, and Fielding adopted him with such a zest that Heartfree, the virtuous foil, was made to appear foolish and weak because he observed the dictates of normal decency. (The reason why Heartfree is an artistic disappointment is, it seems, that the irony will not work in inverse. If villainy is acclaimed as excellence and strength, virtue must be disparaged as stupidity and weakness; but though to undermine by sarcastic praise is easy, to eulogize by sarcastic disparagement is another matter.)

The ironic manner expresses itself, as so often in Fielding, in terms of the mock-heroic. The details of Wild's ancestry and birth, the deeds of his forefathers and the portents which accompanied his nativity are elaborated with a sufficiently broad parody of pedantic scholarship; stock epithets and heroic similes abound. Fielding is a master of these absurd inflations and deflations. Wild finds his "chaste Laetitia" in the arms of Fireblood, and after a burst of inarticulate rage, says Fielding,

> the following accents leapt over the hedge of his teeth, or rather, the ditch of his gums, whence those hedge-stakes had long since by a patten been displaced in battle with an amazon of Drury.*

* The beginning of this speech is lost.

One notes throughout the significant grandiloquence, the shifts of language toward the heroic and formally dignified, which are in keeping with two other qualities to be mentioned shortly—the careful show of logical method and the imposition of formal pattern on the characters' behavior. It is akin also to the skilful periphrasis; Mr. Snap, we hear, "would sometimes relax his mind from the violent fatigues of his employment" by playing cards—Mr. Snap was a Bow Street runner. The grandiloquence is persistent:

> Men of great genius as easily discover one another as freemasons can. It was therefore no wonder that the Count soon conceived an inclination to an intimacy with our young hero, whose vast abilities could not be concealed from one of the Count's discernment.

A good many of Wild's conversations are in the same tone, heightened by a pretence at philosophy; he discusses with the Count the proper subjects of human ambition, and with Bagshot the rights of the Great Man; he discourses on honor to the quarrelling card-sharpers, soliloquizes superbly on statesmen and thieves, argues with Blueskin on political theory, calls on the prisoners of Newgate to submit to his authority—always with a formal elevation which implies Fielding's reference to the circles of court, where such grandiloquent theorizing of "Great Men" would be more at home. Fielding does not directly *state* an intention of making such a reference through the medium of the style; yet one cannot help feeling it as a potent means of implying the equivalence of court and gaol.

To turn to another point: we are often struck by the success with which Fielding indulges in elaborate proof of the blindingly obvious, with the transparent suggestion that the world so flatly denies the dictates of sense and reason that even the self-evident must be supported by a Euclidean clarity of proof. Swift, too, makes stinging implications about social behavior by putting common sense as though it were a startlingly original idea. The Houyhnhnms, for example, are unable to comprehend the practice of lying since it contravenes the most fundamental functions of communication. With more rough-and-tumble, less coolly perhaps and with more obvious sarcasm, Fielding demonstrates patiently that a justice of the peace should have some knowledge of the law (*Tom Jones*, VII, ix; *Amelia*, I, ii); that even two beaux rolled into one, with all the advantages of rank and fashion, will hardly benefit mankind as much as a single Shakespeare, Milton, or Newton (*Jonathan Wild*, I, x). In Swift, of course, the deliberation with which the should-be-obvious is expounded is the means by which radical hypocrisies are laid bare; the success of the process is a commonplace of Swiftian criticism. In Fielding the hypocrisies are nearer the surface; something, the reader feels, could be *done* about the social errors and stupidities which they reflect. The main point about such a mannerism, however, is not the surprise caused by the disparity between the solemn proof and the ironically obvious conclusion, but the way in which the formal gravity suggests a preference for firm outlines and controlled purposes so typical of Fielding's whole method as a novelist. It is a kind of pattern imposed deliberately yet spontaneously both on the characters' behavior and on the circumstances which control their behavior. Having told how Wild flung himself into the sea from a small boat, Fielding writes a whole chapter to account for his getting back into the boat again, on the ground that it was Nature's intention that he should be hanged and not drowned, and that her purposes are not to be thwarted. The transformation of a spontaneous and impromptu action into one performed to accord with a formal pattern is one of Fielding's most frequent ironic devices; at times it links arms with farce, but generally it is a source of strength. Blueskin, brought into court, makes an attack on Wild and wounds him; the deduction is drawn with a formal gravity reinforced by a grip over rhythm:

This accident, however, was in the end attended with worse consequences: for, as very few people (those greatest of all men, absolute princes, excepted) attempt to cut the thread of human life, like the fatal sisters, merely out of wantonness and for their diversion, but rather by the so doing propose to themselves the acquisition of some future good or the avenging of some past evil; and as the former of these motives did not appear probable, it put inquisitive persons on examining into the latter.[2]

That sort of "realism," which is one of the staple methods of the novels, imposes on the unthinking or spontaneous actions and deductions of the characters a strong suggestion of deliberation and definite intention; the instinctive and intuitional become conscious and purposeful, and so contribute to the epic tone.

And this deliberation leads to the imposition of formality on the normal spontaneous behavior of the characters themselves. The advantages which this ironical deliberation allows can be seen by considering the difference of tone between Fielding's and Dickens' treatment of the deception of honesty by villainy,—say in *David Copperfield* or *Oliver Twist*. The controlled tension in the one case keeps the emotions close to human reality and fact; the hysteria and exaggeration in the other make Uriah Heep and Fagin figures of nightmare. The farcical supernatural in *Jonathan Wild* serves just this purpose; Wild's life is lived in accordance with some formal intention of Nature which heralds his birth with portents and guides him unerringly through life to his destined end of the gallows. Fortune wards off the physical effects of Blueskin's attack; Nature makes sure Wild is not drowned; divine power superintends him:

> He was enabled to provide himself with a place in the stage-coach; which, as God permitted it to perform the journey, brought him, at the appointed time, to an inn in the metropolis.[3]

So, not perhaps with great subtlety, but with an admirable firmness, Fielding relates together the grandiose formality which is the mask and which raises *Jonathan Wild* to art, and the unsavory reality on which it is moulded.

Art imposes pattern. The pattern in Fielding has the healthy discipline and strength, the poise and vigor of really central writing in the eighteenth century. It knows its distance from the object and spontaneously maintains it, even in the process of making direct comment. It is essential in Fielding's adoption of the heroic manner, not only in *Jonathan Wild* but in *Joseph Andrews* and *Tom Jones*, too, that we should notice the manipulation of his characters and the interference, the deliberate gestures, he imposes on them. This deliberation, whether serious or comic, frequently coincides with a shift toward the "heroic." [4] It is a characteristic of the typically "heroic" or mock-heroic. Cervantes and

---

[2] *Jonathan Wild*, IV, i.

[3] *Jonathan Wild*, II, xiii.

[4] It is, incidentally, one reason for the crude psychology of the heroic play, in which the hero's dignity would be compromised by complex or undisciplined states of mind.

Scarron, among Fielding's models, practice it frequently. Sidney uses it as a valid heightening of the romance:

> It was in the time *that the earth begins to put on her new aparrel against the approach of her lover,* and that the Sun *running a most even course becums an indifferent arbiter* betweene the night and the day; when the hopelesse shepheard Strephon *was come* to the sandes which lie against the island of Cithera; where, *viewing the place with a heavy kinde of delight,* and *sometimes casting his eyes to the Ileward,* he called his friendly rivall, the pastor Claius unto him; and *setting first downe in his darkened countenance a dolefull copie of what he would speake:* "O my Claius," said he, "hether we are now come to pay the rent, for which we are so called unto by overbusie Remembrance, Remembrance, restlesse Remembrance, which claymes not only this dutie of us, but for it will have us forget our selves." [5]

The italicized words give a hint of the formal deliberation so typical of the "heroic" idealized characterization; Fielding does exactly the same thing for his "inverted heroic" satire:

> Our hero, finding himself in this condition [*i.e.,* adrift in a small boat], *began to ejaculate* a round of blasphemies. . . . *He then accused* the whole female sex . . . as the unhappy occasion of his present sufferings. . . . *At length, finding himself descending too low* into the language of meanness and complaint, *he stopped short, and soon after broke forth* as follows; "Damn it, a man can die but once, what signifies it? What signifies fear? I shall die whether I am afraid or no; who's afraid then, damn me?" *At which words he looked extremely fierce,* but *recollecting that no-one was present to see him, he relaxed a little the terror of his countenance* and . . . repeated the word "Damn." [6]

By this careful definition of the various stages of Wild's feeling, Fielding gives a dignified order to the grumblings of a ruffian. Let us, he says on another occasion, "keep our attention fixed on our hero, whom we shall observe taking large strides towards the summit of human glory." Again there is the formalization, grand though grotesque.

This is largely the reason why the ironic manner is so successful. Fielding so obviously has his eye firmly on the characters, the outlines are so notably prominent, the behavior deliberate, the control strongly exercised even when the outlines are farcical. His method deals particularly well with sharp formal oppositions of character or with symmetrical points of view in distinct antithesis. Molière, to whom he owed so much, was an adept in the same mannerism: the disputes between the *Maître à Danser* and the *Maître de Musique* before M. Jourdain are

---

[5] *Arcadia,* the opening paragraph.
[6] *Jonathan Wild,* II, xi.

representative. Here is Fielding dealing with the rivalry of Thwackum
and Square:

> Square held human nature to be the perfection of all virtue, and that vice
> was a deviation from our nature, in the same way that deformity of body
> is. Thwackum, on the contrary, maintained that the human mind, since
> the fall, was nothing but a sink of iniquity, till purified and redeemed by
> grace. . . . The favourite phrase of the former was the natural beauty of
> virtue; that of the latter, was the divine power of grace. The former
> measured all things by the unalterable rule of right, and the eternal fitness
> of things; the latter decided all matters by authority.[7]

> Though they would both make frequent use of the word Mercy, yet it
> was plain that in reality Square held it to be inconsistent with the rule of
> right; and Thwackum was for doing justice, and leaving mercy to heaven.
> The two gentlemen did indeed somewhat differ in opinion concerning the
> objects of this sublime virtue; by which Thwackum would probably have
> destroyed one half of mankind, and Square the other.[8]

The briskly formal-antithetical style is Fielding's chief weapon for reducing both propositions to absurdity; it suggests the inhumanity of the
logic-chopping mind unilluminated by charity—and such a feeling underlies all his attacks on theoretical and hypocritical morality. He suggests
a narrowness of mind by the very narrowness of the phrases. The most
familiar instance is probably Thwackum's famous definition of religion
as synonymous with the Church of England:

> Honour . . . is not therefore manifold, because there are many absurd
> opinions about it; nor is religion manifold, because there are many sects
> and heresies in the world. When I mention religion, I mean the Christian
> religion; and not only the Christian religion, but the Protestant religion;
> and not only the Protestant religion, but the Church of England. And
> when I mention honour, I mean that mode of divine grace which is not
> only consistent with, but dependent upon, this religion; and is consistent
> with and dependent upon no other.[9]

By this "pattern" of speech Fielding ironically presents his comment
upon moral pedantry. The contrasts between precept and practice also
become flatly clear and recognizable. Philosophers, he says, differ only
in theory from other men:

> They know very well how to subdue all appetites and passions, and to
> despise both pain and pleasure; and this knowledge affords much delight-
> ful contemplation, and is easily acquired; but the practice would be vexa-

[7] *Tom Jones*, III, iii.
[8] *Tom Jones*, III, x.
[9] *Tom Jones*, III, iii.

tious and troublesome; and therefore, the same wisdom which teaches
them to know this, teaches them to avoid carrying it into execution.[10]

The same vital and alert outlines which he employs in revealing the
antithetical hypocrisies of Thwackum and Square Fielding uses, too, in
the conduct of the incidents. He has already implied the unreality of
Square's pretensions by the very primness with which he expounds them:
all that is left to do is to show them shattered by real life—and behold,
we find Square hiding behind the curtain in Molly Seagrim's bedroom.
The angular caricaturing outlines and the unmasking turns of event are
supplementary indices of the strongly precise way in which Fielding
grasps his comic world.

Again and again we notice the effectiveness of the irony in reducing
complex behavior to a deliberate formalization—it is not too much to
call this Fielding's favorite mode of psychological analysis. In some cases
it is so prominent as to suggest that the Good and Bad Angels of the
morality have been conscripted for the purposes of comedy. His practice
as a dramatist impelled him in this direction, for plays, especially of his
own farcical kind (and, strictly speaking, of any kind whatever) demand
a clarification of behavior; we are normally aware that things are being
made much simpler for us; the pattern of action is far more sharply de-
limited than it ever is in real life; intentions and motives are more
decisive. This, after all, is a fundamental condition of the reduction of
life to literature, but in farce or comedy it is peculiarly pronounced. The
*locus classicus* is perhaps the rumination of Launcelot Gobbo in *The
Merchant of Venice*, ii, ii, which starts:

> The fiend is at mine elbow, and tempts me, saying to me, "Gobbo, Launce-
> lot Gobbo, good Launcelot . . . use your legs, take the start, run away."
> My conscience says, "No, take heed, honest Gobbo, honest Launcelot . . .
> do not run, scorn running with thy heels."

The conflicts in the mind of Mrs. Honour when she wonders whether
to be true to Sophia or to betray her flight to Squire Western, and in
the mind of Black George when, having already stolen £500 which belonged to Tom Jones he was tempted to conceal a further sixteen
guineas, are presented similarly as a comically precise battle, duly for-
malized.

> His conscience . . . began to upbraid him with ingratitude to his bene-
> factor. To this his avarice answered, That his conscience should have con-
> sidered this before, when he deprived poor Jones of his £500. . . . In
> return to which, Conscience, like a good lawyer, attempted to distinguish.
> . . . Avarice presently treated this with ridicule. . . . In short, poor Con-

[10] *Tom Jones*, V, v.

science had certainly been defeated in the argument, had not Fear stepped
in to her assistance, and strenuously urged, that the real distinction between the two actions did not lie in the degree of honour, but that of
safety. . . . By this friendly aid of Fear, Conscience obtained a complete
victory in the mind of Black George, and after making him a few compliments on his honesty, forced him to deliver the money to Jones.[11]

The patterned deliberation shifts the tone tacitly toward the heroic
—one reason, no doubt, why Fielding and most of his critics have saluted
the "epic" qualities of *Tom Jones.* The most jovially absurd example is
perhaps the description of Tom's meal:

. . . three pounds at least of that flesh which formerly had contributed to
the composition of an ox was now honoured with becoming part of the
individual Mr. Jones.

The incident of the unfortunate sentinel frightened by the appearance
of the swathed and bandaged Tom runs it close in this respect:

When the sentinel first saw our hero approach, his hair began gently to
lift up his grenadier cap; and in the same instant his knees fell to blows
with each other. Presently his whole body was seized with worse than an
argue fit. He then fired his piece, and fell flat on his face.[12]

The effective rhythms assure us, even in the middle of farcical exaggeration, that there is nothing slipshod about this mode of comedy, that the
genuine and powerful intellectual discipline behind it sets Fielding above
his contemporary rivals and above all but two or three later novelists. It
is this persistent impression of assurance and adequacy which, over and
above matters of characterization and incident, which have been sufficiently praised, continues to evoke admiration through a succession of
readings.

[11] *Tom Jones,* **VI,** xiii.
[12] *Tom Jones,* **VII,** xiv.

# Fielding's Early Aesthetic
# and Technique

### by Winfield H. Rogers

During his apprentice years from 1729 to about 1740,[1] Henry Fielding developed the aesthetic and techniques upon which his great works were written. Particularly important were: (1) his impatience with the restrictions of comedy and his consequent developing of farce as a satiric and moral medium for a criticism of life, (2) his adapting of the commonplace "humour" as a basis for the study and analysis of the springs of human action, (3) his developing of words as symbols, which in context often carry allegorical meaning, (4) his developing of a genuinely comprehensive and inclusive allegorical method of interpreting life, in which farce, "humour," and other word symbols, played an integral part.

## I

The assumption has been that nearly all of this early work of Fielding's was hastily and thoughtlessly executed. Yet the plays were Fielding's major consideration for about eight years, during which time he also had varied journalistic experience. And, indeed, much of his work bears the unmistakable evidence of considerable thought; some of it is obviously the result of hard and conscientious work. *Tom Thumb*, for example, could not have been written without care, precision, and some study based on a well-stocked memory. *The Grub-Street Opera* went through three significant versions; a man who looked upon his playwriting as only a trade would not have given this much attention to a single work.

Furthermore, the critical theory in Fielding's early work is evidence that he thought long and carefully about whatever phase of writing he was practicing, that in general he was an assiduous student of his prede-

"Fielding's Early Aesthetic and Technique." From *Studies in Philology*, XL (1943), 529-551. Reprinted by permission of *Studies in Philology*.

[1] 1740, because *Jonathan Wild* was probably written about this time. The date of the composition of *Jonathan Wild* has been variously argued, and a Ur-J. W. has been posited by Digeon as early as 1737. None of his arguments is convincing, not even that for a third version.

cessors and of his contemporaries, that he looked to them for methods which he might adapt to his particular ends.[2]

The most striking characteristic of Fielding's thought in his early work —a way of thought of permanent importance—is its analogical nature. He was constantly seeing analogies between people and phenomena apparently dissimilar. This characteristic or faculty, the result of a lively and discerning intelligence, was of prime importance in the development of Fielding's art. Upon it rests his justification of farce, a justification contrary to the then current theory of comedy. Comedy, we will recall, aims at entertaining and teaching by a faithful representation of certain aspects of life-characters put into situations that reveal their essential absurdity or lack. Farce aims at raising laughter and teaching by exaggerating to the point of outrageous absurdity. Professor Bond defines burlesque in this manner:[3]

> Burlesque consists . . . in the use or imitation of serious matter or manner, made amusing by the creation of an incongruity between style and subject. This inconsistency between form and content, this opposition between what is said and the way it is said, is the necessary qualification of burlesque. As a species of indirect satire burlesque achieves its end by creating a sense of the absurd because by serious standards the form does not fit the theme, because the flesh and the spirit are not one.

Fielding's plays are associated with the terms burlesque and farce, little distinction being made between the two terms. Fielding's talent certainly was in farce rather than in regular drama. Furthermore, his talent was not in burlesque. Indeed, I question if Fielding ever wrote a pure burlesque in the sense that the *Rehearsal* is one, with the possible exception of *The Tragedy of Tragedies*. We must remember that Fielding indicates contempt for pure burlesque in the Preface to *Joseph Andrews*. Critics have tended to treat the period in Fielding's literary career that begins with this work as an artistic and philosophic *volte face*. On the contrary, I am convinced that Fielding's theory in *Joseph Andrews* is merely an expression of what had long been his view. Here he speaks of his comic intention, which includes the satiric, and in which may be admitted the burlesque in diction, but not burlesque proper.

While *The Author's Farce, The Tragedy of Tragedies*, and *Pasquin* are obviously "rehearsal" drama, fundamentally they are farce. From one point of view, and that quite obviously Fielding's, farce is a discernment, by the wary and penetrating observer, of the extreme incongruities in

---

[2] The catalog of his library (see Ethel M. Thornbury, *Henry Fielding's Theory of the Comic Prose Epic* ["Studies in Language and Literature," No. 30 (Madison: University of Wisconsin Press, 1931)]), pp. 168-189, shows him a serious student of the drama. In addition, all the more important writers of his time had a place in his library.

[3] See Richmond P. Bond, *English Burlesque Poetry* ("Harvard Studies in English," VI [Cambridge: Harvard University Press, 1932]), p. 1.

actual life. Fielding's burlesques tend to make contact with life, rather than merely to ridicule a particular type or piece of literature. The "farcical" situations in Fielding's works—in his novels as well as his plays —are of this nature. One of the reasons why Fielding had some difficulty with the "regular comedy" was that his observations and experiences would not fit into the pure genre; his liking for farce was a part of his analogical thinking. The farce carried on by great men, for example, in the great world, the farce of a village election, with its incongruities between profession and action, and the farce of a puppet show, all seemed to him analogous.

I think it significant that Fielding called *Pasquin*, "A Dramatic Satire." Fielding was writing with one eye upon the practice and theory of those late renaissance satirical comedians who allowed farce if the farce had satirical point. The point of the *Author's Farce* is not in the rehearsal idea; in fact, this is merely a means by which to get the audience to accept the "lowness" of the farce that they are to witness. And in *Pasquin* the audience is made to accept the political farce because of its "rehearsal" framework. Trapwit speaks to his fellow, Fustian. Fustian's little piece is to come on later, after we have been regaled with a drinking-bribery-corruption scene, in which Fielding characteristically blames the voters as much as the candidates. Trapwit says:

> I am afraid, Mr. Fustian, you have hitherto suspected that I am a dabbler in low comedy: Now, Sir, you shall see some scenes of politeness and fine conversation amongst the ladies. Come, my Lord, come, begin.

Then follows a scene picturing false refinement and female politics (vote for the Lord because he is your Lordship). *Pasquin* is characteristic of Fielding's art; in no way is it more characteristic than in its use of farce through which to maintain satiric contact with reality in a theatrical medium that had become highly stylized.

Fielding, furthermore, was willing to admit frankly by statement in the titles that five of his plays were farces. True, he was ostensibly apologetic in his Prologue to the *Author's Farce*. Farce, the genre of laughter, in contrast to the spurious heroic, has appeared frequently in borrowed dress; here she is without disguise. He hinted that he was laughing at the public's literary taste, and the piece makes it quite clear that he is laughing at their politics also; for this British public responds to the heroic actor who

> —stares you in the face
> And cries aloud with emphasis that's fit, on
> Liberty, freedom, liberty, and Briton.

Under such conditions, "What generous Briton can refuse his hand?" Thus he pointed his joke of presenting to this same audience a farce based on the political corruption they countenance while applauding bombastic celebration of "liberty and Briton":

> Bred in Democritus his laughing schools,
> Our author flies sad Heraclitus' rules:
> No tears, no terror plead in his behalf;
> The aim of Farce is but to make you laugh,
> Beneath the tragick or the comick name,
> Farces and puppet-shows ne'er miss of fame,
> Since then, in borrow'd dress, they've pleased the town,
> Condemn them not, appearing in their own,
>
> > Smiles we expect from the good-natur'd few;
> > As ye are done by, ye malicious, do;
> > And kindly laugh at him, who laughs at you.

In *The Lottery* Fielding clearly showed his attitude toward farce and differentiated it from comedy as narrowly defined. I think his Prologue indicates that he chafed under the restrictions of narrow aesthetic *genres*. In this respect it is to be noted that "low" characters play an important part in some of the dramatic pieces that Fielding entitled, not farce, but comedy, such as the *Intriguing Chambermaid*. The opening of the Prologue to *The Lottery* reads:

> As Tragedy prescribes to passion rules
> So Comedy delights to punish fools;
> And while at nobler games she boldly flies,
> Farce challenges the vulgar as her prize.
> Some follies scarce perceptible appear
> In that just glass, which shows you as you are.
> But Farce still claims a magnifying right,
> To raise the object to the sight,
> And shew her insect fools in stronger light.

Farce, then, is a legitimate satiric method, and as such was later to be fused with "straight comedy" in *Joseph Andrews*, where we find the comic, the farcical, the mock-heroic (closely akin in essential nature to the farcical). In Molière Fielding found satiric-farce that appealed to him. And thus his very obvious indebtedness and his translations or adaptations, *The Mock Doctor*, and *The Miser*, in 1732 and 1733. Fielding's first play was an attempt in the conventional comedy of manners, his third and fourth satirical farces, and thenceforth his plays, even when entitled comedies, were to have strong farcical elements.

Fielding turned to farce because of his analogical way of looking at the phenomena of life. His aesthetic of farce, which defined anew the term, caused him to be misjudged by his contemporaries, and especially by the critics who judged on the basis of the comedy of manners, or on the basis of sentimental comedy. What these critics, and modern critics as well, did not realize was that Fielding derived his theory of farce and his concept of its relation to satire from the new satire of the period, which in turn went back to renaissance "comicall satyre" and in some respects to medieval farce.

Fielding on January 3, 1739-40 in *The Champion*, adumbrating his theory of satire, wrote:

> When wit hath been used, like that of Addison or Steele to propagate virtue and morality; when like that of Swift, to expose vice and folly; it is then only that these become commendable, and truly worthy of our praise and admiration.

The century, and Fielding with it, demanded wit in its satire. Wit referred to the handling of particulars to get a happy, telling combination of words and a general frame or allegory that would point the moral and establish the necessary references. In comedy and satire the age worked on the background of the restoration, on the theory and practice of restoration comedy and satire. The strongest tradition was that of dramatic satire, which conflicted, however, in the early part of the century with sentimental comedy. This dramatic satire in the eighteenth century was merged with a satire softened by sentimentalism.

In the theory of dramatic satire inherited from the renaissance and from the derivative eighteenth century theory, Fielding found his *apologia* for satirical farce.[4] In the twenty-third *Spectator* Addison states:

> There is nothing that more betrays a base, ingenerous Spirit, than the giving of secret Stabs to a Man's Reputation. Lampoons and Satyrs, that are written with Wit and Spirit, are like poisoned Darts which not only inflict a Wound, but make it incurable.

As in other matters, here the age turned to Horace. Addison in a later paper (No. 209) developed his theory. It is remarkably like Fielding's: avoid lampoons, attack the corrigible only, concentrate upon the culpable in a profession and class rather than mistakenly to satirize the class itself; vice and folly "ought to be attacked wherever they could be met with, and especially when they were placed in high and conspicuous Stations of Life" (No. 34). In this last is the resolution of the apparent discrepancy between theory and practice, a resolution which made it possible to reconcile the professions of the age that the individual should not be attacked with the practice of attacking, for example, Walpole. An in-

---

[4] See Oscar James Campbell, *Comicall Satyre and Shakespear's "Troilus and Cressida"* (San Marino, California: Huntington Library, 1938), pp. 12-13.

dividual's prominence (in "high and conspicuous station") released the satirist from his obligation to avoid personal satire.[5]

On a similar satiric aesthetic Fielding wrote his early as well as his late satires. Those who derogated his plays in his own time, as well as his later interpreters, did not and have not fully appreciated this. Nor have they seen the essential nature of burlesque and especially its relation to the mock-heroic. Indeed *comedy, farce,* and *burlesque* when used under an aesthetic that demands more than amusement, are but three modes of achieving the same thing. Under such an aesthetic each is satire.

In this lies the real connection between farce and burlesque, the essential difference being in the starting point: in the case of farce, with life, in the case of burlesque, with some piece of literature or literary style. The end may be the same, as it mostly was in the eighteenth century. For in the eighteenth century the end was frequently a criticism of life or attitude toward life that had been expressed in a particular work or group of works. Certainly in Fielding one discerns the tendency to bring the two together. The fondness of Fielding and the eighteenth century for *Don Quixote* is a case in point, for *Don Quixote* is at once burlesque and farcical satire. The satire justifies the burlesque. Fielding in his later career put the matter in another way when he said that the burlesque may be permitted in the comic epic in prose only in diction. He apparently made a distinction between the burlesque and the mock-heroic mood, which was characteristic of contemporary theory. Quite obviously, either was justifiable only in the interests of moral-social satire. Farce as here defined, burlesque, or the mock-heroic mood depend on analogy if they are to have moral or social significance; indeed they approach allegory and symbolism.

## II

Fielding's third play, *The Temple Beau,* significantly leans toward a kind of symbolism. It is a characteristic manifestation of the eighteenth century predilection for a dominant symbol under which to treat human nature. The vicissitudes of the word humour in English literature need not concern us here; it is sufficient to say that "humour" and "ruling passion," stemming from classical theory and from medieval medical lore through the Elizabethans, came to be used interchangeably. The recrudescence of the term "ruling passion" was no doubt a result of the

---

[5] The existence of this satiric norm in the aesthetic of the time is shown by the professions of Swift. In Number III of "Intelligencer," for example, Swift states: "It is certainly the best Ingredient toward that Kind of Satyr, which is most useful, and give the least Offence; which instead of lashing, laughs Men out of their Follies, and Vices, and is the Character which gives Horace the Preference to Juvenal." The age leaned to allegorical satire, rather than to satire in the narrower sense.

loose uses to which "humour" gradually came to be put. Fielding's idea of comedy is inextricably related to his concept of satire with its proper base in the "humours." This idea was later to become intrinsic to his interpretation of human nature. To Fielding comedy, or the comic, emanated from three sources, from farce, from the humours, from the mock-heroic (which Fielding called attention to under the phrase "the burlesque in diction" in the preface to *Joseph Andrews*). Farce was heightening through isolation or through the creation of incongruous situations. It is not concerned with following character traits to their roots but with revealing the follies and foibles of character that they may appear ridiculous. Inherent in the humour idea was the desire to come to grips with the springs of human action. The "humour" might be, of course, either tragic or comic. The humour idea, as I have pointed out, was only one way of expressing the age's interest in the balanced man. Fielding saw fit to clarify his mind on this matter at the time when he was working on his first great prose work, *Joseph Andrews*.

Fielding's second play, *Love in Several Masques*, though conventional, shows his early interests (most of them permanent) in Cicero, Epictetus, Plato, Aristotle, and Swift. Fielding, in keeping with the aesthetic of the time, called for humour free from indecency, with nothing to offend the fair, no private character, and aimed at vice, not at the vicious. This is quite possibly merely an echo of contemporary opinion, yet the play, derivative as it is, shows in its brilliant imitativeness a genuine interest in the humour idea. Indeed Fielding was conservative in his use of the word humour. He always used the word in some sort of connection with the older and more traditional connotation. His third play, *The Temple Beau*, symptomatic of so much of Fielding's art, tries to give new life to the humour idea by different terminology. Each of the main characters in *The Temple Beau* is a humour character whose overemphasis causes him to be ridiculous. That Fielding derived this play from Addison and from Steele,[6] and maybe from Swift, shows the age searching for symbols by which to indicate the deviation from the balance of the golden mean.

In *The Tragedy of Tragedies* Fielding ridiculed the false wit that had abounded in his first comedy, especially, and to a lesser extent in *The Temple Beau*. He had naturally fallen into imitation of the wit-similes of his immediate predecessors in comedy. With characteristic perspective Fielding turned about and mocked the falsity into which he had fallen. We may read here that he had come to value the humour play that relied on character more than the play that relied on witty dialogue. Fielding began, I think, to hit his stride in *The Temple Beau*, actually fell into it in *The Author's Farce* and in *Tom Thumb*, the early version of *The*

---

[6] In this play Fielding took the symbol *pedant* from Addison's *Spectator* paper 105, to give new significance to the humour point of view. See Winfield H. Rogers, "The Significance of Fielding's *The Temple Beau*," *PMLA*, LV (1940), 440-444.

*Tragedy of Tragedies.* In the former he used, in the after piece, *The Pleasures of the Town,* the word humour in an indicative manner. Joan, speaking of her husband's inclination to song, despite his poor voice, says: "But he keeps his old harmonious humour even in the shades." And throughout the plays he almost always used the word in its older and more exact sense.

*The Coffee-House Politician,* for example, has "political humour" to describe the individual derived from Addison's "Upholsterer."

> I recollect the dawnings of this political humour to have appeared when we were at Bath together; but it hath risen finely in these ten years. What an enthusiasm must it have arrived to, when it could make him forget the loss of his only daughter! The greatest part of mankind labour under one delirium or other: and Don Quixotte [*sic*] differed from the rest, not in madness, but the species of it. The covetous, the prodigal, the superstitious, the libertine, and the coffee-house politician, are all Quixottes in their several ways.
>
> > That man alone from madness free, we find,
> > Who by no unruly passion blind,
> > To reason gives the conduct of his mind.

This is the germ of his *Essay on The Characters of Men,* presumably written in 1743, some thirteen years after *The Coffee-House Politician,* in which he developed his differentiation between good-humour and good-nature. The passage from *The Coffee-House Politician* is a fair sample of eighteenth century psychology, the basis of Fielding's character portrayal in his novels. These "humours," in general, seem to have been corrigible. Surely there is a real relation between the humour idea and his development in *The Champion,* February 2, 1739-40, of the medieval and Elizabethan commonplace that the body is a battleground, which one passion might become master of, and his comparison of the economy of the body to that of a state, both comparisons leading to the idea of self-discipline. There are some character bents, of course, so strong that they cannot be corrected. Yet the aesthetic (and philosophy) of the time took an optimistic view of human frailties, believing that, with the general inclination in human nature toward goodness, under the proper treatment and circumstances, the individual might free himself from the madness of a wild unruly passion by the use of reason. The difference between the humourous character and the serious character in much of eighteenth century literature may well lie in this: when corrigible the character might be satirized, when incorrigible he must be held up as an object of detestation.

In some instances, of course, the humour idea is a mere device of comedy, as in *The Letter Writers,* when Mrs. Wisdom tries to rid herself of Mr. Softly by affecting a humour in order to keep Softly from discovering Rakel in her closet; and again in his adaptation of *L'Avare*, when Lappet is building up the idea that Mariana has a preference, "a humour," for elderly gentlemen, preferring them above the younger. Once, at least, Fielding used the word in the sense of capricious, when he had Fustian in *Pasquin* speak of "the Muses, who are humourous ladies, and must be attended; for if they take it into their head at any time to go abroad and leave you, you will pump your brain in vain. . . ."

Yet, despite his occasional use of the word in its less special signification, the contemplation of the humour idea in Fielding's work brings us into touch with the fundamentals of his art. His very real concern with the humours is one strong indication of his protest against the artificial interpretation of life in his times. Trapwit's speech to Fustian in *Pasquin* characteristically strikes in several directions, at Trapwit, at the audience, at decadent wit. One might suppose, on the evidence of this speech, that Fielding had been considering, with Congreve and others, the differentiation between wit and humour.

> Mr. Fustian, you'll observe I do not begin this play like most of our modern comedies, with three or four gentlemen who are brought on only to talk wit; for to tell you the truth, Sir, I have very little, if any, wit in this play: No, Sir, this is a play consisting of humour, nature, and simplicity: It is written, Sir, in the exact and true spirit of Moliere; and this I will say for it, that except about a dozen, or a score, or so, there is not one impure joke in it.

There is, he observed in his *Champion* essay for June 12, 1740, great difference of opinion concerning all works of wit and humour. The variety of his readers' palates causes an author much difficulty. "If he be serious, one half of his readers cry he is dull; if ludicrous the other half call him ridiculous, foolish, farcical." For Fielding's period was one of many different points of view on aesthetic matters and Fielding was one of the few who cared to and was able to make a synthesis of the disparate trends. The unique quality of Fielding's satire lies in the application of a theory compounded from satirical commonplaces of the period, and his giving this intellectual and ethical rationalization.

Fielding's view of the humours constitutes an important part of his satirical code as it was forming in the years from 1732 to 1740. For the relation of the foolish, farcical and the ridiculous caused him to come out definitely for satirical comedy that admitted purposeful farce, or farcical elements. For farce could be righteous, a part of ethical satire. Vice, not the vicious; the follies and foibles of mankind, not man—against those a fearless ethical wielding of the satirical lash. "But while I hold the pen, it will be a maxim with me, that vice can never be too great to be lashed, nor virtue too obscure to be commended; in other words, that satire can never rise too high, nor panegyrick stoop too low" (Epistle to Mrs. Clive, prefaced to *The Intriguing Chambermaid*).

"Lively representation of the calamities brought on a country by general corruption, might have a very sensible and useful effect on the spectators," stated Fielding in the Dedication to *Don Quixote in England*. Again in this Dedication he spoke of the effectiveness of satire, at the same time protesting against its abuse:

> Socrates, who owed his destruction greatly to the contempt brought on him by the comedies of Aristophanes, is a lasting instance of the force of theatrical ridicule: here, indeed, this weapon was used to an ill purpose; but surely what is able to bring wisdom and virtue into disrepute, will, with great facility, lay their opposites under a general contempt. There are among us who seem so sensible of the danger of wit and humour that they are resolved to have nothing to do with them: and indeed they are in the right on 't; for wit, like hunger, will be with great difficulty restrained from falling on, where there is great plenty and variety of food.

Fielding developed these ideas more completely during 1739-40. On December 4, 1739, Captain Hercules Vinegar published a letter in which his correspondent begged him to "infuse gall in your ink, and, instead of morality, wit, and humour, deal forth private slander and abuse." Thus Fielding ironically stated his case. Shortly thereafter, on December 22, 1739, Fielding wrote that "whatever is wicked, hateful, absurd, or ridiculous, must be exposed and punished. . . ." On March 13, 1739-1740, he published an essay against "roasting," quite in keeping with Addison's stricture on lampoons. In the course of his discussion, he quoted from Shaftesbury's essay in support of this destructive and injurious practice. He also follows Addison and Shaftesbury in believing that there is "nothing so unjustifiable as the general abuse of any nation or body of men," and in condemning the custom of throwing scandal on a whole profession for the vices of some particular members. On the other hand, a profession, "should give no more security to the man than the man should bring a disgrace on his profession." From this we may conclude that those humours affecting in general the characters of men, the transgressions of a particular group, and lastly the vanities of men, are the proper objects of satire:

> Vanity, or the desire of excelling, to cast it in a ridiculous light (for it may be seen in one very odious, being perhaps at the bottom of most villainy, and the cause of most human miseries) may be considered as exerting itself in two ways; either as it pushes us on to attempt excelling in particulars, to which we are utterly unequal, or to display excellence in qualities which are in themselves very mean and trivial.

This latter, he said, exerts itself in mean, indifferent, and sometimes vicious habits. Thus Fielding's satire on fox-hunters, adepts in horse-racing and cock-fighting, and "Knights of the Trencher."

These are vain persons. And Fielding came to associate the words "vanity" and "'affectation." Affectation proceeds, he wrote in the Preface to *Joseph Andrews,* from the closely related causes, vanity or hypocrisy. To Fielding the tracing of these connections had considerable importance. They were matters basic to one who was interested in the springs of human action.

This concern with affectation was not extraordinary. But as Fielding said, no one, not even the great Aristotle, had made the basic connection between the ridiculous and affectation. There is a suggestion of interest even as early as *The Temple Beau,* in Bellaria's advice to Clarissa: ". . . for believe it, my dear Clarissa, a pretty face, over-affectation, pride, ill-nature, in a word, over-coquetry, is but a gilt cover over a volume of nonsense, which will be despised by all wise men. . . ." This is affectation from vanity. Two years later, in 1732, in the *Modern Husband,* Gaywit and Bellamant talk of Lord Richly's voluptuous arrogance. Bellamant speaks:

> Insolent vanity! I wonder the spirit of mankind has not long since crush'd the tyranny of such lordly wolves; yet believe me, Gaywit, there generally goes a great deal of affectation to compose this voluptuous man. He oftener injures women in their fame, than in their persons .This affectation of variety, discovers a sickly appetite; and many mistresses, like many dishes, are often sent away untasted.

Fielding's thought on these matters may be seen in *The Miser,* when Lovegold rationalizes the hypocritical affectation in Mariana, as described by Lappet.

> That is a good sign, tho'; Lappet, let me tell you, that is a good sign; right habits as well as wrong are got by affecting them. And she who could be thrifty a whole fortnight, gives lively hopes that she may be brought to be so as long as she lives.

On the other hand, affectation may lead one to pretend to greater hypocrisy and evil than he actually possesses, as it did Captain Hercules Vinegar's correspondent in *The Champion* of December 11, 1739.

In his apprenticeship, Fielding's concept of the humours, then, led inevitably in his hands to a careful consideration of the basic springs of actions, especially as they related to affectation and hypocrisy and thus to his theory of satire.

### III

It has been thought sufficient to label Fielding a realist. This is to belittle him, for, though a realist, he was only satisfied when he had gone behind appearance or surface reality. This highly critical and analytic quality, leading frequently to generalization, caused him to mould words, by giving them new connotations, into effective tools for a satirical or ethical interpretation of reality. His use of words as satiric or ethical symbols is at once a part of his predilection for symbolism and of his desire for exact expression. To this last his revisions of his most important works, *Jonathan Wild*, *Joseph Andrews*, and *Tom Jones*, attest, as well as his devastating criticism of Colley Cibber's sloppy English in his *Apology*.[7]

In his use of words, Fielding was greatly stimulated by John Locke, whose discussion of semantics was the most significant to date. Again Fielding showed himself one who made the applications and synthesis. Apparently Fielding studied Book III of the *Essay Concerning Humane Understanding* with great care.

Twice in *The Champion* he referred to Locke for his authority on the use and abuse of language. On January 17, 1739-40, he stated that the manner in which we employ speech differentiates man from other worldly inhabitants. He quoted Locke, "Of the Remedies of the Imperfections— and Abuses." [8]

> That whoever shall consider the errors and obscurity, the mistakes and confusion, that are spread in the world by an ill use of words, will find some reason to doubt, whether language, as it has been employed, has contributed more to the improvement or hindrance of knowledge amongst mankind.

He then stated the abuses: in compliments, in expletives, in swearing, and in the language of the various professions and stations. Again on March 27, 1740 he quoted Locke: "Those gross and confused conceptions which men ordinarily have, and to which they apply the common words of their language may serve them well enough in their ordinary discourses and affairs; but this is not sufficient for philosophical inquirers." Further, Fielding said, following Locke, that all one "can find in all the volumes and varieties of controversies with which the world is distracted, is that the contending learned men of different Parties do, in their arguings with one another, speak different languages."

There are many references to Locke in Fielding's works, in the plays, in the novels, and in the periodicals. In the *Covent Garden Journal*, No. 4, he quoted Locke again on the use of general words by those who have "no determin'd ideas laid up in their Minds" about these words. Surely Fielding had determined ideas laid up in his mind! In the sixth section, Chapter X, of the third book, Locke spoke of an abuse in language that Fielding might be accused of perpetrating, if his work is judged superficially. This is "applying old words to new and unusual significances, or introducing new and ambiguous terms, without defining either."

[7] See *The Champion*, April 22, 29, 1740.
[8] *Essay Concerning Humane Understanding*, Book III, chap. xi, sec. 4.

Fielding never introduced new and ambiguous terms; he commonly applied old words in new and unusual significations. Always, or nearly always, he carefully defined these symbols. It was ethically, and frequently satirically, effective to show what terms had, might, or should stand for.

He began very early to experiment with the content of words. In his second play, *The Temple Beau,* he hit upon an extended meaning of the word "pedant" to signify the lack of intellectual poise. Even before this he had toyed with the application of "Quixotism," for at Leyden he had sketched a few scenes in an attempt to adapt Don Quixote and Sancho to a satire on English life. Fielding returned to the theme when he took up his early Leyden sketches and produced his play *Don Quixote in England.* To the essentials of Fielding's interest in *Don Quixote,* I must return elsewhere in an interpretation of *Joseph Andrews.* Here it is sufficient to point out that part of Fielding's definition of "Quixotism" has not been realized. The key is in Constant's soliloquy in *The Coffee-House Politician.*

> I begin to be of that philosopher's opinion, who said, that whoever will entirely consult his own happiness, must be little concerned about the happiness of others. Good-nature is Quixotism, and every princess Micomicona will lead her deliverer into a cage.

"Good-nature is Quixotism"! The well-intentioned man, concerned about the happiness of others, has a hard time in this selfish world. Fielding jockeys back and forth between "Quixotism" and good-nature. And it is to be kept in mind that *Joseph Andrews* was "in the manner of Don Quixote."

"Good-nature" was one of the words that Fielding redefined and made into a significant word-symbol. The emphasis in *Don Quixote in England* is slightly different from that in *The Coffee-House Politician.* The "good-natur'd man" is "one, who seeing the want of his friend, cries he pities him." The Don is called mad because he genuinely wants to relieve people, and he says: "Sancho, let them call me mad." *The Champion* of March 27, 1740, in which Fielding quoted Locke on gross and confused conceptions, outlines good-nature, defined as true magnanimity. Concerned with the whole rather than the particular, it delights in the happiness of mankind: good-nature implies judgment (an early version of the prudence that was not Tom Jones'); good-nature is the quality of the mind that urges the individual to listen to revealed Christianity. It is concerned with the extirpation of vice and villainy, and thus if rightly directed there is nothing ill-natured in satire. Sweetness and light, benevolence and intelligence, are the marks of good-nature. Good-nature is the most satisfactory attitude, for the good-natured man can never carry his enjoyments too far, and good-nature is "the only affection of the human mind which can never be sated." Fielding sketched here his ideal

man under one symbol; later he was several times to put this type into
narrative, i.e., concrete allegory. In the sixth number of *The Champion*
he had published six lines on the same subject that later appeared, with
some changes, as part of the poem *Of Good-Nature*. The poem sets forth
the same ideals as the *Champion* essay. Apart from his novels Fielding
made one other attempt to bring to life this symbol of good-nature, in
the late comedy *The Fathers, or the Good-Natur'd Man*, the manuscript
of which was lost, a play revised and acted by Garrick.

Fielding eagerly grasped another symbol, again a redefined commonplace of the time, and a symbol that should be appreciated by ours. This
was that of the "great man." Fielding in his usual manner took an idea
that was in nearly every one's mind, and by continuous application, new
definition, and emphasis, made it an effective symbol. The age had become interested in the old commonplace of the iniquitous conqueror because of the prominence of Louis XIV, and Charles XII of Sweden. Vol-
taire wrote Charles XII's history and Fielding translated one by Adlerfeld.
The contrast, too, between the ideal of the enlightened despot and the
usual character of kings and conquerors, plays its part. The contrast became one between goodness and greatness; the problem one of the reconciliation or fusion of these. To this problem Fielding later turned in
the preface to *The Miscellanies*, in the meantime weaving the idea into
the texture of *The Tragedy of Tragedies*. The symbol of the great man
was in and out of Fielding's mind for many years, until he brought it to
its ultimate development in *Jonathan Wild*.

From the first Fielding seemed to think of "greatness," that is, prominent success, as spurious:

> Have you not heard
> (What ev'ry Corner of the Court resounds)
> That little *Thumb* will be a great man made.

Even in 1730 Fielding had well in mind the ambiguity of greatness.

> Where art thou Grizzle, where are now thy Glories?
> Where are the Drums that waken'd thee to Honour?
> Greatness is a lac'd Coat from Monmouth-Street,
> Which Fortune lends us for a Day to wear,
> To-morrow puts it on another's Back.

In the next scene, in a dialogue between Grizzle and the Queen, the
Queen speaks:

> Wherefore, Oh Blood and Thunder! hav't you heard
> (What ev'ry Corner of the Court resounds)
> That little *Thumb* will be a great Man made.

Tom Thumb (Tom Thumb, the great) is the symbol for greatness, physically representing the spiritual insignificance of greatness. *The Tragedy of Tragedies* is closer to *Jonathan Wild* than is commonly thought.

As the symbol lay with Fielding it gradually took on richer connotations. Risque says, for example, in *The Letter Writers*: "If you were but as like a great man in your riches, as you are in your promises——." Fielding approached the idea again in *Pasquin*, but from 1739 to 1741 he gave the most explicit statement of the content of the word, outside of *Jonathan Wild*, in the *Champion* and in a poem afterwards published in the *Miscellanies*, "Of True Greatness. An Epistle to the Right Honorable George Dodington, Esq." In the *Champion* of January 17, 1739-40, he again spoke of the insincerity, here especially in speech, of great men. More important, however, is the poem "Of True Greatness," in which he brought *true* greatness together with goodness and nobility of mind. The *truly* great is the good-natured man; the good and the great come together.[9] Later in the essay on the "Knowledge of the Characters of Men," he spoke of political great men.

From one point of view, *Jonathan Wild* was an attempt to bring together several different symbols or sets of symbols (great, good-nature, good-breeding), a fact which Fielding partly indicated in the preface to the *Miscellanies*. The symbols "well-bred" and "ill-bred" play an important part in the irony of *Jonathan Wild*. As with great and good-nature, Fielding had played with defining well-bred and ill-bred, supplying new content, opposed in general, he felt, to that accepted by the world. Fielding had not concerned himself with this symbol, however, to any great extent. He had used it in *The Coffee-House Politician, The Grub-Street Opera*, and in *The Modern Husband*, as a casual instrument and in a manner that shows he had definite concepts of the nature of what breeding should mean. To this he returned again in the *Essay on Conversation*, in *Tom Jones*, and he continued his interest in it until his death.

In his early plays we see Fielding developing his equipment of symbols, by definition and redefinition of word-symbols which were to become a part of more embracing methods of interpretation, the integration resulting ultimately in his masterpieces.

## IV

Although Fielding started with conventional comedy, he soon turned to farce and burlesque. *The Author's Farce; and the Pleasures of the Town* was written under the threefold influence of the dialogue of the dead, of burlesque, and of the contemporary satire on learning and letters by

[9] Among Fielding's verbal symbols one might also mention "madness" and "liberty."

the Scriblerus group, recently enforced by the variorum *Dunciad.* The play is really two loosely connected pieces, held together only by the "rehearsal" idea. The whole is a satire on Grub Street, on the theatrical managers, on false taste in literature, on taking nonsense for wit (Charon remarks, "I had forgot to tell your ladyship [the Goddess of Nonsense], I hear rare news; they say you are to be declared Goddess of Wit." To which the Goddess replies dryly, "That's no news, Mr. Charon"). The play was Fielding's declaration of war. Henceforth, he will attack the false, no matter what its cloak. He began, here, to develop the technique of the dialogue of the dead which he was to use over and over again, with varying degrees of success, culminating in *The Journey From This World to the Next,* and which he finally dropped, I surmise, because of its inherent limitations.

In *The Author's Farce* Fielding was attempting *inclusiveness,* always his desire, as his redefinitions and analogies have indicated. He had not yet found the completely satisfactory methods. In the first place the piece broke into two (complementary, it is true) parts; it was not integrated. Nevertheless, we see Fielding working typically in what we may call multi-directional allegory (or satire) or multileveled symbolism. Suggested here, this sort of thing was more thoroughly developed in *The Tragedy of Tragedies.*

In *Tom Thumb* he gave over the rehearsal idea. *Tom Thumb* immediately followed *The Author's Farce.* When first presented, Fielding and the public quickly caught the undeveloped possibilities, and Fielding enlarged and revised the play until it became, not merely *Tom Thumb* but *The Tragedy of Tragedies, or the Life and Death of Tom Thumb the Great as It is Acted at the Theatre in the Hay-Market, with the Annotations of H. Scriblerus Secundus.* From a fairly simple piece of burlesque foolery, the work became a rather elaborate satire. In general it is in the mock-heroic mood. Tom Thumb is the noble tragic hero, acting and talking rhodomontade. The general manner of the heroic is here, with a most amusing discrepancy between manner and characters. The play parodies, also, a large number of particular passages from various heroic tragedies. In addition, Fielding supplied, in good Scriblerus manner, elaborate editorial paraphernalia.

But this was not all. This much is an amusing burlesque that combines several of the methods of that mood. Fielding's analogical mind could not leave it at this. In the revised version, *The Tragedy of Tragedies,* he reached out for more and more of contemporary life. Tom Thumb has become the *Great,* and is thus taken from literature into life. One even wonders if Fielding meant his new title to point the irony of the fact that we entrust our worldly affairs to spiritual Tom Thumbs,—this the tragedy of tragedies. Dollallolla and Huncamunca are more defined: they become much more like those irreproachable ladies in *Jonathan Wild,* symbols of what passes in the world. Noodle, Doodle, Foodle become symbols of party politics, and it is possible that the figure of Walpole flitted through Fielding's mind and that Fielding smiled for a moment when he inscribed Tom Thumb, the great. The new scenes in the finally revised play show that Fielding felt somewhat confined by his literary framework. He obviously felt the need of symbols that would allow him to comment at once on literature and life.

Fielding's difficulty was that plays were not as readily adaptable to the three-directional satire or symbolism as were prose allegories. With his eye on Swift, for example, he was attempting to write that he might be understood in several different ways. Because of this, as I have already pointed out, Fielding was interested from a very early date in the symbol of Quixotism and had connected it with that of good-nature. The general formula of Cervantes' book had a natural appeal to Fielding, It allowed for inclusive comment on life. It supplied the various contrasts and comparisons, the analogies, that he valued so much in his art. In fact, contrast and comparison became with him a narrative principle in *Jonathan Wild, Joseph Andrews*, and in *Tom Jones*. The *Don Quixote* formula, however, though its symbolism was congenial, was difficult to adapt to the stage. In the *Tragedy of Tragedies* there had been some opportunity for contrast and comparison. This tendency becomes especially clear with *The Grub-Street Opera*, and thereafter remains prominent in Fielding's technique.

*The Grub-Street Opera*, written, of course, under the influence of Gay's *The Beggar's Opera*, emphasizes the high-low comparison that Gay had suggested. The juxtaposition, by various methods, for the purposes of satiric comparison and contrast, became a permanent characteristic of Fielding's technique. As a corollary to this he was able to make one symbol stand for several things or persons; this ability Miss Hessler finds the principal reason for the brilliance of the plays. Miss Hessler says:[10] ". . . the brilliance of the plays is in a large part due to Fielding's ability to make one symbol stand for several things or persons—to satirize, in the same lines, the mismanagement of the theatre, the maladminstration of government; Theophilus Cibber, and Sir Robert Walpole." Sometimes the symbolism is even more complicated than this. Even in the *Grub-Street Opera*, Robin is the quarrelsome, thieving, lying servant, a low-life replica of the reprehensible aristocrat, Sir Robert Walpole. The realization of the complicated allegory of the plays suggests that the interpretation of novels, on which Fielding spent a great deal of care, has been far too facile.

This three-directional satire that Fielding found so useful, he managed to adapt to the rehearsal idea again in *Pasquin, a Dramatic Satire on the Times, Being the Rehearsal of Two Plays, viz., A Comedy call'd The*

[10] Mable Dorothy Hessler, *The Literary Opposition to Sir Robert Walpole, 1721-1742. Fielding's Attacks on Walpole* (Chicago: The University of Chicago Libraries, 1936), p. 140.

*Election, and a Tragedy call'd, The Life and Death of Common-Sense.*
The comedy is farce, the tragedy is mock-heroic. Both are comments on
actual life. *The Election*, though ostensibly political, is an indictment of
the general moral state of the nation from the highest to the lowest, a fact
pointed by Fielding when he says that, after all, it takes two to make
bribery. Yet Fielding manages to keep several objects in view at once, as
shown by Trapwit's answer to Fustian.

> Fust.   Is there nothing but bribery in this play of yours, Mr. Trapwit?
>
> Trap.   Sir, this play is an exact representation of nature; I hope the
> audience will date the time of action before the bill of bribery and cor-
> ruption took place; and then I believe it may go down; but now Mr.
> Fustian, I shall shew you the art of a writer, which is, to diversify his
> matter, and do the same thing several ways. You must know, Sir, I dis-
> tinguish bribery into two kinds; the direct, and the indirect: the first you
> have seen already; and now, Sir, I shall give you a small specimen of the
> other.

The obvious irony here needs no comment.

*The Historical Register for the Year 1736* is again in the "rehearsal"
manner, but with the analogical-comparison method carried even further.
It is built in part on the analogy between the theatre and politics. Medley says: "When my politicks come to a farce, they very naturally lead
me to the playhouse, where, let me tell you, there are some politicians
too, where there is lying, flattering, dissembling, promising, deceiving,
and undermining, as well as in any court in Christendom." *The Historical
Register* impudently mocks all the conventions of the eighteenth century
theatre, including Fielding's own work—fine dialogue, rehearsal plays
themselves, the comical satiric opera, pretence of moral seriousness, dialogues of the dead. With all, a deal of seriousness underlies the whole
potpourri—even bitterness, for example, in the auction scene. Only five
pounds is bid for "a most curious remnant of Political Honesty," a
thousand for "a very considerable Interest at Court."

*The Historical Register* is an inclusive, almost bewildering, kaleido-
scopic satire, shifting rapidly from political satire to literary, to moral
indictment ("a man of great parts, learning, and virtue, is fit for no employment whatever"). Primarily it shows the integration of Fielding's
mind, that by 1737 his mind had matured to the point of seeing life
whole. Untimely though Fielding's death was, he had had his say by then.
He had worked out means for complete expression; if he had lived to
write more novels he would have repeated himself, though never dully.
In his novels he freed himself from basically uncongenial influences
which, because of time-circumstances, he could not for some time escape.
We have seen him breaking the bounds of dramatic art as conceived
in his time. When he was forced by the Licencing Act into nondramatic

expression he had to begin over again. He had, in short, to adapt the allegorical and analogical method to his new medium (in this I think the well-known "preparation" *really* consists).

I should like to emphasize further the allegorical nature of Fielding's artistic method by abstracting the discussion of allegory by Dr. R. V. Redinger, presented in the course of her unpublished study of Swift.[11] The allegorist follows one of four methods: (1) abstract qualities are symbolized by people or animals, as in the morality play, or as the epic hero who embodies a concept of virtue; (2) a normal individual is set in the midst of symbolic happenings, as in Dante and Bunyan; (3) a humour-character is subjected to a series of adventures that reveals his representative quality, as in *Don Quixote*; (4) some part of reality is symbolized by a different plane of reality, as in the *Battle of the Books*, or *The Purple Island*. Fielding used three of these, and frequently three at once, in his dramas, (only by special pleading can we get number (2) in the plays). In his prose-fiction he used all of them, and sometimes various combinations. I think, finally, that Fielding was fully conscious of his allegorical tendencies. Certainly the passage in *The Champion* of January 24, 1739-40, where he spoke of the attractiveness with which the lady, vice, is set forth before the world, indicates this: ". . . several treatises were written showing how men might attain the full possession of the former lady; or, to drop the allegory, rules were prescribed to make us complete rogues." Again in the paper of April 22, 1740, he used the word in the same sense, following an elaborate figurative indictment of Colley Cibber.

The same paper of April 22, 1740, illustrates his allegorical tendency; here he uses the fourth method of representing one plane of reality by another, in this case the comparison being life to the stage, or rather to Mr. Rich's pantomime entertainments. Having initiated his comparison, he draws his conclusion:

> In the same manner we are deceived in the grand pantomimes played on the stage of life, where there is often no less difference between appearances and reality of men and things, and where those who are either strangers to the springs of political action, judging by habits, posts, or titles, have actually mistaken men for heroes, patriots and politicians, who have been in fact as mere machines as any used by the aforesaid Mr. Rich: for when a man is absolutely void of capacity, it matters not whether his skin be stuffed with guts or straw, or whether his face be made of wood or brass.[12]

A straight political pantomime cannot be found to equal that told by Suetonius in his life of Caligula. From such considerations Fielding came to modern historians and to Colley Cibber.

The nondramatic writers whom Fielding most admired—Lucian, Cer-

---

[11] An untitled, unpublished Ph.D. dissertation in the Western Reserve University Library.

[12] This passage anticipates at least two in *Tom Jones*.

vantes, Swift—were allegorists. No wonder, then, that working as he was in a medium established by sentimentalists, he should find himself in very considerable difficulties. And it is no wonder that we find him trying to adapt the methods of the allegorist to the periodical. The allegorical "imaginary voyage," "Voyages of Mr. Job Vinegar," is in the direct Scriblerus-Gulliver tradition, with a leaf or two taken from Lucian. Again in the two papers of February 21 and March 11, 1739-40 the proposal for a home for fools would seem to result from the influence of "Laputa." Withal, Fielding was forced to speak out in straight didacticism, though even then his style tended to be analogical, and to enforce his ideas, he gave the other side of the picture in an elaborate ironic answer that would do credit to Swift (January 26 and 29, 1739-40).

## V

Coincidentally and providentially, Fielding was forced into nondramatic writing a few years before Richardson's example made it clear to him that prose narrative offered the real opportunity for inclusive humorous satiric farce, replete with far-reaching verbal symbols, employing contrast and comparison throughout. Fielding had to be true to the observed fact and to the vision of what seldom is but may be; implicitly Fielding's principal works after *The Champion*— *Jonathan Wild, Joseph Andrews, Tom Jones*—are like all great art, realistic and symbolic. These works, I think we shall be able to show, with his early developed artistic propensities in mind, are far more complicated artistic units than has been commonly thought.

# Shamela

## by Ian Watt

*Pamela: or, Virtue Rewarded* was published on November 6th, 1740. It immediately became the sensation of the literary season, and a swarm of attacks, parodies, and spurious continuations soon appeared to sour Richardson's remarkable and unexpected triumph; of these the first and easily the best was the eighteen-penny pamphlet *An Apology for the Life of Mrs. Shamela Andrews,* published on April 4th, 1741, under the name of Mr. Conny Keyber.

That Fielding was the author is indisputable. Horace Walpole and several other contemporaries privately recorded it as his in terms that do not suggest that there was any doubt about the matter; and in the last fifty years or so the labors of Austin Dobson, Wilbur Cross, Alan D. McKillop, Charles B. Woods,[1] and many others, have strengthened the attribution with a great deal of internal and external evidence. There is always an element of uncertainty about the authorship of any work that was published pseudonymously, remained unacknowledged by its author, and was not publicly attributed to him in his lifetime.[2] In the case of *Shamela,* however, these things are natural enough: Fielding was soon to become prominent as a novelist, journalist, and reforming magistrate, and was naturally unwilling to avow so indecent a work, especially once he knew, which he apparently did not when he wrote *Shamela,* that *Pamela* had actually been written by Richardson, whose *Clarissa* he was later to admire, and who was, moreover, a friend of his sister Sarah's; as

"Shamela." Introduction to Ian Watt's edition of *An Apology for the Life of Mrs. Shamela Andrews,* "Augustan Reprint Society," No. 57 (Los Angeles: William Andrews Clark Memorial Library, 1956), pp. 1-11. Reprinted by permission of the author and publisher; and slightly revised by the author.

[1] Whose excellent article, "The Authorship of *Shamela,*" *PQ,* XXV (1946), 248-272, gives full references to previous work on the subject.

[2] With one exception: the catalogue of books and copyrights offered at the bankruptcy sale of the bookseller Francis Cogan, July 10th, 1746, shows that his half interest in "Shamela, by Fielding" was sold to Andrew Millar (Alan D. McKillop, *Samuel Richardson: Printer and Novelist* [Chapel Hill: University of North Carolina Press. 1936], p. 74).

for the public, it was not likely to be very interested in the authorship of a minor squib which, after the three editions of 1741, was not reprinted until 1926.

One might have expected that the question would have been settled in 1804, when Mrs. Barbauld published her edition of Richardson's correspondence; for it made public a letter to Lady Bradshaigh naming Fielding as the author.[3] Nevertheless, the issue was avoided for nearly a century more, a fact which can perhaps best be explained as the result of the misplaced zeal of nineteenth century editors and scholars for Fielding's reputation or our morals, both matters, of course, which might more properly have been assumed to be no less invulnerable than Pamela's virtue.

I

*Shamela*, then, is Fielding's, and it is therefore his first prose fiction. The tale itself is accessible enough: the only facts it requires of its reader are those of life. Nor is the main range of satiric allusion much more recondite: it demands only a nodding acquaintance with *Pamela*, such as college easily supplies. The book opens and closes, however, with a series of secondary allusions which may call for some explanation. Any readers of the title page, for example, who do not have the works of Cibber and Middleton at their fingertips, may well wonder who is Mr. Conny Keyber?

Colley Cibber, actor, dramatist and Poet Laureate since 1730, was a very old enemy and butt of Fielding. His *Apology for the Life of Mr. Colley Cibber, Comedian, Written by Himself*, had been one of the best sellers of 1740; the title of *Shamela* is closely modeled on it, and there is, further, some similarity between Cibber's air of ingenuous self-satisfaction and the innocent self-revelation of Fielding's heroine. Here, however, the connection stops; and it is probable that Fielding used Cibber's name for his parody mainly because it would add to its topicality, and to the further discredit of a celebrity whom everyone would recognize under the patent and already established sobriquet of "keyber."

The "Conny" of "Conny Keyber" is a conflation of "Colley" and "Conyers," with the added appropriate suggestions of "coney," a dupe, and possibly of "cunny," latin "cunnus." Conyers was the given name of Dr. Middleton, Fellow of Trinity College, Cambridge, whom grateful colleagues had made "Principal Library-Keeper" of the University as some compensation for his vigorous, unsuccessful, and ruinously expensive attacks on the Master of his college, the redoubtable Dr. Bentley. Middleton had published a *Life of Cicero* early in 1741, and we know from *Joseph Andrews*[4] that Fielding had little regard for the work itself; but what drew his fire in *Shamela* was the adulatory inanity of Middleton's "Epistle

---

[3] *Correspondence of Samuel Richardson*, IV, 286; probably written late in 1749.
[4] Bk. III, chap. vi.

Dedicatory" to his patron, John, Lord Hervey. This courtier and poetaster, Pope's Sporus, was the Lord Privy Seal of Walpole's crumbling administration; and his effeminacy, which had already excited a good deal of satiric comment, explains the terms of Fielding's dedicatory letter "To Miss Fanny, &c."—an appellation Pope had already established. The letter is actually a very close parody of Middleton's effusion; compare, for instance, its third, sixth, and final paragraphs with these passages from Middleton:

I cannot forbear boasting, that some Parts of my present Work have been brightened by the Strokes of your Lordship's Pencil.

That singular Temperance in Diet, in which your Lordship perseveres . . .

It was Cicero who instructed me to write; your Lordship who rewards me for writing.

[*First*, then, Madam, I must tell the World, that you have tickled up and brightened many Strokes in this Work by your Pencil.

[*Fourthly*, You have a Virtue which enables you to rise early and study hard, and that is, forbearing to over-eat yourself, and this in spite of all the luscious Temptations of Puddings and Custards, exciting the Brute (as Dr. *Woodward* calls it) to rebel. This is a Virtue which I can greatly admire, though I much question whether I could imitate it.

[. . . it was *Euclid* who taught me to write. It is you, Madam, who pay me for Writing.]

Middleton had also commended Hervey's habit of early rising, of "spending a useful day, before others begin to enjoy it," and had recorded his own matutinal visits "when I have found you commonly engaged with the classical writers of Greece and Rome." The vignette was irresistible, and in the fifth paragraph of his dedicatory letter Fielding delightedly developed the opening afforded by the ambiguity of "engaged" into the kind of sexual innuendo appropriate to Hervey's reputation. We must agree with the verdict of Thomas Dampier, later Dean of Durham, who writes in a private letter of 1741 that "the Dedication to Lord Hervey has been very justly and prettily ridiculed by Fielding in a Dedication to a Pamphlet called 'Shamela' which he wrote to burlesque . . . 'Pamela,' a Romance in low Life." [5]

So much for the title page and dedicatory letter: the second of the "Letters to the Editor" introduces yet another polemic note. Unlike Fielding, Cibber and Middleton were both Administration supporters, and this was no doubt an added reason for Fielding's mockery: but the political issue is not specifically raised until John Puff's letter. There

[5] McKillop, *op. cit.*, p. 73.

Fielding ironically suggests that the talents of the creator of *Shamela* might even be equal to no less a task than writing a biography of "his Honour"—Walpole, and follows this insult with an injurious explanation of that politician's notorious complaisance about his wife's infidelities. The political aspect of *Shamela*, however, is very minor, and we must pass on to the letters of the two parsons which serve as introduction and conclusion to the narrative itself if we are to get to grips with Fielding's main intentions and appreciate *Shamela* as—among other things—a topical literary, religious, and moral satire.

When Parson Oliver, who bears the name of Fielding's early tutor, speaks of "an epidemical Phrenzy now raging in Town" over *Pamela*, we are confronted with yet another example of the Augustan rearguard action against the swelling ranks of the Grub-Street Dunces. It was bad enough that Cibber should make 1500 pounds from his *Apology* and Middleton much more from his *Cicero*,[6] especially when Fielding himself was in the literary and economic doldrums, the dramatic career ended, that of the novelist and magistrate not yet begun; but the simultaneous furor over *Pamela* must have looked like the most dangerous conspiracy of all against the Republic of Letters, since the clergy seemed to be the ringleaders.

Fielding probably had two things mainly in mind when he made Parson Oliver attack "the confederating to cry up a nonsensical ridiculous Book, (I believe the most extensively so of any ever yet published)." There was, first, Richardson's insertion of some thirty pages of laudatory letters in the second and subsequent editions of *Pamela*: puffing was ancient enough, but never had it been so copious and shameless, and Fielding could make his satirical point merely by culling the riper fatuities from the original—the passages in quotation marks in Tickletext's first letter are all, with one brief exception,[7] cited verbatim from the prefatory matter to *Pamela*.[8]

The second, and much more important thing that Fielding had in mind in attacking "the confederating to cry up" *Pamela* was the unprecedented and enthusiastic collaboration of the clergy. Dr. Benjamin Slocock had even recommended it from the pulpit of St. Saviour's Church, Southwark, and, it was rumored, had received ten guineas for the favor. When

---

[6] Richard H. Barker, *Mr. Cibber of Drury Lane* ("Columbia University Studies in English and Comparative Literature," No. 143 [New York: Columbia University Press, 1939]), p. 194; Conyers Middleton, *Miscellaneous Works*, 1755, I, 397.

[7] On p. 3, l. 21, "innocent story" is changed into "&c"; cf. *Romeo and Juliet*, Act II, scene I, line 38. The "dear Monysyllable" toasted on p. 30, l. 29, is glossed in Eric Partridge, *Dictionary of Slang and Unconventional English*. [References are to the text of Mr. Watt's edition, which is a facsimile of the second edition of November 3, 1741. Ed.]

[8] The passages, which were actually written by Aaron Hill, can conveniently be compared in the Augustan Society's valuable reprint of the Introduction to *Pamela* (ed. Sheridan W. Baker, Jr., No. 48, 1954).

Fielding, therefore, put the rubric "Necessary to be had in all Families" on the title page of *Shamela*, and made Tickletext compare the *Whole Duty of Man* unfavorably with *Pamela*, he was only going a little further than Richardson's clerical *claque*. Pope himself, incidentally, had been numbered in the chorus, and in the charming eulogy "The Editor to *Himself*" Fielding seems to be embroidering his no doubt intentionally ambiguous encomium that *Pamela* "would do more good than many volumes of sermons."

One other religious aspect of *Shamela* perhaps calls for brief explanation. Shamela, we notice, is like her avatar in owning a little library of devotional as well as other reading; and she twice mentions *A Short Account of God's Dealings with the Reverend Mr. George Whitefield*. Whitefield had published this work in 1740 as a reply to an attack on Methodism and on him personally by Dr. Joseph Trapp in the previous year; and when Parson Williams takes as his text "Be Not Righteous Overmuch" he is following Trapp in his first sermon, which had provided the keynote for the subsequent polemics.[9] Public interest in the rise of Methodism, then, supplied Fielding with yet another set of topical allusions: and it is also, no doubt, partly responsible for the expansion of the role of Parson Williams, who is a very minor figure in Richardson, but who in *Shamela* becomes a caricature of a canting and hypocritical enthusiast.

Fielding's religious target in *Shamela*, however, is certainly not the Methodists as such, but rather those of any persuasion who are governed by what in *Joseph Andrews* he called "the detestable doctrine of faith against good works."[10] This emphasis on the social and moral virtues is typical of Fielding; and it is the central idea in *Shamela*, since it brings together Fielding's two main polemic purposes—the attack on those who had puffed *Pamela* as a book likely to promote the cause of virtue and religion, and the attack on Richardson's interpretation of his heroine's character. The domain of faith is inward and subjective: those who profess it may be deceiving themselves, or they may intentionally be deceiving others; we cannot test their professions any more than we can test the oft-protested purity of Pamela's motives; but we have a right to be suspicious, and a duty both to warn those who are duped and to expose those who sham.

## II

These dual intentions give *Shamela* its basic narrative strategy. Fielding very ingeniously outdid Richardson in his pretense that he was only the editor of authentic letters: for he provided two independent sets of cor-

---

[9] See Sheridan W. Baker, Jr.'s Introduction to his edition of *Shamela* (Berkeley and Los Angeles: University of California Press, 1953), pp. xv-xx.

[10] *Joseph Andrews*, Bk. I, chap. xvii.

respondence. We begin with a discussion between two clergymen about *Pamela*; then, once the framework of moral and literary criticism has been built up, Oliver discovers the real letters which prove his view of the case; and when these have been given, the two parallel actions—the disabusing of Tickletext and the unmasking of Shamela—are brought together in the final letter where Tickletext acknowledges that he had grievously misunderstood the whole matter, before telling us in his last postscript that justice has at last overtaken Shamela and her paramour.

Fielding's retelling of the *Pamela* story for his own purposes keeps very close to the original incidents; but gives them a contrary psychological explanation. Shamela feigns virtue only because Booby's inexperience makes her see that instead of "making a little Fortune by my Person" she can easily make "a great one by my Vartue." What changes Fielding makes are not without warrant in the original: Mr. B., for example, had noted Pamela's "lucky Knack of falling into Fits when she pleases"—it was easy enough to show that it was not luck but cunning; and even Shamela's intrigue with Parson Williams is licensed by Mr. B.'s suggestion that his interest had been amorous rather than pastoral.

This aspect of Shamela is obvious enough to any reader of *Pamela*, and has often been analyzed. But some other elements of the satire have perhaps met with less notice. Fielding parodies Richardson's manner as cruelly as his moral. He is particularly successful in hitting off the incongruity between Pamela's pretensions to literate gentility and the rusticity, not to say boorishness, of much of the dialogue: some of the badinage between Pamela and her "Angel" is not far removed from such a report on her master's courtship as the following from Shamela: "Says he . . . Hussy, Gipsie, Hypocrite, Saucebox, Boldface, get out of my Sight, get out of my Sight, or I will lend you such a Kick in the —— I don't care to repeat the Word, but he meant my hinder part." The juxtaposition of exalted sentiments and inconsequential domestic details, which was a characteristic Richardsonian innovation in making the narrative seem real, is also very nicely taken off by Fielding: "And so we talked of honourable Designs till Supper-time. And Mrs. Jewkes and I supped upon a hot buttered Apple-pie." Excellent, too, is the hit at Richardson's use of present-tense narration in highly improbable circumstances: "Mrs. Jervis and I are just in Bed, and the Door unlocked; if my Master should come—Odsbobs! I hear him just coming in at the Door. You see I write in the present Tense, as Parson Williams says."

In general, then, Fielding unerringly selects the most dubious aspects of *Pamela*, and drives home its crucial moral and psychological ambiguities. The eighteenth century was a great age of burlesque; there is much to be said for the view that the best of Fielding's previous works had been burlesques such as *The Tragedy of Tragedies* and *The Grub-Street Opera*; and *Shamela* may be seen as the happy fruit of Fielding's own long experience in the genre.

But of course *Shamela* also looks forward. Like Hemingway's *Torrents of Spring*, it goes far beyond its original intention as parody, and takes on a life of its own. Not only so: Fielding, again like Hemingway, is ridiculing someone from whom he has learned much, more, perhaps, than he knows: for there is substantial truth in Richardson's assertion that "Pamela, which [Fielding] abused in his Shamela, taught him how to write to please. . . . Before his Joseph Andrews (hints and names taken from that story, with a lewd and ungenerous engraftment) the poor man wrote without being read. . . ." [11]

*Shamela*, of course, is not a faultless performance. Some of the details show signs of its hasty composition—there is some confusion, for example, about the extent of Mrs. Jewkes's complicity in Shamela's designs. It may also be questioned whether Shamela's very conscious hypocrisy about sexual matters is in harmony with the apparently unconscious nature of her religious hypocrisy; and there is perhaps an analogous contradiction between Tickletext's main role as a foolish dupe, and his conscious and unashamed revelation to Oliver of the aphrodisiacal effects of reading *Pamela*. At other times Fielding's love of the facetious tends to interfere with his main intention; and it is difficult to reconcile his many scabrous innuendoes with the serious didactic purpose he puts into the mouth of Parson Oliver.

*Shamela*, then, has many diverse elements: in matter, both coffee-house polemic and timeless satire on human folly; in manner, both precise stylistic parody and uproarious burlesque. This diversity naturally puzzles the literary historian, who is called on to place a work that is both a footnote to the *Dunciad* and a prologue to *Tom Jones*; while the critic, recognizing much of the brilliant invention, the lively narrative pace, the human insight, and the fortifying gusto found in Fielding's novels, may well have difficulty in determining how successfully the varied aims and methods of *Shamela* have been combined. There is a further difficulty: the ultimate criteria by which so bawdy a work can properly be judged have not, to my knowledge, been satisfactorily established. Grave moral reservations are doubtless mandatory. But perhaps I should leave them to my betters, and end instead by revealing that, if perfect honesty in these matters were to be made possible by some guarantee of academic immunity, I could find one reader of *Shamela* at least willing to testify that—to use a metaphor dear to Fielding—this salty *hors d'oeuvre* is more to his taste than some of the more imposing dishes on the Pierian buffet.

[11] See note 3.

# Joseph Andrews and Pamela

## by Maynard Mack

### I

Henry Fielding's first novel, *Joseph Andrews,* was published in 1742, partly in parody of Samuel Richardson's first novel, *Pamela,* which had appeared two years before. Pamela is the story of a servant girl who relates to her parents in a series of meticulously detailed letters how her chastity is laid siege to by her master Mr. B., how she passionately resists his stratagems, and how, at last, having gradually fallen in love with her tormentor, as he with her, she becomes his lawful wife. On the slim thread of this action, Richardson had suspended a full-dress psychological study of his heroine, the first such study in English fiction, where he manifested somewhat fumblingly a talent for minute interior delineation of female character that was to make his next novel *Clarissa* (1747-1748) a work of enduring, and somewhat tedious, power.

If this innovation in character had been the merit Richardson claimed for *Pamela,* it would probably never have awakened Fielding's comic muse. But as the book's preface as well as its original title made clear— *Pamela: or Virtue Rewarded. Now first published in order to cultivate the Principles of Virtue and Religion in the Minds of the Youth of both Sexes. A Narrative which has its Foundation in Truth and Nature*— Richardson attributed to his work certain virtues of ethical insight and general truthfulness which it simply did not have. The story, intended as a moral exemplum, was actually a rather vulgar bourgeois success story, matching at some essential points Richardson's own rise (from an industrious and prudent apprenticeship in a printing house to marriage with his master's daughter and succession to the firm) and in fact the rise of the business classes generally in the century in which he wrote. Likewise his Pamela, intended as a model woman, was in many respects simply a pioneer capitalist, a middle-class *entrepreneur* of virtue, who

*"Joseph Andrews and Pamela"* (Editor's title). Introduction to Maynard Mack's edition of *Joseph Andrews* (New York: Holt, Rinehart and Winston, Inc., 1948), pp. ii-xxiv. Copyright © 1948 by Maynard Mack. Reprinted by permission of the author and Holt, Rinehart and Winston, Inc.

looked on her chastity not as a condition of spirit but as a commodity
to be vended for the purpose of getting on.

From Fielding's point of view, Richardson was equally short of general
truth. Though still a young man (thirty-four), Fielding had seen a good
deal more of the world than Richardson, now a prosperous middle-
aged printer, who had always been confined to his trade. Fielding had
been educated at Eton and Leyden and had spent most of his adult life
in the rough and tumble of literary London, carving out a career for
himself, first, as a comic dramatist, and now more recently, in journalism
and the law—the latter sometimes taking him as circuit justice into that
vivid and barbarous life of country inns and alehouses which forms the
basis of both *Joseph Andrews* and *Tom Jones*. To an observant mind,
thus experienced, Pamela was bound to seem a falsification of the world of
fact. Apart from the initial improbabilities—improbable less in Pamela's
extraordinary virtue than in the clumsiness of her persecutor, which is
always just great enough to allow her to escape, and the number, length,
and literacy of her letters—there was the distortion and disproportion resulting from Richardson's intense magnification of one character and one
theme. The sprawling diversified life of eighteenth century humanity (so
it must have struck Fielding) was pared down in *Pamela* to one silly
gentleman and a handful of (mainly) genteel servants. The multifarious
conflicts of good and evil were shrunk to a purely physical struggle
against the snares of Mr. B. Large and complicated issues of moral behavior were diluted to the single question of female chastity, and in fact
more precisely, middle-class respectability. While of those elaborate *self-
deceptions*, on which, as Fielding knew, much of the world's evil turns,
Richardson showed no consciousness at all.

These are the weaknesses that engage Fielding's comic imagination in
*Joseph Andrews*. Instead of Pamela's amazing literacy, he supplies a
heroine who can neither read nor write. Because of Pamela's alarms about
her chastity, he supplies a man as hero, whose chastity will be always in
his own power. Since Pamela betters herself by her virtue, Joseph refuses
to better himself by his—in fact, keeps himself pure, and poor, for the
sake of Fanny, who is yet lower in the social scale than he. Pamela is
assaulted with monotonous regularity by Mr. B. (a name Fielding expands
to Mr. Booby); therefore Fanny will be often attacked, but with the
difference of being thoroughly afraid. Pamela fancies herself on her
gentility; Fielding's Slipslop and Grave-airs will fancy themselves on
theirs. Pamela affects virtue; the same affectation, in *Joseph Andrews*,
will be dealt out with a liberal hand. But these are surface connections
only. Fielding's serious criticism of *Pamela*, whether or not he intended
it as such, is the kind of world that *Joseph Andrews* creates. With its
squires, ladies, waiting women, doctors, lawyers, parsons, innkeepers,
prudes, and rogues, it is a more inclusive world than Richardson's, and
also a more profoundly familiar one, being motivated not by sex alone

but also by the humdrum motions of avarice, stupidity, vanity, courage, and love. More important, as Coleridge emphasized when he said that picking up Fielding after Richardson was like emerging from a sick room heated with stoves to an open lawn on a breezy day, Fielding's world is wholesome, spontaneous, and alive. In contrast to Richardson's method-ized morality, Fielding can contemplate a goodness that does not always know how to be consistent with itself, that rarely announces its advent in pious clichés, that acts as often from impulse as from principle, and that embodies itself, typically, not in "exemplary" characters like Pamela and Clarissa, but in the postilion who gives Joseph his coat—though he was transported for robbing a hen roost the next year, the Tow-wouses' good-hearted maid Betty—who has no virtue in Richardson's sense at all, and Parson Adams, whose decorum is as tattered as his cassock but whose dignity nothing impairs.

II

Though *Pamela* supplied the occasion for *Joseph Andrews*, the impor-tant features of Fielding's novel came to him from other sources—from habits of craftsmanship acquired while writing for the stage, from the mock-heroic style with which he had experimented in his plays, and from the *Don Quixote* of Cervantes, where he could find fully elaborated, out of an impatience with high-flown romances that was fully equal to his own, a telling formula for combatting them. The serious danger in romancing, Cervantes seems to have felt, lay in diverting moral idealism into tilts with sensational or merely apparent evils—giants who are only windmills —when all about real evil walks unchallenged in homelier shapes. To illustrate this situation, he launched his crack-brained hero, and *ingénu* idealist whose ideas of the world had been entirely formed on tales of villainous giants, distressed damsels, and miraculous rescues (the ancestors of *Pamela*), on the actual roads of sixteenth-century Spain, and derived from the resulting collision a rich ambiguous comedy. Partly the comedy is from the discomfiture of Quixote as the real world breaks about his ears, but partly, in the background, it is from the discomfiture of the world as it finds it cannot break his spirit.

Fielding's treatment of Parson Adams is based on this. Adams, too, has built a dream world, in his case from the tenets of a simple Christianity and the Greek and Roman moralists, which collides head-on with the real one, and he is therefore, like his forebear, partly hero and partly dupe. But he is dupe and hero in a peculiarly complicated way. Dupe at one level, like Quixote, when we see him put upon by every rogue whom he encounters, he is dupe at quite another when we see him self-deceived by a theoretical ideal of conduct that his own nature will not support. Thus his theory is pacific, but he is always in the thick of fights; his theory preaches Stoic insulation, but when the news comes that his little boy is drowned he dismisses Joseph's comfort while the tears trickle down into his bosom—just as, a moment later, when the report proves false, he dances about the room like a man possessed. In the same way, while Adams is a hero like Quixote in having a fund of idealism that no mis-adventures can exhaust, he is also a hero in the respect that his illusory world is closer than Quixote's to a reasonable facsimile of what ought to be. We fall in love with Quixote, but we could not choose his world to live in; Adams' world we might. This fact makes Adams an unusually effective instrument of social criticism. His education in the world's ways is to a large extent a criticism of them by a higher standard, the standard that he asserts so appealingly when threatened by Lady Booby with the loss of his place. Thus in a sense his career can be looked on as a parable of the eighteenth-century conscience uncovering some realities to which it has been blind, or even (to give the parable its broadest terms) the good in human nature uncovering the bad. Yet at the same time he represents like Quixote those naïve innocencies of goodness—its tendency to identify itself with partial platforms (Adams' classical, Quixote's romantic theo-ries), or to miscalculate the number and quality of its foes—which con-tinually blunt its force.

Fielding's dramatic training shows itself in his method of structuring his story. Book IV and the London scenes in I are hardly more than translation into prose fiction of contemporary comedy of manners and stage farce; while in Books II and III Fielding avoids the narrative monotony inseparable from previous picaresque and adventure tales by breaking his action into scenes. He is able in this way to segregate im-portant incidents from less important ones and to juxtapose them, as in drama, so that they comment on each other; the impassioned clerical debate of I, xvii, interrupted by the low lay conduct of Betty and Mr. Tow-wouse, is a case in point. Stagecraft also taught Fielding to delineate his characters primarily through idiom. Adams' Latin tags, Slipslop's malapropisms, Trulliber's "I caal'd vurst," Mrs. Tow-wouse's "Common charity, a f—t!" Lady Booby's "did ever mortal hear of a man's virtue!" Pounce's "How can any man complain of hunger in a country where such excellent salads are to be gathered in every field?" remind us that there is only a little exaggeration in the saying that you can open Fielding anywhere and tell who is speaking by the accent. More important, Field-ing uses structure, as a playwright does, to articulate his theme. The two poles of value in *Joseph Andrews* (as later in *Tom Jones*) are the country-world and the city, neither perfect, but the former superior to the latter because more honest. In the first book the relative honesty of the country penetrates to the city in the person of Joseph and, having re-sisted corruption there, is reinforced in its withdrawal by another of its representatives, Adams. In the last book the relative hypocrisy of the city-world (Lady Booby, Beau Didapper, and the rest) invades the country and is again defeated, the action alternating back and forth between

country and city symbols: Lady Booby's house, where everybody is both
lickerish and affected (and even Adams stumbles into other people's beds);
and the parson's own dwelling, where the vexations, follies, and little
triumphs of unpretentious human nature keep their homely course. In
the meantime, throughout the story, these basic poles of value have been
kept before us, not only in the adventures to which Joseph and Adams
are subjected, but in the two symbolic narratives (foreshadowings of the
stories of Mrs. Fitzpatrick and the Man of the Hill in *Tom Jones*) which
treat the fortunes of Leonora and Mr. Wilson.

As Fielding's preface shows, he was quick to see that the tradition of
mock-heroic offered one of the best positions from which to underscore
those modes of the ridiculous that arise from affectation. Affectations
being, in one possible way of looking at them, the adoption of heroic
stances by persons not entitled to them (the pretense that *our* natures,
passions, acts are profound, irresistible, deliberate, like those of heroes),
the easiest way of deflating them is to let them, like Aesop's frog, inflate
themselves a little more. Fielding accomplishes this inflation, like all the
great practitioners of mock-heroic, primarily through his style. He includes, of course, for what he calls his classical reader, a multitude of
explicit mock-epic jokes—ranging from Homeric similes through the
epic genealogy of Joseph's cudgel to the hilarious and surprisingly cir-
cumstantial travesty of *Oedipus* at the close—where the humor is largely
at the expense of epic forms and the heroic attitude toward life. But
the subtler and more characteristic type of mock-heroic in Fielding is
that which is illustrated in passages like the following. "Curse his
beauties," says Lady Booby of Joseph, ". . . which can basely descend
to this despicable wench, and be ungratefully deaf to all the honours I do
him. And can I then love this monster?" In passages of this sort, the
mock-heroic style is fully functional, enabling the author to put before
us in a single dimension both the character as it understands itself and
as he wants us to understand it.

### III

The difference in their methods of characterization that Johnson
noticed when he said that Fielding saw only the hands of the clock,
Richardson the wheels (the remark was intended to disparage Fielding),
seems to be in reality a quality of the difference between the comic mode
in fiction and what, for want of a better name, may be called the tragic
one. Character in the tragic mode, though it need not end in death,
always inhabits, like Richardson's Clarissa, a world of choices followed
by consequences. The logic of events always involves this kind of character, and at the close of its story one is compelled to say of it in one sense or
other what Shakespeare's Falstaff says over the body of Sir Walter Blunt:
"There's honor for you." For the tragic emphasis seems to be on the

uniqueness and finality of human experience, as man the transient individual moves through his world from a situation which is a datum to a destiny developing from himself. The curve of tragic action, in other words, is a curve of self-discovery. On the other hand, the comic curve is one of self-exposure. Here the emphasis is on the permanence and typicality of human experience, as projected in persistent social species whose sufficient destiny is simply to go on revealing themselves to us. For this reason, the great comic characters of literature, whether Shakespeare's, Fielding's, or Dickens', do not *essentially* change. They are enveloped in events without being involved by them, and they remain immutable like Fielding's lawyer, who has been "alive . . . these four thousand years" and seems good for as many more. Thus at the close of *Joseph Andrews*, Lady Booby, on the one hand, and Parson Adams, on the other, are as self-deceived as they were at the start; they have uncovered others, but they have not discovered themselves. Had they done so—had Fielding allowed them to do so, in any of the senses which matter in art—they would have lost precisely that perpetual possession of being well-deceived in which their comic essence consists.

The same distinction affects the nature of Fielding's plots. In tragic life, to paraphrase Meredith, passions spin the plot; it is the web which the tragic character weaves unwittingly for his own ensnaring, and in the great tragic fictions one is hardly aware of it except as pointing the lines of growth. In comedy, plot is likely to be felt as something imposed; it is the author's net whose function is to arrest character and display it. Hence we find in both *Joseph Andrews* and *Tom Jones* a calculated tripartite system—country, road, and city—designed to house and interrelate a wide range of characters who do not fundamentally develop. Hence, too, the surprises and reversals of these novels do not offend us, because they do not rupture character but help exhibit it. Joseph's elevation to the gentry, though as improbable intrinsically as Pamela's (which it satirizes), is acceptable for the reason that it brings all the characters into new and comic postures vis-à-vis each other, yet does not require a readjustment in our understanding of them. On the other hand, Pamela's marriage with a master she has always thought a villain and a boor shocks us; it is a denouement thrust upon a development which it contradicts.

These features of Fielding's plot and character seem to be dictated by the distinctive nature of the comic point of view. If we are usually aware with comic characters that we are looking around them as well as at them, the reason seems to be that comedy presents us with life apprehended in the form of spectacle rather than in the form of experience. In the tragic mode, since the meaning lies in the protagonist's consciousness of the uniqueness of this moment, this choice, this irreversible event for him, our consciousness must be continuous with his, and we are given a point of view inside that consciousness, or at any rate inside the consciousness of some other character who can interpret it for us. But in comedy the case is different because there the consciousness that matters most is ours and is a consciousness of the typicality of *all* moments, choices, and events. Again and again in life-as-spectacle (though only once in life-as-experience), the same moments, choices, and events recur: a Lady Booby lays her hand "accidentally" on a Joseph's and asks if he has ever been in love; or an Adams descants half the night with an acquaintance on contempt of riches while both lack money to pay their bill. For this kind of vision we must be not inside the character but outside him, in a position that compels us to observe discrepancies between the persuasive surfaces of personalities as they see themselves and these personalities as they are. Thus the point of view that ours must be continuous with in comedy is not the character's but the author's. Laughter, Bergson says, implies a complicity with other laughers. This is only another way of saying that the comic artist subordinates the presentation of life as experience, where the relationship between ourselves and the characters experiencing it is the primary one, to the presentation of life as spectacle, where the primary relationship is between himself and us as onlookers. The imposed plot, the static character are among the comic writer's surest means of establishing this rapport, and these are implemented in Fielding's case by devices of comic irony and mock-heroic, which always imply complicity, by serious essays and reflections, which poise him and us outside the action, and by the formality of his highly articulated prose, whose elegant surface keeps us coolly separated from the violences, grotesqueries, and postures that it mirrors. The result of all this, in novels like *Joseph Andrews* and *Tom Jones*, is the continuous conversion of act into reflection and experience into spectacle, which seems to be the secret of the comic art. Our reactions to reality, we may remind ourselves, depend upon the context. Even a rabbit, were it suddenly to materialize before us without complicity, could be a terrifying event. What makes us laugh is our secure consciousness of the magician and his hat.

# Comic Resolution
# in Fielding's *Joseph Andrews*

## *by Mark Spilka*

### I

Though the night adventures at Booby Hall are among the most memorable scenes in *Joseph Andrews*, many scholars tend to ignore them or to minimize their importance. Generally speaking, they pluck the adventures out of context and file them away—out of sight, out of mind—among even more colorful bedroom antics within the picaresque tradition. Thus J. B. Priestley writes:

> Such chapters of accidents are very familiar to students of the *picaresque*, and all that need be said of this one is that there is some slight relation to character in it . . . but that it is not enough to make the episode anything more than a piece of comic business of a very familiar type. Smollett could bustle through such rough-and-tumble business just as well, if not better. . . .[1]

Priestley is right as far as he goes, but he forgets that *Joseph Andrews* is more novel than picaresque tale and that the novel requires special handling. In the picaresque tale there is little or no dramatic connection between one episode and the next, and the critic can lift things out of context to his heart's content. But with the more fully developed novel form he must show how an episode—lifted *from* a tradition—has been fitted *into* the scheme of a given book. Certainly this is the proper approach to the escapades at Booby Hall, the last major comic scenes in *Joseph Andrews*—scenes which involve all the major characters in the book and both aspects of the central theme, the lust-chastity theme. Yet with all this in mind it may still be argued that the Booby Hall affair is a simple comic interlude, or diversion, which Fielding inserted at

"Comic Resolution in Fielding's *Joseph Andrews*." From *College English*, XV (1953), 11-19. Reprinted by permission of the author and the National Council of Teachers of English.
[1] "Parson Adams," in *The English Comic Characters* (New York: Dodd, Mead, 1925), p. 113.

the most crucial point in the novel to increase suspense and at the same time to vary the fare. On the surface there is some truth to this assertion: the night adventures are sandwiched between the all-important chapters in which the incest problem is first introduced then happily solved. But the argument breaks down before a simple comparison: in the famous knocking-at-the gate scene in *Macbeth*, the commonplace is used (according to De Quincey) to offset and heighten the essential strangeness and horror of murder; if the "diversion" argument holds true, the same function should be performed by the bedroom scenes in *Joseph Andrews*; but as any honest reader will admit, these scenes perform precisely the opposite function—that is, they neither increase nor heighten the dramatic intensity of the incest plot; rather, they lessen its seriousness and achieve a special importance of their own. In the next chapter, for example, the company are "all very merry at breakfast, and Joseph and Fanny rather more cheerful than the preceding night"; it becomes obvious that some sort of emotional purgation has occurred and that the resolution of the main plot will be anticlimactic.

All this seems normal enough for a comedy based on character rather than on situation. As Aurélien Digeon points out, "The ending is necessarily the weak point in works of this kind. It is almost always engineered from without; for passions never stop working nor come to an 'end.'" [2] Unfortunately, Digeon fails to add here that if passions never stop working, they are sometimes resolved, and that it is the business of a good comic writer to resolve them. In the night adventures at Booby Hall, Fielding has done just that; with the aid of condensed, violent action, he has stood his book on its head, shaken out all the themes and passions, and resolved them through warmhearted laughter. If this interpretation seems farfetched, its essential soundness may become evident as we pay more attention to the lust-chastity theme, to Fielding's theory of humor, to the role of nakedness in the novel, and, finally, to two of the most comic figures in the book, Parson Adams and Mrs. Slipslop. As for the other relevant characters—Joseph Andrews, Fanny Goodwill, Lady Booby, and Beau Didapper—we need only note here that the first two embody all the natural health, goodness, and beauty which Fielding admired, while the last two embody much of the vice and artificiality he deplored.

## II

In order to parody Richardson's *Pamela*, Fielding built *Joseph Andrews* around a central moral problem: the preservation of (and the assault upon) chastity. On the one hand, Joseph Andrews must protect his virtue from such lustful creatures as Lady Booby, Mrs. Slipslop, and Betty the chambermaid; on the other, Fanny Goodwill must withstand

[2] *The Novels of Fielding* (London: Routledge, 1925), p. 60.

the attacks of a beau, a squire, a rogue, and a servant. But as most writers have observed, the scope of the novel is much broader than this. Fielding saw affectation in two of its forms, vanity and hypocrisy, as the "only source of the true Ridiculous," and he hoped to expose these qualities wherever he found them. Accordingly, he also designed his novel along more general lines: three virtuous, good-natured persons—Joseph, Fanny, and Adams—must be thrust through every level of society as exemplars or as touchstones and instruments for exposing vanity and hypocrisy, and, just as important, goodness and kindness, in whomever they meet. Adams will be the foremost touchstone, since his religious position and his personal traits—innocence, simplicity, bravery, compassion, haste, pedantry, forgetfulness—will always pitch him into a good deal of trouble; yet, once in trouble, his virtues will make him stand out in complete contrast to those who take advantage of him. Finally, in his perfect innocence he will always be the main instrument for exposing his own mild affectations.

But, as these remarks indicate, Adams' position is somewhat ambiguous with regard to Fielding's formula for the ridiculous in humor. Like his predecessor, Don Quixote, he cuts a bizarre figure outwardly, but, at the same time, his inner dignity remains unassailable: as *Joseph Andrews* tells us, true virtue can never be ridiculed, and we know that Adams, however outlandish, is truly virtuous—so that he stands half within Fielding's theory of humor and half without.[3] But this theory is, after all, static and reductive rather than organic. Through shrewd analysis Fielding has called attention to the affectations, the *particular* qualities which make men appear in a ridiculous light. But through his admiration for Cervantes he has unconsciously seized on the principle of the *comic figure*—the whole man who is at once lovable and ridiculous, whose entire character is involved in each of his humorous actions, and whose character must be established through time and incident, in the reader's mind, before he becomes "wholly" laughable. To put it in different terms, when someone we know and like is involved in a ridiculous action, then the humor of the situation broadens and quickens to include our identification with and sympathy for that person. A sudden or prolonged juxtaposition of his inner dignity with his outer "awkwardness" produces a state of mixed emotions in us—love, sympathy, and identification, as well as condescension—and this state is released or resolved, in turn, through laughter.[4] The point can be made clearer perhaps through a

[3] In Book III, chap. vi, Joseph says, "I defy the wisest man in the world to turn a good action into ridicule. . . . He, who should endeavour it, would be laughed at himself, instead of making others laugh."

[4] Fielding's (and Hobbes') theory of humor depends upon the reader's feeling of superiority toward the person ridiculed. But in practice Fielding tapped a second psychological source by working upon our sympathies: all of us know how it feels to be misunderstood or defeated, and such feelings help us to maintain a close identification with likable comic figures—Adams, Quixote, Chaplin. If, as Maynard Mack insists (in

modern analogy: the amorphous Keystone Cops amuse us (at least they used to) in accord with Fielding's theory of the ridiculous—that is to say, they lose their false outer dignity in falls and madcap fights; yet when Charlie Chaplin puts up a magnificent bluff in the boxing ring (as in *City Lights*), our laughter becomes much warmer and far more sympathetic in quality—Chaplin's bluff may be ridiculous, but the man who bluffs is brave, and we have learned something of this through time, situation, and the development of character; we are prepared, that is, for his simultaneous display of inner dignity and outer vanity in the boxing ring, and our laughter is accordingly that much richer. One Keystone Cop is much like the next, but Chaplin has become a unique and appealing figure in our eyes—and in a similar manner so has Parson Adams. Our respect, love, and admiration for Adams continue to grow through the length of *Joseph Andrews*. And only when his character has been firmly established in our minds (and in the same vein, only when the lust-chastity theme has been worked for all it is worth) can the night scenes at Booby Hall occur. Place these scenes earlier in the book and they will strike us as meaningless horseplay; but at the end of the book we are prepared for them—Parson Adams is now familiar to us as a well-developed comic figure, and his nakedness strikes us with symbolic force.

As a matter of fact the spectacle of nakedness is significantly common (though not always symbolic) in *Joseph Andrews*. Fanny, Joseph, Adams, Lady Booby, Mrs. Slipslop, Beau Didapper, Betty the chambermaid, Mr. Tow-wouse—all appear at one time or another and for various reasons, in a state of partial or complete undress. In the early chapters, for example, Joseph is beaten and stripped by robbers and left on the road to die; when a carriage passes, Fielding "tests" each of the passengers by his willingness to accept Joseph *as he is,* for what he is—a defenseless human being. And late in the book, when Adams appears in a nightshirt (the usual eighteenth century equivalent for nakedness), Fielding tests, in effect, *our* willingness, as good-natured readers, to take Adams for what he is. It should not surprise us, therefore, that a definite symbolic equation between nakedness, on the one hand, and innocence and worth, on the other, occurs in other portions of Fielding's work: Squire Allworthy also appears in his nightshirt, for example, in the opening pages of *Tom Jones;* and in *The Champion* for January 24, 1740, Fielding even cites Plato to the effect that men would love virtue if they could see her naked. This platitude is put to good use in *Joseph Andrews*, though the problem there is to "expose" or "lay bare" both virtue and affectation, often in the same man.

---

*Joseph Andrews*, ed. Maynard Mack [New York: Rinehart, 1948]), we view comedy from the outside, as a spectacle, this is only our conscious point of view; at the deeper emotional level we are actively engaged in the spectacle. Of course, all art demands some form of audience participation at this level, but the point deserves re-emphasis, since, in our current (and much-needed) passion for analysis, we have partially deadened our sense of the unity of aesthetic experience.

With regard to affectation, Fielding's theory of the ridiculous fits in well with our "nakedness" theme. Affectations are "put on," and it is the humorist's job (or more properly the satirist's) to "strip them off." This much Fielding knew by rote from his earliest published work, a poem against masquerades, to his attack on masquerades in his last novel, *Amelia*: take off the mask, remove the outer pretense, and expose the "bare facts" which lie beneath—vanity, hypocrisy, smugness. But his chief accomplishment, as well as his chief delight, was to distinguish between a man's defects and his essential goodness; and we think in this respect of Adams, Tom Jones, Captain Booth, and dozens of the minor creations. If a man is good-natured "at bottom," then the problem for the novelist is how to get to the bottom. Fielding usually arrives there by playing off the man's faults against his virtues, as when Adams first cautions Joseph against immoderate grief, then grieves immoderately, like any compassionate man, at the news of his son's supposed drowning. But a more pertinent example occurs in one of the inn scenes in *Joseph Andrews*, when Fanny faints and Adams, in his haste to rescue her, tosses his precious copy of Aeschylus into the fire. Here Adams has literally stripped off an affectation while revealing his natural goodness—the book is a symbol, that is, of his pedantry, of his excessive reliance upon literature as a guide to life, and this is what is tossed aside during the emergency. Later on, when the book is fished out of the fire, it has been reduced to its simple sheepskin covering—which is Fielding's way of reminding us that the contents of the book are superficial, at least in the face of harsh experience. Thus the whole incident underscores the fact that Adams' faults, like his torn, disordered clothes, are only the outward, superficial aspects of his character and that the essential Adams, a brave, good man, lies somewhere underneath; his heart—not his Aeschylus, not his harmless vanity—is his true guide in all things of consequence.[5]

Mrs. Slipslop is another matter. She is usually praised by critics as the well-rounded comic foil to Lady Booby. But she is something more than this, since her lust for Joseph, and for all manner of men, is more natural and appealing than Lady Booby's hot-and-cold passion. To begin with, Mrs. Slipslop is an unbelievably ugly maidservant who, after an early slip, has remained virtuous for many years. Now, at forty-five, she has resolved to pay off "the debt of pleasure" which she feels she owes to herself. Though Fielding heavily ridicules her vanity and hypocrisy throughout the book, he also brings out the pathetic strain in her makeup, and at times he even reveals an author's fondness for a favorite creation. Mrs. Slipslop may rail at Joseph, for example, but unlike Lady Booby she will never turn him out into the street; in fact, she saves or

[5] Consider in this respect what a poor showing Partridge makes as a comic figure in *Tom Jones*; like Adams he is vain, pedantic, and superstitious, but he lacks the nobility of heart which great comic figures—at least in the quixotic tradition—must possess.

aids him on several important occasions; but, more than all this, there is something almost touching, as well as ridiculous, about her faulty speech, her grotesque body, and her foolish dream of becoming "Mrs. Andrews, with a hundred a-year." All in all, she is a comic figure in her own right, as well as a comic foil, and if Fielding deals her a sound drubbing in the night scenes at Booby Hall, he also "deals" her a last warm laugh.

III

Fielding beds down his entire cast at Booby Hall in preparation for the night adventures. Then, when the household is asleep, he sends Beau Didapper off to ravish Fanny through trickery, and the round of fun begins. By mistake, Didapper enters Mrs. Slipslop's pitch-dark room and, posing as Joseph, tells her that the incest report was false, and that he can delay the enjoyment of her charms no longer; then he climbs into bed with her. She receives him willingly enough—her dream come true —but the two of them soon discover their mutual error. Ever-prudent, Mrs. Slipslop now sees her chance to win back her reputation for chastity, which she had damaged through recent conduct with Lawyer Scout; so she hugs Didapper even more firmly, calls out for help, and Parson Adams comes running to her rescue from the next chamber. But in his haste Adams has forgot to put on any clothes, and this action is far more characteristic of him than any we have yet seen in the novel. For Adams has now become his own true symbol: he stands there as God made him, all courage and kindness, with his affectations, his clothes, left in a heap behind him. He is now the naked truth, quite literally and lovably, and he is never more himself than at this moment, not even while throwing his Aeschylus into the fire to save Fanny. He is brave, true virtue on the march now, stripped clean of all encumbrance and far beyond the reach of ridicule—for true virtue, as we have already seen, can never be ridiculed. Of course, Adams is laughable because he is naked and imprudent and we are not; but mainly he arouses those feelings to which we have been conditioned, with regard to him, from the beginning of the novel. For as Fielding and Plato have told us, men will love virtue if they see her—or in this case him—naked. We see him naked now, and we laugh, to a great extent, out of love. But let us return for a moment to the goings-on in Mrs. Slipslop's bedroom.

Obeying, of all things, the dictates of common sense, Adams now passes over the small, whimpering body—obviously the woman—and proceeds to grapple with the large bearded one—obviously the man. Here Fielding ridicules, in Slipslop and Didapper, that vanity by which one poses as a seducible woman and the other as a virile man. For the small body (Beau Didapper) escapes, and Slipslop receives an almost fatal beating. But Lady Booby, attracted by all the noise, enters the room in the nick of time with lighted candle in hand. At which point Adams discovers both his error and his nakedness and leaps under the covers with Mrs. Slipslop. We have then, in one corner of the bed, Vice posing as Virtue, which is hypocrisy; and in the other corner, Virtue hiding its "lovable" nakedness and apparently acting as Vice—which is false, foolish modesty at the very least. And we also have, as Lady Justice with the Lighted Candle, Lady Booby, the far from blinded villainess of the novel.

Shall we stop a moment to straighten things out? We have already seen that vanity has been exposed to ridicule—a normal enough procedure. But now we can see that virtue itself has been exposed to some sort of laughter; moreover, it has been exposed in a worthless cause—until Adams arrived and began pummeling Mrs. Slipslop, no one was in any real danger. This reminds us at once of Don Quixote, and the comparison enables us to see that virtue has been confounded rather than ridiculed and that we laugh once more, in the main, out of sympathy for a brave man in an awkward fix.[6]

There is more to it than this, however. We have been neglecting Mrs. Slipslop, who at long last has had not one but two men in her bed (simultaneously!), but who has been forced by circumstance to reject them both. The sex-starved maiden, with her mountainous breasts and her spur-of-the-moment virtue, has been soundly trounced. In a very real sense this is Waterloo for the prudent gentlewoman, and for the lust half of the lust-chastity theme as well. All, all is resolved through a burst of laughter, though again through laughter of a special kind. In a parody on *Pamela*, one of two lusting ladies (both foils for Richardson's clumsy Mr. B) was bound to receive a severe comeuppance. Fielding, the sure comic artist, chose the more comic figure; but the very condition which makes Slipslop appear so ridiculous in our eyes—the extreme distance between her desires and her qualifications—also makes her appeal to the warm side of our (and Fielding's) sense of humor. She is a far less harsh figure than Lady Booby and therefore the more proper bed companion for the equally harmless, "sexless," but virtuous Parson Adams.

Nevertheless, we must return to Lady Booby, at the scene of the alleged rape, for the key to all these resolutions and reversals. After berating Adams as a wicked cleric, the stern hostess spies Didapper's telltale cuff links on the floor. Then, when she hears Adams' story, when she takes in "the figures of Slipslop and her gallant, whose heads only were visible at the opposite corners of the bed," she is unable to "refrain from laughter." For once, then, Lady Booby appears in a good light: until

---

[6] This is also Adams' first "real" windmill and therefore the most quixotic moment in the book. Until now Adams' rescues have been much to the point and more or less successful, since Fielding always attempted to show that virtue can be a successful way of life—hence Adams' vigor, his robust strength, his eventual muddling through. As a knight-errant, he is generally far more effective than the gallant Quixote.

now she has behaved in a completely selfish manner, but the kind of laughter which we cannot withhold, *in spite of ourselves,* stems more from the heart than the ego. Even the opinionated Mrs. Slipslop now checks her tongue, and it becomes apparent that evil itself has been dissolved by some strange power. We can say, of course, that Lady Booby laughs at a maid and a parson who are far too old and ridiculous for zealous modesty; but, more to the point, she laughs at Adams' lovable innocence, and perhaps she laughs at herself as well, at her own defeat; for, as we have observed, Mrs. Slipslop is in part her comic foil, and Parson Adams now lies in the place where Joseph Andrews might have lain, if her own hopes had been fulfilled.

At any rate, a general absolution has obviously just occurred: through elaborate contrivance (the creation of Beau Didapper as catalytic agent, the convenient rainstorm, the crisis in the main plot, Slipslop's affair with Lawyer Scout, and so on) Fielding has brought Adams before us in all his nakedness. The good parson has never seemed so ridiculous, nor has he ever been burdened so heavily with the guilt which rightfully belongs to those around him—to Slipslop, to Didapper, to Lady Booby, and even to you and me, as we stand behind the bold hostess in judgment of the scene and see our own sins revealed by flickering candlelight—yet Adams emerges untarnished from under this double burden of guilt and ridicule, and, like the true comic hero, he absolves us all with his naïve triumph over circumstance: for good and bad men alike have a common stake in that perfect, naked innocence which can force a Lady Booby, or even a Peter Pounce, to grin or laugh from some buried store of benevolence.[7] All this is nicely underscored, I think, when the lady retires once more and the scene at hand, which opens with naked Adams running characteristically to the rescue, now closes with naked Slipslop sliding lustfully, pathetically, characteristically, and as Fielding puts it, "with much courtesy," across the bed toward Parson Adams, who takes the hint and quickly leaves the room. One cannot help thinking that at long last, among all those thorns, Fielding has placed a rose for Mrs. Slipslop— for the last warm laugh is hers, in a madcap world where virtue is masked as vice, and vice as virtue, while, in the unmasking, warmheartedness prevails over all morality.

In the next half of the chapter things begin to settle down. Adams, in his haste, inadvertently takes the wrong turn; he climbs quietly into what he thinks is his own bed and prepares for sleep. But in reality the poor man has moved directly from the bed of the ugliest, most indiscriminately lustful woman in the book to that of the loveliest and most chaste. On the other side of him lies Fanny "Goodwill" Andrews (not

---

[7] In Book III, chap. xii, the normally severe Peter Pounce is also forced to grin at the sight of Adams' bedraggled figure. In the same manner, a misanthrope might grin at a mud-spattered child: the outer ridiculousness is reinforced by inward innocence in both Adams and the child, and the responsive grin or laugh is basically sympathetic.

yet Joseph's wife but his supposed sister) in profound, peaceful, naked slumber; and Fielding promptly reminds us that Adams has done what every red-blooded man in the novel has been trying to do, unsuccessfully, since Book II, chapter ix: he has climbed into bed with Fanny:

> As the cat or lap-dog of some lovely nymph, for whom ten thousand lovers languish, lies quietly by the side of the charming maid, and, ignorant of the scene of delight on which they repose, meditates the future capture of a mouse, or surprisal of a plate of bread and butter, so Adams lay by the side of Fanny [writes Fielding], ignorant of the paradise to which he was so near.

The book has now come full circle, for not only Fanny's incomparable charms but her priceless chastity as well are treated with the utmost indifference by the one man who has succeeded, so far, in sharing her bed; nor is she in any real danger, for this man, this cat or lap dog, neither knows nor cares, nor would care if he knew, about the "paradise" beside him; he simply wants to go to sleep. We can safely say, then, that the lust-chastity theme has been fully and ironically resolved or, if you will, stood on both its ears.

But it is daybreak now, and Joseph Andrews has come for an innocent rendezvous with Fanny. When he raps at the door, the good-natured, hospitable parson calls out, "Come in, whoever you are." Consternation follows, and for the first time in the novel the three paragons of virtue, the three touchstones, are at complete odds with one another. Adams is again burdened with undeserved guilt and can only blame the affair on witchcraft; but, once he recounts his story, Joseph explains to him that he must have taken the wrong turn on leaving Slipslop's room. Then Fielding makes a significant emendation: he has already told his readers that the naked Adams is wearing a nightcap; now he reminds them that he is also wearing the traditional knee-length nightshirt—all this in deference, perhaps, to Fanny's modesty but nevertheless a sign that things are back to normal once more and that the naked truth no longer roams through the halls of night. Fanny and Joseph forgive the parson with the indulgence one shows to an innocent child, and again the scene ends on a benevolent note.

What are we to make of night adventures which serve as a kind of parody on the whole novel; which apparently involve no real problems but in which lust and self-love appear, momentarily, in an almost friendly light; in which chastity is ignored, brave virtue confounded, and a whole comic method thrown thereby into reverse? One solution seems obvious: by sending his beloved parson from bed to bed, Fielding has put a kind of comic blessing upon the novel; he has resolved the major themes and passions through benevolent humor. Or to push on to a more inclusive theory, the comic resolution in *Joseph Andrews* depends for its warmth upon the flow of sympathy which Fielding creates between his readers and his comic figures; for its bite, upon his ridicule and deflation of those figures; and for its meaning, upon the long-range development of character and theme, as well as the local situation at Booby Hall. Apparently Fielding, like Parson Adams, did not always practice the simple theories he preached. But as Adams insists at the close of the night adventures, there is such a thing as witchcraft, and perhaps this is what Fielding practiced upon Adams and upon his readers, and with a good deal of awareness of what he was doing.

# Jonathan Wild

## by Aurélien Digeon

The third volume of the *Miscellanies* is entirely occupied by the *Life of the late Jonathan Wild the Great*. It is the only first-class work which they contain. The *genre* to which it belongs, the biography of thieves and vagabonds, was an old one in England, as the well-known books of Nash and Greene testify. But during the course of the seventeenth century the indigenous stock of romances of roguery was enormously enriched by the advent of the Spanish novelists and of their successor and popularizer, Le Sage. From 1600 to 1740, twelve editions of *Guzman d'Alfarache* appeared. Rogues became popular. Their picturesque life and ingenious tricks charmed the public, and their biographies were soon enriched by incidents borrowed from the picaresque novels. A special literature thus kept their glory alive; Abbé Le Blanc who traveled in England about 1738, was quite surprised to find that thieves were there regarded as heroes. Every notorious gallows' bird was the subject of a broadsheet or ballad; his memoirs (more or less apocryphal) and his last confidences to the Newgate Ordinary were published. There was a whole literary *genre*, and a very abundant one, which pandered to the same sort of curiosity as the columns of police court news in our daily papers.

We know how easily parody came to Fielding. It is not impossible that his first intention was to parody the grandiloquence and pretentiousness of these biographies of rogues, and indeed some of the works of which we have been speaking may even have given him the idea; for some of them, as we shall see, were not devoid of irony.

Jonathan Wild, who was executed in May, 1725, is an important figure in this police court literature. The numerous biographies in the British

*"Jonathan Wild."* From *The Novels of Fielding* by Aurélien Digeon (London: Routledge & Kegan Paul Ltd, 1925), chap. iii: "Jonathan Wild the Great (and the Miscellanies)," pp. 96-128. Copyright George Routledge & Sons. Originally published in France as *Les Romans de Fielding* (1923). Reprinted by permission of Routledge and Kegan Paul Ltd. All footnotes have been omitted, except when needed to document a reference in the text; passages that are not strictly necessary for M. Digeon's argument (biographical and bibliographical information, and lengthy quotations) have also been omitted.

Museum are not always consistent, and legend is often mingled with history. The most significant was published in Northampton in 1725, under the following title: *The Life of Jonathan Wilde, Thief-Taker General of Great Britain and Ireland, from his Birth to his Death, containing his Rise and Progress in Roguery; his first acquaintance with Thieves, by what arts he made himself their Head, or Governor; his Discipline over them; his policy and great cunning in governing them; and several Classes of Thieves under his Command. In which all his Intrigues, Plots, and Artifices, are accounted for, and laid open. Inter-mix'd with variety of diverting Stories; taken chiefly from his own private Journals, and daily transactions of his Life, as found amongst his papers since his first being apprehended.* The preface states, with a somewhat ironical enthusiasm:

> We need make no apology for collecting these Materials, and offering them to the Publick. For here they will meet with a system of Politicks unknown to Machiavel; they will see deeper Strategems and Plots form'd by a Fellow without Learning or Education, than are to be met with in the Conduct of the greatest Statesmen, who have been at the Heads of Governments. And, indeed, when Things are rightly compared, it will be found that he had a more difficult game to play; for he was to blind the Eyes of the World, to find out Tricks to evade the Penalties of the Law; and on the other Side, to govern a Body of People who were enemies to all government.

It is true that the paradox of the brigand-genius and the comparison between the criminal and the statesman are rather clumsily handled, but they are present, all the same, and that is the main point. Elsewhere the author assumes an attitude of mocking admiration of his hero. "He show'd early signs of a forward Genius, and, whilst a Boy, would commit a thousand little Rogueries . . . in which he discover'd a ready Wit, and a Cunning much above his Years" (p. 6). "It was not long after this, that he found the making of Bucklers too mechanick an Employ-ment for him; his Soul was too great to be confin'd to such servile Work. . . ." Finally, after a very clever forgery, he is put in prison and "here he laid the Foundation of all his future greatness" (p. 12). He becomes the chief of a gang and then, very cleverly, plans to act as inter-mediary between the robbers and the robbed, to whom he returns, for a monetary consideration, the goods which have been stolen from them. At the same time he publicly declares himself an informer, and hands over his rebellious "subjects" to the police.

It is strange to observe how this worthless pamphlet, written almost immediately after Wild's execution, foreshadows the ironical attitude of Fielding. The thing was, however, of fairly frequent occurrence. "Faith, Sirs," cries the Guzman of Le Sage, "ye are still but apprentices in your trade. I will show you that a superior genius has far better lights than yours. If you so desire it, I will take charge of this enterprise" (V, i). The "enterprise" is a carefully organized swindle.

It was a part of the tradition that tales of thieves should be told with a smile. Their life ended in a ballad, and thus the public avenged itself for having feared them. Because Jonathan Wild had been considered one of the most formidable of thieves, he was one of the most widely mocked. His biographers are pleased to jest; they tell how he asked, upon the eve of his execution, how the great men of Rome and Athens behaved on similar occasions; they relate his matrimonial misfortunes at length. Many dialogues and ballads were composed in his honor. Swift dedicated some verses to him and Defoe wrote his biography. He won such a lasting fame that thirteen years after his death Pope could still refer to him as a well-known character.[1]

Such was the historical personage whom Fielding makes his hero. No finer hypocrite could be found than this informer, honorably known as "thief-catcher," and secretly at the head of a gang of thieves. Being a hypocrite, he is, therefore, odious and not merely ridiculous (we must remember the theories set forth in *Joseph Andrews*); so he will not be let off lightly. From the very beginning Fielding adopts toward him a determined attitude of severe irony. He is about to relate the history of a "great man"; and the very terms in which men are wont to speak of an Alexander or a Caesar, will serve him for his rascal.

Once more we are faced with a parody. It is really remarkable what a fascination parody, or, more generally, satire has for realistic writers, either at the beginning or the end of their careers. It would seem that they take a certain time before they perceive that reality will suffice them, or else that a moment comes when reality suffices them no longer. Thus Marivaux begins by burlesquing the *Iliad* and *Télémaque*, and Flaubert ends with *Bouvard et Pécuchet*. In the same way Fielding's first two novels are parodies.

Jonathan Wild is a "great man," a complete "great man." He is even more perfect than Alexander; for whereas Alexander is reported to have acted sometimes with comparative goodness, the wickedness, nay, the greatness of Wild is unblemished. His life from his birth to his death on the scaffold, is a perfectly harmonious work of art, unmarred by a single good action. Such is the philosophical basis of the book; a simple, clear and accessible idea, a development familiar to rhetoric.

The idea of the criminal conqueror is a commonplace, which is found here and there throughout antiquity. It occurs again in Boileau (Satire VIII) and the French classics; Mandeville (*Fable of the Bees*, 6th ed., 1732, I, 40) and Pope (*Essay on Man*, IV, l. 222) call Alexander "Macedonia's madman." The classical commonplace, however, acquired a new vogue in England about 1720. To what was this vogue due? Alarm had

---

[1] Swift, *Newgate Garland;* Defoe, *The Life of Jonathan Wild, by H.D., late clerk to Justice R . . . ,* London, 1725; Pope, *Epilogue to the Satires,* dialogue II, ll. 38-39.

already been aroused by the danger to public security involved in the
ambitions of a Louis "the Great." But upon English minds the deepest
impression seems to have been made by Charles XII. . . . Thus revived,
the idea that "great" conquerors are criminals pursued its way. It cor-
responded so closely to the general aspirations of the time and to the
development of liberal ideas, that it could not fail to be accepted with
enthusiasm. The mere conqueror became more and more unpopular.
The really great man must henceforth be a good man. A lady, later on,
wrote to Richardson to thank him for showing in Grandison that "greatness and goodness are synonymous terms." The question was in the air;
indeed it was at the core of all the speculations of a philosophic era
which was to conceive an "enlightened despotism." Fielding alluded to
it on more than one occasion. . . .[2]

.  .  .

Genius is often a personal arrangement of pre-existing data. Fielding
found himself faced with two literary traditions: on the one hand, the
joking tone of rogues' biographies, on the other, the commonplace of
the criminal conqueror. He was the first to combine these two hitherto
isolated elements into a new and consummate creation. The low joke,
in the service of a general idea, is transmuted into philosophical irony,
while the commonplace ceases at once to be banal.

Moreover, Fielding gives it a personal twist. The comparison of the
conqueror to the thief was a convention of the school, but he reverses
it. He gives us the inversion of the travesty *à la Scarron*, of which everyone was tired. No longer is Aeneas a rogue, it is the rogue who is
Aeneas.[3] The irony thus gains in subtlety. Mr. Jonathan Wild is treated
all through as a fine gentleman. The joke is aimed straight at him, but
it rebounds from the poor devil, and strikes the fine gentleman, his
neighbor. The stone is not cast at the great man, but it is he who is
bespattered with the mud which splashes from it.

But none of this is yet enough to account for the virulence of the
outburst. What was the point of attacking Jonathan Wild? He was dead.
Or Charles XII? He was dead, too. One does not become as indignant as
this, against two corpses. Behind them Fielding envisaged a living figure,
and that living figure was without any doubt the Minister, Walpole. . . .

.  .  .

[But] we should do but scant justice to so philosophical an irony were
we to see in it merely a vulgar libel. The irony may have been roused

---

[2] See the Preface to the *Miscellanies*, as well as the poem, "On True Greatness," "A
Dialogue between Alexander and Diogenes," etc. [Editor's note.]

[3] I do not forget *The Beggar's Opera*, the success of which was immense (1728).
Several of its characteristics may have influenced Fielding but its laughter is very gay
and far removed from the deep and severe irony of *Jonathan Wild*.

by the ephemeral actions of a Prime Minister, but it soon went further and higher. Even so, Pascal, scribbling down thoughts on the foundations of justice, was reminded of the Fronde which he had witnessed and the dangers to which it exposed public order; but very soon the Fronde was to him only a fragment of eternal history. Fielding begins by caricaturing Walpole in the figure of Wild, a notorious thief; but his personal anger is quickly transformed into a universal anger, the anger of humanity. One day he thinks of the great massacrer of men, Charles VII, whom he despises; then his thoughts turn to Charles I and he speaks of Wild in terms analogous to those which Clarendon applied to his king, making the thief leave, after his death, certain Maxims on greatness, which Fielding himself compares with those which the author of *Eikon Basilike* claims to have found after the execution of Charles I.

But this is not all. After the elections of 1741, the fall of Walpole began to appear imminent. And now his great adversary, the journalist of the *Champion*, the pamphleteer of so many virulent attacks, published a poem entitled *The Opposition: a Vision*, in which he expresses infinitely more moderate opinions. Here he predicts that the principles of patriotism in the name of which the Prime Minister has been opposed will soon be forgotten, that there will be place-hunting, and ingratitude toward the good fighters who have won the victory. At last in February 1742, Walpole falls. Would Fielding, who had written his *Jonathan Wild* with this "great man" in mind, now vent his rage upon the dead? No, for suddenly the satire takes a new direction. When Jonathan Wild arrives at Newgate he finds a certain Roger Johnson, who is king of the thieves. Wild makes an inflammatory speech, demanding "the liberties of Newgate," overthrows Johnson and takes his place. The prisoners soon find to their disgust that the new master is worse than the old. Wild even wants to dress himself in the spoils of his predecessor but the fine velvet cap is too heavy for his head and the embroidered waistcoat is so big for him that it hangs in folds. Walpole has now become Roger Johnson and Wild represents Wilmington. The same mask now conceals another face. Walpole's successor was proverbially a nonentity. With what interest must Fielding have watched the scenes which accompanied the fall of a ministry which had lasted so long! Can we wonder at the political scepticism which we encounter in *Jonathan Wild*?

It is a difficult and complex book, for those who would decipher and follow all the author's intentions. If it were worthwhile to look for them and if we could know the whole secret history of the period, a hundred other allusions might be discovered. We have only pointed out the most obvious, those which could not be neglected without mistaking the real character of the book. A famous thief, Charles I, Charles VII, Walpole, Wilmington, and others still, these are not contradictory interpretations; they are all gathered into Fielding's Jonathan Wild. We can, we ought even to read the book without thinking of them, but we needs must

study them if we would understand why it is that this book is not the
mere cold development of an abstract topic; its whole life and strength
is mysteriously drawn from a thousand actual realities. By fathoming
these realities we fathom the deep secret of its life.

The miracle is that from all these scattered elements, there should
emerge the harmonious unity of a book; a unity so vigorous and so
perfect that some have thought that the book was written "at a sitting." [4]
Again let us try to surprise the secret of this artistic synthesis. "My design," says the author, "is not to enter the lists with that excellent historian, who from authentic papers and records, etc., hath already given
so satisfactory an account of the life and actions of this great man."
Fielding will take Wild as a type and will depict, he tells us, "roguery
and not a rogue." This claim immediately places him on a different plane
from Defoe. As we observed in the case of *Joseph Andrews*, he is writing
a novel and not pseudo-memoirs, a pseudo-correspondence or a pseudo-
biography. Nor does he make use of any of these pretenses which are
designed to give an air of reality to such works; his aim is rather to
reject reality when it proves a hindrance, to add to it at need, to be more
true than nature. "My narrative is rather of such actions which he might
have performed, or would or should have performed, than what he really
did; and may in reality as well suit other such Great Men as the person
himself whose name it bears." Nor does the author hesitate, as Coleridge
profoundly observes, to put into the mouth of his hero speeches which
the real Jonathan Wild would never have uttered, for these speeches and
reflections conform to the author's secret purpose of making his story un-
real in order to give a transcendental reality to the truths which he
wishes to convey.[5] Everything which idealizes Wild, everything which lifts
him out of the crapulous mediocrity of the real man, serves but to give
more weight and universality to his example. This is a clear use, and
possibly the first conscious one in literary history, of the synthetic method
employed by the great realistic novelists of the nineteenth century.

Fielding must thus choose from the true history of Wild only those
few characteristics which will enable him to bring out clearly his conception of the "great man." For example, he keeps the attempt at suicide
whereby Wild aspires to imitate the heroes of antiquity. He keeps the
public stoning at the execution. Such a circumstance is well-suited to this
hero, so misunderstood by the crowd. Other features are modified. Wild
had been married several times and had shown himself at once brutal
and lascivious toward women. Fielding keeps only the lasciviousness and
his hero is deceived by the women whom he loves. Such is often the fate
of great men! Again, according to history, Wild was accused of stealing
a box of lace and of helping to steal another and was condemned on

    [4] Cf. G. T. Bispham, "Fielding's Jonathan Wild," in *Eighteenth Century Literature,
an Oxford Miscellany* (Oxford: Clarendon Press, 1909).
    [5] Coleridge, *Miscellanies, aesthetic and literary* (London, 1885), p. 339.

the evidence of a certain Margaret Morphew, who asserted that she had
gone one morning about midday to Wild's house to give his wife a pair
of shoes and had heard him speaking of the theft. None of this appears
in Fielding's work; such an end would have been too undignified for
so great a hero. Life does not grant each man the fate which his character deserves, but the novel can correct this and in this respect is "more
philosophic than history."

Fielding thus chooses and *composes* the life of his hero. Jonathan Wild
has inherited every quality which constitutes heroism. Of noble birth,
since his genealogy goes back as far as one of Hengist's companions, many
of his ancestors have been remarkable for their expert thieving; and his
mother's fingers possessed a certain "glutinous quality" which was most
useful. Formed by these examples, giving in his schooldays indications of
a precocious genius, young Wild one day meets at the house of his uncle,
the bailiff, a certain Count La Ruse whom a ruthless tailor is keeping in
prison for debt. Wild plays cards with him and cheats. The count, instead
of being annoyed as a meaner spirit might have been, congratulates himself on having found someone more ingenious than himself. The two
men begin a conversation, a noble conversation in alternate speeches, a
conversation worthy of tragic heroes.

> You cannot, I apprehend, Mr. Wild, be such a stranger to your own ca-
> pacity as to be surprised when I tell you I have often viewed, with a
> mixture of astonishment and concern, your shining qualities confined to
> a sphere where they can never reach the eyes of those who would introduce
> them properly into the world and raise you to an eminence where you may
> blaze out to the admiration of all men . . . for those abilities which would
> entitle you to honour and profit in a superior station, may render you only
> obnoxious to danger and disgrace in a lower. (I, v)

There follows a most philosophical debate. The count exhorts Wild to
work in a sphere worthy of the "greatest genius of the age," for the same
qualities that make a good "prig" or thief often make a Prime Minister.
But, objects Wild, is it more profitable to be a Prime Minister than a
thief? Certainly, answers the count, there is less risk of being punished,
and "there is a crowd oftener in one year at Tyburn than on Tower-Hill
in a century." But in an extremely sarcastic speech Wild weighs the two
professions in the balance and ends by proving that the thief is the
happier of the two. His last argument—very characteristic of Fielding—
is that the thief's conscience can never prick him for the theft of a few
shillings, while that of the Prime Minister may reproach him for having
"betrayed a public trust and ruined the fortunes of thousands, perhaps
of a great nation." But the count has fallen asleep during this noble
discourse, and Wild picks his pocket before leaving him.

This splendid education continues. Even travel, traditionally necessary
to the formation of a gentleman, is not omitted. And His Gracious

Majesty finds an opportunity of sending Mr. Wild to see his American plantations.

So Wild's character is formed. He is none of your dull pickpockets who steal without finesse. He only likes a masterly and well-planned fraud. We find him trying his method first in a small deal. One evening the count, adept in giving fortune a helping hand, has reaped a fine harvest "at the hazard-table"; Wild arranges for a certain Bagshot to rob him as he leaves the gaming-house. When the time comes to divide the booty Wild proves irrefutably that the whole sum belongs to him . . . (I, viii). At last, after a scene of alternate intimidation, doubtless inspired by the interview between Maître Jacques and Valère, Bagshot yields to threats and gives up his booty. What a comic string of deceptions! La Ruse, who has thieved at the gaming table, is despoiled by Bagshot, Bagshot in turn by Wild, Wild . . . one might continue, and Fielding actually does so, but Wild is not robbed vulgarly. He hurries to place the money at the feet of Miss Laetitia Snap to whom he pays "urgent addresses." Indeed he becomes so urgent and brutal that "to confess the truth," Laetitia was "more indebted to her own strength for the preservation of her virtue than to the awful respect or backwardness of her lover." But there is yet another surprise in store for us. The rejected lover has scarcely left the room before Miss Laetitia liberates another wooer from his hiding place, and grants him everything that she has just refused our "great man." The series of robbers robbed ends with Wild himself.

By the end of the first book Wild's system is complete. He has observed that men are divided into two classes: those who work themselves, and those who make others work. Wild, of course, wishes to take up his position in the second class. This comprises two subdivisions according to whether one makes others work for the common weal or for one's own interest. The first section includes merchants and the second "conquerors, absolute princes, Prime Ministers and prigs (thieves)." So Wild must recruit a gang which will work for his benefit.

Such is the first book. The figure of Wild is harshly drawn, with a cruel and naked irony; the execution is that of an engraver rather than of a painter. For it is necessary to avoid any possibility of a misunderstanding on the part of the reader. In a certain passage of *Tartuffe*, Molière has thought it advisable to add a note that a hypocrite is speaking, "*c'est un hypocrite qui parle.*" The heavy lines in which Fielding draws his hero fulfil the same function as Molière's note.

Wild alone fills the first book. And the figure which Fielding has made of him is so deeply impressed upon us from the beginning that a few reminders in the rest of the novel suffice to keep him vividly before us. The second and following books are enriched by new characters and different adventures, a few honest men even appear upon the scene, the novel flows in a wider and more complex stream, but, from time to time,

there reappear pages and chapters written in the same vein as the first
book. Just as a geologist finds a stratum appearing in a sudden outcrop
and then reappearing once again further away, so does this vein of sharp
irony reappear from place to place with great distinctness in the midst
of the more abundant flow of the other pages. With a little care it is
easy enough to isolate these chapters. There is only one in the second
book, the chapter entitled "of Hats"; . . . chapters iii, vi, vii, viii, ix,
xiii-xiv, of the third book, which deal with Wild's marriage; and in the
last book, chapters ii, iii (the mutiny in Newgate) and xiii-xv (Wild's last
hours) are successive outcrops of this vein. In addition to their peculiar
quality of cynical and implacable irony they have another characteristic
in common. They are concerned with Wild's personal destiny. None of
the events which they narrate are ever referred to in the other chapters,
while on the other hand they are never concerned with episodes related
in the other chapters (*i.e.*, mainly the Heartfree swindle) with the exception perhaps of some connecting link at the beginning or end of a
chapter. If one were to take out of the whole work the first book and
the few chapters which I have enumerated in the others only a few links
would be needed to make of them a complete and self-sufficient novel,
a simple biography, mordant and restrained, of Jonathan Wild.

I am convinced that we should then possess the primitive vein, the
original form in which Fielding conceived his novel, and probably the
form in which he first drafted it.

. . .

The most violent political allusions are to be found in this original
nucleus of the novel, or rather in what remains of it in the final version.
But in the meantime Fielding's talent was maturing, he was developing
into the author of *Joseph Andrews*. And the pages which remain to be
described are undoubtedly the work of the hand which produced *Joseph
Andrews*.

It was the new Fielding who feared to weary his readers by such continuous villainy, such unrelieved and inexorable irony. The moment has
come when he discovers his true genius. Onto the picaresque biography
which he had begun, he now grafts a novel according to his own fashion.
And this is why, parallel to the fate of Wild, we are told the story of
his victim, Heartfree. A few remarks will enable us to appreciate the
consummate art with which this story is connected with the other and
woven intimately into the very texture of the work.

Observe, first of all, that as soon as Heartfree and his wife are presented
to us at the beginning of the second book, above all, as soon as they are
clearly portrayed as the future victims of Jonathan Wild, we are given
the impression that everything which preceded was mere preparation and
that we are now about to witness the central incident of the novel. The

whole development of Wild has become nothing more than the first act
of a four-act drama. The second "binds" the plot, and sets Wild at grips
with his victim Heartfree. Wild, with the complicity of Count La Ruse,
robs Heartfree and then has him imprisoned, abducts his wife and carries
her away on a ship. Privateers seize them and abandon Wild to the mercy
of the sea; but "Providence" watches over the hero and brings him safely
back to England. The third book, despite several shadows in the picture,
shows the progress of Wild's greatness. He is on the point of victory and
Heartfree on the eve of being condemned to death; Wild is still posing
as Heartfree's intimate friend. With the fourth book comes the catastrophe. Wild is arrested. Mrs. Heartfree who has been lost for a long
time, returns and confounds him by her evidence. His wife and his old
friends desert him; and Jonathan Wild wins the glorious death which
should be that of all "great men," present and future; he is hanged by
the neck till he is dead.

Directly the unfortunate Heartfree is introduced into the novel, it
no longer seems possible to do without him. He acts as a foil to the
figure of Wild, gives it its true value, and buttresses it. Heartfree is a
jeweler. He is one of those men (like Parson Adams) "whom experience
only, and not their own natures, must inform that there are such things
as deceit and hypocrisy in the world." He suffers from

> several great weaknesses of mind, being good-natured, friendly, and generous
> to a great excess: he had, indeed, too little regard to common justice, for
> he had forgiven some debts to his acquaintances only because they could
> not pay him. . . . He was withal so silly a fellow that he never took the
> least advantage of the ignorance of his customers, and contented himself
> with very moderate gains on his goods.

The irony is a little heavy, but nevertheless we have here already
Fielding's characteristic method, which is to be resumed with a finer sense
of humor in *Tom Jones*. This method consists essentially in painting two
contrasting figures: an honest man persecuted, and a rascal prospering.
The malice of fate and the naughtiness of the world will have it that the
good seems always wrong and the wicked right. The final catastrophe,
however, sets everything straight and the hypocritical rascal is unmasked
in the end. Yet the catastrophe is only there to satisfy man's conception
of justice; from the very beginning of the story, in the midst of his
greatest misfortunes, the honest man has never ceased to be happier than
the successful rascal, for his conscience brings him joys which are greater
than any material prosperity.

* * *

The novel does not flow with a smooth and equal tide toward its
close. It rises and billows like a wave; Wild becomes greater and greater:
he will have the further to fall. Similarly Heartfree grows in importance,

as he must if he is really, as we have seen, the counterpoise of Wild. Indeed, Heartfree is, at first, only described in relation to the principal hero; then Fielding becomes interested in the honest jeweler; Heartfree is described for his own sake and we hear about his family and his apprentice. Little by little the author grows so attached to them that he sometimes forgets his original design. At the beginning, whenever he addresses the reader, he apologizes for introducing a character as stupid and as deficient in "greatness" as this worthy man. But as the denouement draws near, he almost allows his irony to relax. If any fortunate incident favors Heartfree he hastens to assure the reader that "there is no passage in this whole story that can afford him equal delight," and he praises the good judge who releases Wild's victim. Thus the mask is sometimes slightly withdrawn, which is a further proof that the work was not written "at a sitting."

Even Mrs. Heartfree who was, at first, nothing more than a "mean-spirited" woman, gradually acquires a more marked personality (particularly in the course of the second book). She is given individual features, and has her peculiarities, which sometimes make us smile. I cannot resist the pleasure of quoting the beginning of a chapter, were it but to show that Fielding is not always a man of big effects, but that his style is often full of wit and delicacy. Mrs. Heartfree who has just been interrupted continues the story of her adventures: "If I mistake not, I was interrupted just as I was beginning to repeat some of the compliments made me by the hermit." "Just as you had finished them, I believe, Madam," said the justice. "Very well, Sir," said she; "I am sure I have no pleasure in the repetition." (IV, xi). Other amusing touches such as Heartfree's continual fears throughout this story for his conjugal honor and his wife's dangerous—and comical—voyages would perhaps almost tend to change the atmosphere of the novel toward the end. But, as we have seen, chapters of pure and incisive irony recur at regular intervals to restore the dominant note, and the very contrast only serves to throw them into stronger relief.

In *Jonathan Wild* the "real" Fielding is not as yet entirely revealed. But the evolution is beginning and, little by little, it alters the earlier man. We have pointed out the parts of this work which seem to us to belong to his youth. On the other hand there are several characteristics which distinctly foreshadow the author of *Tom Jones* and *Amelia*. To begin with, there is the general construction of the novel, the two complementary figures, the good and the bad man. The difference is that in *Tom Jones* the proportion will be reversed. Of the two characters introduced in *Jonathan Wild* it is the bad man who attracts all the artistic and moral interest. The book remains a satire. On the contrary, of the two personages depicted in *Tom Jones*, the weak and theoretical figure will be that of the wicked Blifil, and the living character, which absorbs all the moral and psychological interest, will be the honest man.

• • •

In *Jonathan Wild* Fielding, the novelist, bids farewell to pure satire.
He has attacked Walpole bitterly, has seen him replaced by another, and
is now heartily sick of these struggles, the sole object of which is to put
one "great man" in the place of another. As for the small and the weak,
they are always oppressed; it is from them that reform must come.

> Nothing sure can be more justly ridiculous than the conduct of those who
> should lay the lamb in the wolf's way and then should lament his being
> devoured. What a wolf is in a sheep-fold a great man is in society. Now,
> when one wolf is in possession of a sheep-fold, how little would it avail
> the simple flock to expel him and place another in his stead. . . . Perhaps
> some would say, Is it then our duty tamely to submit to the rapine of the
> *prig,* who now plunders us, for fear of an exchange? Surely no: but I
> answer, it is better to shake the plunder off than to exchange the plunderer.
> And by what means can we effect this but by a total change in our man-
> ners? (IV, iii)

So says the "grave man," drawing his lesson from the revolt at Newgate
which has replaced Johnson by Wild. Henceforward Fielding hopes far
more from moral reform than from any political change. The moralist
emerges more and more clearly from the pure satirist.

• • •

We cannot, however, complete this chapter without pausing before one
other consideration. Many of Fielding's readers, among them Walter
Scott, and even Coleridge, have not been able to avoid a certain feeling
of discomfort in reading *Jonathan Wild.* It is true that this book, by
reason of its very depth, is cruel. It belongs to the type which Bernard
Shaw calls "unpleasant." Is the cause to be sought in its advanced democratic aspirations, which had struck Byron? [6] I think not, for all Fielding's
readers, whatever their opinions, experience this uncomfortable feeling
in a greater or less degree. Neither is it due to the crudity of certain
expressions; the realistic novelists have taken the edge off our susceptibili-
ties in that matter. No, I am inclined to think that the undeniably uncomfortable sensation which may still come over the modern reader of
*Jonathan Wild* arises from the character of the book, which is at bottom
purely anarchical. It probes deep down into our souls and there, like
Swift, stirs up certain beliefs which we neither dare nor desire to disturb.
It is an intellectual pastime, a lawyer's game, wherein the concepts of
honor, virtue, and social distinctions are roughly handled. Judged as
dangerous by those who believe in "necessary prejudices," it may also
shock those who accept them without believing in them, or who deem
it imprudent to destroy them. Like Pascal's, his [Fielding's] doubt sometimes leads us into depths which terrify the ordinary swimmer.

[6] *Works,* ed. Murray, 1904, *Letters and Journals,* V, 465.

# Notes for a Preface
# to Fielding's *Tom Jones*

## by *André Gide*

He admires only spontaneous virtue. All striving toward perfection —if it is not attained effortlessly by love—is motivated by pride and achieved only by loss of common humanity. His antipathy to sanctity is like that of Molière. I do not mean that neither is incapable of understanding and appreciating a saint, but neither portrays a character who consciously aspires to self-perfection, self-conquest, painful self-denial— in short, to mortification of the flesh.

Tom Jones' most flagrant misdeeds never occasion remorse or repentance; if he worries at all, it is because they may have distressed Sophia.

> Good nature is that benevolent and amiable temper of mind, which disposes us to feel the misfortunes, and enjoy the happiness of others; and, consequently, pushes us on to promote the latter, and prevent the former; and that without any abstract contemplation on the beauty of virtue, and without the allurements or terrors of religion. ("Essay on the Characters of Men," *The Works of Henry Fielding, Esq.*, ed. W. E. Henley (London: Heinemann, 1903), XIV, 285)

> For admitting, that laughing at the vices and follies of mankind is entirely innocent (which is more, perhaps, than we ought to admit), yet surely, their miseries and misfortunes are no subjects of mirth; and with these *Quis non vicus abundat?* the world is so full of them, that scarce a day passes without inclining a truly good-natured man rather to tears than merriment. (p. 286)

"Notes for a Preface to Fielding's *Tom Jones*" ("Notes pour une préface au *Tom Jones* de Fielding"). From the "Feuillets" in *Oeuvres complètes* (Paris: La Nouvelle Revue Française, Librairie Gallimard, 1937), XIII, 412-416 (reprinted as "Notes en manière de préface," in Henry Fielding, *Tom Jones*, tr. Defauconpret, Paris, 1938, [vii]-ix). Copyright 1938 by Gallimard. Translated by William H. McBurney. Reprinted here by permission of Librairie Gallimard. All rights reserved. For an excellent elucidation of this essay, see William B. Coley, "Gide and Fielding," *Comparative Literature*, XI (1959), 1-15.

Squire Allworthy: a dubious creation. Any attempt by a novelist to impose on the reader a paragon of virtue is risky—for example, Grandison. Even Prince Myshkin barely escapes the potential dangers and only the brilliant adroitness of Dostoevsky could save him. It is interesting to note, therefore, that Fielding, who disliked paragons (of vice as well as of virtue) has diluted Allworthy's perfect benevolence with a certain obtuseness. He endows him with a theoretical perceptivity but he allows him to be constantly duped. Allworthy tends to believe that everyone is as charitable as he is and so is incapable of understanding the artifices and malice of others—for we can only comprehend what we, in essence, are.

Even more interesting is the fact that Allworthy was an actual person, a benefactor whom Fielding meant to thank. If Allen, the prototype and model, was (as we are told) very pleased to recognize the tribute, probably it was because he knew himself to be less perfect than Fielding had portrayed him.

Nowadays since we are almost too well-aware that piety need not always be hypocritical, the descriptions of _____ seem less striking.

But is it not curious that Fielding only chose to portray pious hypocrites and that true virtue is never associated with real piety in his novels (perhaps I am theorizing too much; this should be carefully investigated).

Early in the novel, we see Tom Jones steal, but he steals for others, not for himself. His rewards are reprimands and whippings; to the gamekeeper's family go the stolen apples and duck.

Then we see Tom lie, but he lies only to protect the same gamekeeper and to take all the blame for a mutual misdeed. Tom, threatened with punishment, has a sleepless night, but not (we are given to understand) because of the anticipated pain but because of the fear that he may weaken and betray what he considers a point of honor to conceal— the name of his fellow offender (who, Fielding tells us slyly, also lies awake worrying about the same problem—Tom's sense of honor).

But Tom does not weaken. He "was contented to be flead rather than betray his friend or break the promise he had made."

Allworthy, who has ordered the whipping, thinks that the punishment exceeds the crime, for he sees in Tom's determination to conceal the truth only a "mistaken point of honour."

"Honour!" cries X. [Thwackum], who here serves as executioner, ". . . Can honour teach any one to tell a lie, or can any honour exist independent of religion?" (Bk. III, chap. ii).

He exposes the workings of certain characters to his readers, but at the same time warns them that "they are deceived, if they imagine that the most intimate acquaintance which they themselves could have had with that divine would have informed them of those things which we, from our inspiration, are enabled to open and discover."

If the event happened contrary to his expectations, this possibly proceeded from some fault in the plan itself;—which the reader hath my leave to discover, if he can. For we do not pretend to introduce any infallible characters into this history; where we hope nothing will be found which hath never yet been seen in human nature. (Bk. III, chap. v)

In reality . . . she certainly hated her own son—of which, however monstrous it appears, I am assured she is not a singular instance. . . ." (Bk. III, chap. vi)

# Tom Jones

## by Arnold Kettle

If *Joseph Andrews* is very different from *Jonathan Wild*, *Tom Jones* is almost as different again. What strikes one most, perhaps, returning to this novel, is how very tentative and experimental a book it is. In spite of all the apparent self-confidence, the easy handling of his puppet master role and the great expertness in plot-construction, Fielding is forever feeling his way, moving from one plane of narrative to another, tentatively exploring the possibilities of his *milieu*.

The immediate impression is the opposite of tentative. Fielding appears to be very much in control of the situation. The plot, as numerous critics have pointed out, is worked out with the greatest skill; it is the job, indeed, of the successful professional dramatist Fielding had been. Even more basic to the impression of assuredness is the nature of Fielding's philosophy, skeptical but optimistic. He takes the world in his stride, always curious, frequently indignant, but never incurably hurt. It is not, in the academic sense, a philosophy at all, certainly not a conscious metaphysical system. Rather is it an attitude of mind, an acceptance of certain standards and approaches. Fielding, like most of the writers of the eighteenth century, is very sure of his world. He is not complacent but he is fundamentally confident—confident that the problems of human society, that is to say *his* society, can and will be solved by humane feeling and right reason. It is this broad and tolerant confidence which gives *Tom Jones* its particular tone and which also (one suspects) alienates those critics who feel less confidence in social man than Fielding, whose optimism they mistake for insensitiveness.

The tentative note can be isolated as emerging from Fielding's constant preoccupation with method. How best to gain the reader's interest? How to project a character on to the page? How to achieve any kind of suspense without either playing a trick on the reader or forfeiting his own position as omniscient puppet master? He is constantly finding that the

"*Tom Jones.*" From *An Introduction to the English Novel* (London: Hutchinson University Library, 1951; paperback reprint, Harper Torchbooks, 1960), I, 76-81. Reprinted by permission of the publisher, Hutchinson & Co. Ltd.

contrivance of his plot does violence to the characters he has created. The truth is that in *Tom Jones* there is too much plot. Scenes take place which do not arise inevitably from character and motive. And the characters themselves are not, in the fullest sense, people. They are almost all "flat" characters in the tradition of the comedy of humours, that useful though unsubtle theory based on the crude physiological psychology of the Middle Ages. The very language of the "humors" tradition lingers on. Tom Jones's "complexion" is referred to when his amorous exploits are under discussion. Mr. Allworthy's name betrays the manner of his conception.

The point, here, is not that the "humours" tradition is invalid but that it does not quite square with the larger claims of Fielding to present a true and realistic picture of "human nature." There is any amount of "life" in *Tom Jones*, but it is not presented with any kind of consistency of convention. Some episodes are fully dramatic, developing through and out of their own internal potentialities, like the scene in which Sophia finds Tom in Lady Bellaston's room; others, like the muddles in the inn, are simply contrivances with no point beyond the exploitation of the farcical moment; others again, like Molly Seagrim's fracas in the churchyard, are realistic narrative which make up the larger panorama, but in which the reader is not at all closely involved. The characters, too, are conceived on various planes. Allworthy is almost an allegorical figure, scarcely individualized at all; Square and Thwackum are like ninepins, put up in order to be knocked down; Mrs. Blifil is a realistic character, essentially a type, not presented in the round, but subtly observed; Tom himself and Squire Western are unsubtle but fully rounded figures; Partridge is a great deal larger than life, a creation conceived and introduced almost in terms of the later music hall.

And yet for all this the novel has a unity and a pattern, which is something beyond the artificial unity of its carefully contrived but entirely nonsymbolic plot.

*Tom Jones* is a panoramic commentary on England in 1745, and it is also the story of Tom Jones and Sophia Western. And what engages our sympathy in that story is (oddly enough, one might suppose, for the two books are otherwise quite dissimilar), just what engages our sympathy on behalf of Clarissa. Tom and Sophia, like Clarissa, are rebels, revolting against the respectably accepted domestic standards of eighteenth century society. By such standards Sophia should obey her father and Tom should be, what Blifil thinks him, an illegitimate upstart who ought to be put firmly in his place.

Now it is true that, for the purposes of the plot (and to placate conventional taste) Fielding makes Tom a gentleman after all; but that is not really important. What does matter, because the whole movement and texture of the book depend on it, is that Tom and Sophia fight conventional society, embodied in the character of Blifil. They fight with every stratagem, including, when necessary, fists and swords and pistols. Unlike Clarissa, they are not passive in their struggle, and that is why *Tom Jones* is not a tragedy but comedy. It is not the conventionally contrived happy ending but the confidence we feel throughout the book that Tom and Sophia can and will grapple with their situation and change it that gains our acceptance of Fielding's comic view of life. It is, of course, no real contradiction that the same reader who is convinced by the tragedy of Clarissa should also be convinced by the comedy of *Tom Jones*. Tragedy and comedy, even in the same situation, are not mutually exclusive.

The struggle of Tom and Sophia against Blifil and all that he stands for is at the very center of the novel. It is neither Allworthy, whose standards are shown to be wanting but who is genuinely deceived, nor the superbly presented old idiot, Squire Western, who is the villain of *Tom Jones*, but Blifil. Indeed, it is the particular weakness of both Allworthy and Western that they are taken in by Blifil, whom they accept at his face value. Blifil, "sober, discreet and pious," is in fact treacherous, lecherous, hypocritical and entirely self-seeking. From the moment he betrays Black George, whom Tom has protected with an admirable lie, we know what Blifil is like. He is forever on the side of conventional respectability, the friend (significantly) of both Square and Thwackum, despite their mutual (and logical) incompatibility. And when his fell schemes—centering as they do upon the orthodox ruling class concern with property and a "good" marriage—are defeated, Fielding's description of him is significant:

> He cast himself on his bed, where he lay abandoning himself to despair, and drowned in tears; not in such tears as flow from contrition, and wash away guilt from minds which have been seduced or surprised into it unawares, against the bent of their dispositions, as will sometimes happen from human frailty, even to the good; no, these tears were such as the frighted thief sheds in his cart, and are indeed the effect of that concern which the most savage natures are seldom deficient in feeling for themselves.

Inevitably our minds are carried back to *Jonathan Wild*, and it is not by a casual stroke. It is relevant to recall that the weakness of *Jonathan Wild* lies in Heartfree; the strength of *Tom Jones* lies to a high degree in Tom. For Tom, unlike Heartfree, *is* able to carry the positive values of Fielding's world. Unlike Heartfree, he is not afraid to fight, if necessary to tell lies. He has all the vigor and spirit that Heartfree lacks. In him Fielding's positives—the values of the open heart—become more concrete and more fully realized. In Tom the prevailing positive is spontaneity: he acts "naturally" and therefore the excesses into which his animal spirits lead him are forgiven. There is an interesting link here with that recurring eighteenth century figure, the noble savage (glimpsed by Mrs.

Heartfree in Africa), a personage who becomes in time (Mrs. Inchbald's *Nature and Art* is a link here) the "natural man" of Rousseau and the Romantics.

The "natural man" (descending from a "golden age") and the "noble savage" are of course sentimental idealizations, but they play nevertheless an important part in the struggle of eighteenth century man to free himself from the limitations of mechanical materialism and the consequences of class society. They are vigorous concepts because they oppose the static world view of the eighteenth century ruling class. Their strength lies in their revolutionary assertion of the capacity of human nature to change itself and the world; their weakness lies in the idealist nature of that assertion.

Now the strengths and weaknesses of Fielding's conception of Tom Jones have precisely these same qualities. The strength lies in the vigor and spontaneity of Tom's reactions; the weakness in the element of idealism implicit in Fielding's simple confidence in the values of the heart. After all, is not Tom just a little too ready to wash his hands of Molly Seagrim and does not the inadequacy here spring from an unwillingness to evaluate the morality of spontaneity within the bounds of a particular social situation? More important, can one happy marriage really justify a world in which the Blifils rule the roost? Are the weapons of Tom and Sophia weapons enough?

It is, nevertheless, the central story of Tom and Sophia that best expresses in concrete form the view of life which Fielding is concerned to encompass in his novel (or, perhaps one should say that it is from the effect on us of the story of Tom and Sophia that we are best able to judge the nature and validity of Fielding's view of life). Yet we do not get very close to Tom and Sophia. Fielding deliberately keeps them at a distance. The ironical opening description of Sophia[1] is really a way of *not* describing her. And later in the novel Fielding writes of his heroine:

> As to the present situation of her mind, I shall adhere to a rule of Horace, by not attempting to describe it, from despair of success. Most of my readers will suggest it easily to themselves; and the few who cannot, would not understand the picture, or at least would deny it to be natural, if ever so well drawn.[2]

Now this deliberate refusal to bring us really close to his characters, so that all the time he tends to describe rather than convey a situation, cannot just be dismissed as a failure in Fielding's art. On the contrary it is essential to his comic method. He asks that the reader should survey life rather than experience it. And so he tends always to approach the particular situation through the general comment. Hence the quality of

---

[1] *Tom Jones,* Book IV, chap. ii.
[2] *Ibid.,* Book IV, chap. xiv.

his style,[3] brimming with abstract nouns which generalize the narrative, remove the particular emotion to a distance and yet—because Fielding's own social attitudes (and therefore his language) are so secure and confident—evoke a response remarkably precise and controlled though not, of course, intimate. It is with English society at large, not with the precise quality of feeling of individual characters, that he is primarily concerned. And between this large panorama, this general interest, and ourselves Fielding himself stands (larger, more insistent than any of his creations) directing our attention, controlling our reactions, imposing the pattern. Henry James, of all novelists perhaps the furthest removed from Fielding in method and outlook, has admirably made the essential point:

> It is very true that Fielding's hero in *Tom Jones* is but as "finely," that is as intimately, bewildered as a young man of great health and spirits may be when he hasn't a grain of imagination: the point to be made is, at all events, that his sense of bewilderment obtains altogether on the comic, never on the tragic plane. He has so much "life" that it amounts, for the effect of comedy and application of satire, almost to his having a mind, that is to his having reactions and a full consciousness besides which his author—*he* handsomely possessed of a mind—has such an amplitude of reflection for him and round him that we see him through the mellow air of Fielding's fine old moralism, fine old humour and fine old style, which somehow really enlarge, make everyone and everything important.[4]

[3] E.g., "Matrimony, therefore, having removed all such motives, he grew weary of this condescension, and began to treat the opinions of his wife with that haughtiness and insolence which none but those who deserve some contempt can bestow, and those only who deserve no contempt can bear" (Book II, chap. vii).

[4] Henry James: *The Princess Casamassima*, Preface.

# Fielding's "Sexual Ethic"
# in *Tom Jones*

## by *John Middleton Murry*

Indeed, the chief indictment brought against Fielding's novels by contemporary criticism was that they were "low." In *Joseph Andrews* he came near to representing, what one of his fictitious correspondents in *The Covent Garden Journal* stated as a fact, "that all the wit and humour of this kingdom was to be found in the ale houses." And not the wit and humor only, but the charity, the generosity, and the honest emotion. Certainly, he did believe, and showed, that the good nature—the natural sympathy and benevolence—which he prized above all other human qualities, was as frequent in low society as in high: more frequent, indeed, according to the testimony of his first novel. Who are Joseph Andrews' real benefactors on his eventful journey homeward? The postilion, who lent him his greatcoat, and was subsequently transported for robbing a hen roost; Betty the chambermaid, who got him the tea he longed for in spite of Mrs. Tow-wouse, but was in some other respects no better than she should be; and the pedlar who lent Parson Adams his all, amounting to six shillings and sixpence? The only one who belongs to a higher walk of society is Mr. Wilson, and he is a man who has deliberately retired from it in disgust of its deceptions as well as of his own follies. No doubt, in *Joseph Andrews* Fielding was giving our betters the worst of it, in reaction against the rather fulsome picture of the upper classes drawn in Richardson's *Pamela*. In his novels taken as a whole he holds the balance pretty level between the classes. Generosity of soul, he seems to say, is rare in either; but where it exists, it reveals class distinction as the accident he asserted it to be.

This was the attitude, one feels, which chiefly earned for Fielding the derogatory epithet of "low," and in particular his insistence that the particular manifestation of generosity of soul, which he believed was essential to the experience of love, was entirely independent of social position. He seems to have come to a full awareness of his own instinctive attitude through the impact upon him of Richardson's *Pamela.* That brilliant, but unsatisfactory book, shocked him profoundly. No doubt he was as impressed as we are by Richardson's narrative skill, and the subtlety with which he delineates the growth of Pamela's passion for her designing and unscrupulous master; but he drew the line absolutely at accepting it for what Richardson claimed it to be, a sound and edifying moral tale. As an example of "virtue rewarded" it stuck in his throat. "Virginity extorts its price," would, in Fielding's opinion, have been a much more accurate subtitle. Pamela's "virtue" was a spurious article. Fielding let himself go about it, merrily and coarsely, in *Shamela* (which is almost certainly his, though he never owned it); but he was not satisfied with that immediate explosion. *Pamela,* whose influence was enormous, was not to be combated effectively in that way.

So he set to again, and this time, in *Joseph Andrews* all his faculties were engaged. It is evident from the book that Fielding began with no particular plan beyond the brilliant and immediate one of giving Pamela a footman brother, who was a prodigy of "virtue" like herself, and representing him as assailed by his aristocratic mistress, whose bodily attractions were equal to her appetite. The opening scenes between Lady Booby and Joseph are magnificent: for verve and comic brilliance they are not surpassed, if indeed they are equaled, by anything that follows in the book. But, obviously, if the story was to be developed from that basis—as a sustained and deadly parody of *Pamela*—it would have had to proceed by a fairly patient exposition of Joseph's skill in leading Lady Booby on until her passion got the better of her pride and she agreed to marry him. Not only would this have made Joseph a character thoroughly uncongenial to Fielding, but, because nature would insist on breaking in, Joseph's character had already, in the Lady Booby scenes, been so presented that such a development was impossible. Her ladyship's person had been made very attractive; and the invitation of her naked bed irresistible to a young man of normal composition. And Fielding, on the whole, agreed with Shakespeare:

> And, when a woman woos, what woman's son
> Will sourly leave her till she have prevailed?

Joseph, in refusing the temptation, would plainly have been revealed as a prig, in Fielding's estimation, had he not been able to set up what Fielding regarded as the one absolutely valid defense against the charge of inflicting upon a comely woman the humiliation of rejecting her offered beauty: namely, the fact that he was already in love.

Not that Fielding would have been very severe on Joseph even if he had succumbed to Lady Booby: he certainly would not have rejected him as a monster, or concluded that it was impossible for him to be genuinely in love with his Fanny. It was obviously for him an interesting and important problem in sexual ethics, for he treated it copiously in both *Tom Jones* and *Amelia*, where the heroes have not the advantage—a real one in Fielding's eyes—of having been educated by Parson Adams. Tom Jones falls three times. His initial amour with Molly Seagrim, which at first made him relatively insensible to the charms of Sophia, does not count; but his resumption of it, at the very moment when, slightly drunk, he had taken out his knife to carve Sophia's name upon a tree, certainly does. His affair with Mrs. Waters at the Upton inn also counts; and so, more seriously still, does his intrigue with Lady Bellaston. Common to them all is that the women make the running. And there is to be said for Tom Jones throughout, that he is never really certain, until the very end of the book, that his love for Sophia is not utterly hopeless. The chief difference between his various amours is that, whereas with Molly Seagrim and Mrs. Waters Tom falls to their physical allure—Mrs. Waters' lovely bosom attracts his eyes at their first encounter—it is otherwise with Lady Bellaston. The process of his and her entanglement is admirably described. Her ladyship is prepared to fall for him by the rapturous account of her maid; the growth of her passion—for passion it becomes—is hastened when she sees him, by Mrs. Fitzpatrick's contrivance; the flame is fanned by his confession to her at the masquerade of his entire devotion to Sophia. Then Tom is in the toils.

> Jones had never less inclination to an amour than at present; but gallantry to the ladies was among his principles of honour; and he held it as much incumbent upon him to accept a challenge to love, as if it had been a challenge to fight.

Lady Bellaston's generosity to him rivets the chain. And though Fielding carries his realism to the point of hinting very plainly that her ladyship's breath, like her character, was no better than it should be, he is obviously not at all unsympathetic to Tom's notion of what his honor required. After enlarging on the fadedness of her ladyship's charms, he says:

> Though Jones saw all these discouragements on the one side, he felt his obligations full as strongly on the other; nor did he less plainly discern the ardent passion from whence those obligations proceeded, the extreme violence of which if he failed to equal, he well knew the lady would think him ungrateful; and what is worse, he would have thought himself so. He knew the tacit consideration upon which all her favours were conferred; and as his necessity obliged him to accept them, so his honour, he concluded, forced him to pay the price. This therefore he resolved to do, whatever misery it cost him, from that great principle of justice, by which the laws of some countries oblige a debtor, who is not otherwise capable of discharging his debt, to become the slave of his creditor.

Naturally, Fielding leaves a good deal to our imagination in this delicate matter: but he means to compel us to imagine. And it is fairly plain that, however irksome it might be for a truly good-natured man "to support love with gratitude," Fielding means us to believe that Tom did. His lack of such positive physical desire for Lady Bellaston as had taken him into the arms of Molly and Mrs. Waters was supplied by his genuine gratitude to her. The defect of the one passion was filled by the fullness of the other. And we are sufficiently convinced of this to feel that the potential sordidness of the relation is dispelled.

It seems that in this affair between Tom Jones and Lady Bellaston, Fielding was deliberately exploring the human reality of the situation which he had adumbrated, as a mere abstract and satirical possibility, in *Joseph Andrews*. Originally it entered his mind simply as the comic converse of the relation between Pamela and her concupiscent master, Mr. B——. That, as it stood, he could not develop with veracity. His plan compelled him to depict Joseph as resisting the very positive charms and seductions of Lady Booby; but, though he had fortified him with a moral education from Parson Adams and a genuine devotion to Fanny, Fielding, it is pretty plain, did not really believe in Joseph's behavior. It was, in the simple sense, too good to be true, when judged by his criterion of the natural behavior of a good-natured young man. On the other hand, it was equally impossible to sustain the satire on *Pamela*, by representing Joseph as cunningly trading his virtue for a marriage with her ladyship. So Fielding virtually dropped the situation altogether: he brought Abraham Adams on to the center of the stage, and deposed Joseph to a merely secondary role, in which the fact of his being rather a lay figure could do no great harm.

In other words, *Tom Jones* consists largely in a realization of possibilities which Fielding had suggested to himself in the course of writing *Joseph Andrews*. Tom is Joseph, as Sophia is Fanny, made real flesh and blood. Such a transmutation was not necessary in the case of Lady Booby, for she was already real—much the most real character in the book, if we except Adams, who belongs to a different order of creation. Lady Bellaston had only to be made different; and perhaps that is the original reason why she is definitely older than the still youthful Lady Booby. But Fielding's invention served him well, for it enabled him to represent his hero as betrayed not again by physical appetite but by his own notions of what gallantry and gratitude and honor required.

It is often forgotten by those who cannot help thinking Tom Jones slightly disreputable that he never lays siege to a woman; it is always the women who beleaguer him. Tom's trouble is that he cannot find it in his heart to repulse them: and this is because he is, fundamentally, an idealist about women. Rightly or wrongly, he discerns generosity in the woman's offer of herself to him, to which if he does not respond, he is self-condemned as ungenerous. This does not fit at all with conventional notions of the virtue of chastity, male or female; but it is not incongruous with a delicate and sensitive humanity. Much of Tom's potent charm for us consists in the real, as distinct from and even directly opposed to the conventional, purity he possesses. He is a really innocent soul, where Joseph Andrews is only abstractly innocent; and though he loses some of his boyish naïveté, he never loses his innocence. With Molly, he is naïve; he entirely fails to see that she is inveigling him. It is not vanity which persuades him he is the responsible party, but his incapacity to conceive that a young woman should be determined to seduce him. And when he has possessed her his reaction is that of a naturally generous soul to generosity. He was, Fielding says, one of those who "can never receive any kind of satisfaction from another, without loving the creature to whom that satisfaction is owing, and without making its well-being in some sort necessary to their own ease."

When he meets Mrs. Waters, he is evidently more experienced: he does not delude himself with the notion that he is the aggressor. He is aware that the lady is offering herself to him; and she knows well that the sight of her bosom has lighted a small flame in him.

> She seemed to be at the least of the middle age, nor had her face much appearance of beauty; but her clothes being torn from all the upper part of her body, her breasts, which were well formed and extremely white, attracted the eyes of her deliverer, and for a few moments they stood silent, and gazing on one another.

She does not hesitate to fan the flame by the same means. She deliberately refused Tom's offer of his overcoat, when he walked her to the Upton inn, and seized every opportunity she could to make him look back at her. Presumably, though Fielding did not record it, she consented to let her devastating bosom be covered, when they reached the village. Finally, she completes her conquest of him by "carelessly letting the handkerchief drop from her neck" and "unmasking the royal battery." Tom really had not much chance.

Nor was Mrs. Waters at all deeply perturbed when she discovered that Tom's heart was already engaged.

> The beauty of Jones highly charmed her eye; but as she could not see his heart, she gave herself no concern about it. She could feast heartily at the table of love, without reflecting that some other already had been, or hereafter might be, feasted with the same repast. A sentiment which, if it deals but little in refinement, deals, however, much in substance; and is less capricious, and perhaps less ill-natured and selfish, than the desires of those females who can be contented enough to abstain from the possession of their lovers, provided they are sufficiently satisfied that no one else possesses them.

Fielding's own sentiment about such women as Mrs. Waters is evident. They are more good-natured and more generous than many nominally more virtuous. He quite likes Mrs. Waters, and so do we. She is completely unmercenary, and she retained sufficient affection for Tom to do him a great service; and we may be pretty sure she made her lover happy, for all that Tom "detested the very thoughts of her" when he learned that Sophia had been at the inn and wanting to see him while he was otherwise engaged.

Behind all this behavior of Tom's is not "the genial tolerance of a man about town" in his creator, but a positive moral conviction, in the important sphere of the ethics of the sexual relation. Tom, his creator believes and convinces us, is fundamentally good: and as much as his appetite it is his goodness that leads him into his entanglements. In a different sphere, he manifests the same delicacy when he refuses to be the instrument for conveying Allworthy's sentence of banishment to Blifil. "What might perhaps be justice from another tongue would from mine be insult." Allworthy is a good man, indeed, but he has not Tom's imaginative sympathy, though he comes to recognize and admire it in Tom. "Oh, my child, to what goodness have I been so long blind!" This moral discrimination in the portrayal of Tom is as sound as it is subtle, but it is seldom explicitly distinguished even by admirers of Fielding: partly perhaps because they are content to accept the naturalness of Tom's character while they are engrossed by his adventures, and partly because Fielding himself seems to play it down by representing it as "good-nature," which has come to mean something different and much more vague than Fielding intended by it. In his essay *On the Knowledge of the Characters of Men*, he drew a distinction which is of cardinal importance to an understanding of *Tom Jones* and its hero. He speaks of "the gross but common mistake of good-humour for good-nature"—

> Two qualities, so far from bearing any resemblance to each other that they are almost opposites. Good-nature is that benevolent and amiable temper of mind which disposes us to feel the misfortunes and enjoy the happiness of others; and consequently pushes us on to promote the latter and prevent the former; and that without any abstract contemplation of the beauty of virtue, and without the allurements or terrors of religion. Now, good-humour is nothing more than the triumph of the mind, when reflecting on its own happiness, and that perhaps from having compared it with the inferior happiness of others.

In short, good nature is a natural and effortless goodness expressing itself as imaginative sympathy with the joys and sorrows of others: as distinct from the goodness which is constrained either by religious fears, or by the pursuit of a rationally conceived idea of virtue: both of which

Fielding holds up to ridicule in Thwackum and Square. He means that both these kinds of goodness tend to hypocrisy (perfected in their pupil Blifil), which is intolerable to him; and, even at their best, he believes them to be essentially inferior to the goodness which is natural and spontaneous, and finds expression in sympathy.

Fielding holds that good nature, in this sense, alone is capable of love. In the prefatory chapter to Book VI of *Tom Jones*, as against the philosophers who declare that there is no such thing as love, but only appetite, he defines love in precisely the same terms as he defines good nature.

> I desire of the philosophers to grant there is in some human breasts a kind and benevolent disposition which is gratified by contributing to the happiness of others. That in this gratification alone, as in friendship, in parental and filial affection, there is a great and exquisite delight. That if we will not call such a disposition love, we have no name for it. That though the pleasures arising from such pure love may be heightened and sweetened by the assistance of amorous desires, yet the former may subsist alone, nor are they destroyed by the intervention of the latter.

Love between man and woman is a particular manifestation of this general disposition.

> This love when it operates towards one of a different sex is very apt, towards its complete gratification, to call in the aid of that hunger which I have mentioned above [sexual appetite]; and which it is so far from abating that it heightens all its delights to a degree scarce imaginable by those who have never been susceptible of any other emotions than what have proceeded from appetite alone.

This consummation of physical passion between a man and a woman of good nature who love one another, Fielding holds, very definitely, to be the supreme felicity attainable on earth. And that is the end of Tom's adventurous pilgrimage. When Sophia and he are in bed together, Fielding declares, quite simply and sincerely:

> Thus, reader, we have at length brought our history to a conclusion, in which, to our great pleasure, though contrary perhaps to thy expectation, Mr. Jones appears to be the happiest of all humankind: for what happiness this world affords equal to the possession of such a woman as Sophia, I sincerely own I have never yet discovered.

It is Fielding's genuine conviction that this is the *summum bonum* for mortals: and Tom shares it. But until the very end of the novel he believes this felicity unattainable by him. He is in love with Sophia and believes she may be with him; but she is determined that she will not marry him without her father's consent, which it is hopeless to expect: and Tom, in disgrace with fortune and men's eyes, accepts it as right and proper that she should not. Doubtless, were he a Galahad, he would refuse all substitutes; but he is not. As Fielding puts it, when Tom falls to Molly the second time, after having caught her with Square, and in the very height and ecstasy of his dream of Sophia, "Jones probably thought one woman better than none"—a sentiment which, if not very exalted, is natural. And Tom, as we have seen, is always grateful to his partners: to Molly and Mrs. Waters for their physical kindness, and to Lady Bellaston for another sort of generosity: while, for their part, the ladies are not a whit behind in gratitude. Mrs. Waters afterwards thinks wistfully of him "to whom I owed such perfect happiness." So that Tom is, very definitely, not one of those "who have never been susceptible of any other emotions than what have proceeded from appetite alone." He is, if anything, rather a backward lover; it is being desired that makes him desire. And it is characteristic of him that, out of a kind of chivalry, he is unjust to himself when, at the end he reproaches himself to Sophia.

"After what is past, sir, can you expect that I should take you upon your word?"

He replied, "Don't believe me upon my word; I have a better security, a pledge for my constancy, which it is impossible to see and to doubt." "What is that?" said Sophia, a little surprised. "I will show you, my charming angel," cried Jones, seizing her hand and carrping her to the glass . . . .

Sophia blushed and half smiled; but, forcing again her brow into a frown,

"If I am to judge," said she, "of the future by the past, my image will no more remain in your heart when I am out of your sight, than it will in this glass when I am out of the room." "By heaven, by all that is sacred!" said Jones, "it never was out of my heart. The delicacy of your sex cannot conceive the grossness of ours, nor how little one sort of amour has to do with the heart."

That was unfair to himself. If grossness there was, which is disputable, the sexes had fairly shared it in Tom's affairs. But it was Tom's habit always to take the blame upon himself in everything, and above all where women were concerned. If he had tried to tell the real truth, as Fielding knew it, to Sophia, it would have been interesting. But she, of course, had to reply to what he actually said.

"I will never marry a man," replied Sophia, very gravely, "who shall not learn refinement enough to be as incapable as I am of making the distinction."

It sounds good; it is good. Yet we wonder what precisely *is* the distinction. But Tom understands.

"I will learn it," said Jones. "I have learnt it already. The first moment of hope that Sophia might be my wife taught it me at once; and all the rest of her sex from that moment became as little the objects of desire to my sense as of passion to my heart."

In short, as soon as Tom knew that his felicity with his beloved was attainable, desire and love became identical: no distinction was possible any more. But so long as this fruition seemed unattainable, desire was kindled for any attractive woman who would be kind. Perhaps it is a difficult sexual ethic to formulate: but, within Fielding's fundamental concept of good nature, conceived as fairly embracing the sexual with all the rest of human relations, it is entirely convincing. In *Tom Jones* Fielding exhibits it in a person and in act, and carries his point triumphantly. Good nature is better than goodness. "There is not in all English fiction, a hero as natural and endearing as Tom Jones"—and few heroines, one must add, more spirited, more feminine and more delightful than Sophia.

# Tom Jones and Clarissa

## by Ian Watt

Literature yields few more interesting *causes célèbres* than the debate over the respective merits of the novels of Fielding and Richardson, a debate which continues today[1] even though during the last century or so the supporters of Fielding have been in almost complete command of the field. The main reason for the vitality of the controversy is the exceptional range and variety of the issues—the opposition is not only between two kinds of novel, but between two kinds of physical and psychological constitution and between two social, moral, and philosophical outlooks on life. Not only so: the dispute has the advantage of a spokesman whose strong and paradoxical support for Richardson acts as a perennial provocation to the supporters of Fielding, who are dismayed to find Dr. Johnson, the authoritative voice of neoclassicism, pronouncing anathema on the last full embodiment of the Augustan spirit in life and literature.[2]

One way of resolving this last difficulty has been to suggest that Dr. Johnson's attitude should not be taken too seriously because it was dictated by friendship and personal obligation—Richardson had once saved him from being arrested for debt. Johnson's critical judgment, however, was not usually at the mercy of such considerations, and the supposition in any case runs counter to the fact that his enthusiastic endorsement of Richardson's novels was accompanied by a merciless awareness of the shortcomings of the man—witness his lethal jibe that Richardson "could not be content to sail quietly down the stream of

*"Tom Jones* and *Clarissa"* (Editor's title). From *The Rise of the Novel: Studies in Defoe, Richardson and Fielding* by Ian Watt (Berkeley and Los Angeles; London: 1957; paperback ed., 1959), chap. ix ("Fielding as Novelist: *Tom Jones*" ), pp. 260-289. Copyright 1957 by Chatto & Windus Ltd. Reprinted by permission of the author, the University of California Press, and Chatto & Windus Ltd.

[1] See, for example, Frank Kermode, "Richardson and Fielding," *Cambridge Journal*, IV (1950), 106-114; and, for a detailed account of their literary reputations, F. T. Blanchard, *Fielding the Novelist: A Study in Historical Criticism* (New Haven: Yale University Press, 1926).

[2] See Robert E. Moore, "Dr. Johnson on Fielding and Richardson," *PMLA*, LXVI (1951), 162-181.

reputation without longing to taste the froth from every stroke of the oar." [3]

We should, then, consider Johnson's preference seriously, particularly in view of the consistency with which he recurred to his main charge. "All the difference between the characters of Fielding and those of Richardson," he maintained, according to Boswell, was that between "characters of manners" and "characters of nature." "Characters of manners," of course, Johnson ranked much lower on the grounds that although "very entertaining . . . they are to be understood by a more superficial observer than characters of nature, where a man must dive into the recesses of the human heart." This distinction between Richardson and Fielding was more memorably expressed when Johnson said that "there was as great a difference between them as between a man who knew how a watch was made, and a man who could tell the hour by looking on the dial plate";[4] and the same idea is present in the even more plainly invidious statement reported by Mrs. Thrale that "Richardson had picked the kernel of life . . . while Fielding was contented with the husk." [5]

This basic distinction does not involve any direct divergence from critical orthodoxy, but it perhaps does so implicitly, since the basis of Richardson's "diving into the recesses of the human heart" was his detailed description of individual states of mind, a description which requires a minute particularity in the presentation of character, and which is therefore contrary to the usual neoclassical bias towards the general and the universal. There is no doubt that Johnson's theoretical presuppositions were strongly in this direction, as he often proclaimed the doctrine that the poet "must not dwell on the minuter distinctions by which one species differs from another." [6] Yet his operative premises for fiction were apparently quite different, since he reproached Fielding for his reluctance to dwell on these very distinctions, telling Mrs. Thrale, for example, that "Fielding could describe a horse or an ass, but he never reached to a mule." [7]

It would seem, then, that Johnson's vigorously independent literary sensibility tended to confirm at least one of the elements of the opposition described in the first chapter between neoclassical theory and the novel's formal realism. As for the discrepancy between Johnson's literary theory and his practical judgment, it need occasion little surprise: any body of doctrine is ambiguous in some of its applications, and especially when it is applied in areas for which it was not originally designed. In any case, Johnson's neoclassicism was not a simple thing (neither, for that matter,

[3] *Johnsonian Miscellanies*, ed. G. B. Hill (Oxford University Press, 1923), I, 273-274.
[4] *Life of Johnson*, ed. Hill-Powell, II (Oxford University Press, 1934), 48-49.
[5] *Johnsonian Miscellanies*, I, 282.
[6] *Rambler*, No. 36 (1750); see also *Rasselas*, chap. x.
[7] *Thraliana*, ed. K. C. Balderston (Oxford University Press, 1942), I, 555.

was neoclassicism); and his divergence from his usual principles in the present instance must surely be regarded as yet another example of how the radical honesty of his literary insight raised fundamental issues so forcibly that later criticism cannot but use his formulations as points of departure; any comparison between the two first masters of the novel form certainly must begin from the basis which he provided.

I

*Tom Jones* and *Clarissa* have sufficient similarity of theme to provide several closely parallel scenes which afford a concrete illustration of the differences between the methods of Fielding and Richardson as novelists. Both, for example, show us scenes where the heroine is forced to receive the addresses of the hated suitor their parents have chosen for them, and both also portray the later conflict between father and daughter which their refusal to marry this suitor provokes.

Here, first, is how Fielding describes the interview between Sophia Western and the odious Blifil:

> Mr. Blifil soon arrived; and Mr. Western soon after withdrawing, left the young couple together.
>
> Here a long silence of near a quarter of an hour ensued; for the gentleman, who was to begin the conversation, had all that unbecoming modesty which consists in bashfulness. He often attempted to speak, and as often suppressed his words just at the very point of utterance. At last, out they broke in a torrent of far-fetched and high-strained compliments, which were answered on her side by downcast looks, half bows, and civil monosyllables.—Blifil, from his inexperience in the ways of women, and from his conceit of himself, took this behaviour for a modest assent to his courtship; and when, to shorten a scene which she could no longer support, Sophia rose up and left the room, he imputed that, too, merely to bashfulness, and comforted himself that he should soon have enough of her company.
>
> He was indeed perfectly well satisfied with his prospect of success; for as to that entire and absolute possession of the heart of his mistress, which romantic lovers require, the very idea of it never entered his head. Her fortune and her person were the sole objects of his wishes, of which he made no doubt soon to obtain the absolute property; as Mr. Western's mind was so earnestly bent on the match; and as he well knew the strict obedience which Sophia was always ready to pay to her father's will, and the greater still which her father would exact, if there was occasion. . . .[8]

Structurally, the scene is based on that typical device of comedy, total ignorance by one character of the intentions of the other as a result of a misunderstanding between third parties—Squire Western has been misled by the ineffable Mistress Western into thinking that Sophia loves Blifil, not Tom Jones. It is perhaps because this misunderstanding must be kept up that there is no actual conversation and little feeling of personal contact between the characters concerned. Instead, Fielding, acting as omniscient author, lets us into Blifil's mind, and the meanness of the considerations by which it is governed: at the same time the consistent irony of Fielding's tone suggests to us the probable limits of Blifil's role: we need not fear that he will ever get possession of Sophia's fortune or of her person, for, although he is cast as a villain, it is patently as the villain in comedy.

Blifil's misunderstanding of Sophia's silence leads on to the next comic complication, since it causes him to give Squire Western the impression that his suit has prospered. Western at once goes to rejoice with his daughter, who of course is unaware of how he has been deceived:

> Sophia, perceiving her father in this fit of affection, which she did not absolutely know the reason of (for fits of fondness were not unusual in him, though this was rather more violent than ordinary), thought she should never have a better second opportunity of disclosing herself than at present, as far at least as regarded Mr. Blifil; and she too well foresaw the necessity which she should soon be under of coming to a full explanation. After having thanked the squire, therefore, for all his professions of kindness, she added with a look full of inexpressible softness, "And is it possible that my papa can be so good as to place all his joy in his Sophy's happiness?" which Western having confirmed by a great oath and a kiss, she then laid hold of his hand, and falling on her knees, after many warm and passionate declarations of affection and duty, she begged him "not to make her the most miserable creature on earth, by forcing her to marry a man she detested. This I entreat of you, dear sir," said she, "for your sake, as well as my own, since you are so very kind to tell me your happiness depends on mine."—"How! What!" says Western, staring wildly. "O, sir," continued she, "not only your poor Sophy's happiness, her very life, her being, depends upon your granting her request. I cannot live with Mr. Blifil. To force me into this marriage would be killing me."—"You can't live with Mr. Blifil!" says Mr. Western—"No, upon my soul, I can't," answered Sophia.—"Then die and be d—ned," cries he, spurning her from him. . . . "I am resolved upon the match, and unless you consent to it, I will not give you a groat, not a single farthing; no, though I saw you expiring in the street, I would not relieve you with a morsel of bread. This is my fixed resolution, and so I leave you to consider on it." He then broke from her with such violence, that her face dashed against the floor; and he burst directly out of the room, leaving poor Sophia prostrate on the ground.

Fielding's primary aim is certainly not to reveal character through speech and action. We cannot be meant to deduce, for instance, that Sophia knows her father so poorly as to entertain any hopes of being able to hold him down to one position by force of logic; what Fielding tells us about Sophia's decision to break the matter to her father is obviously mainly aimed at heightening the comic reversal that is to follow. Similarly we cannot consider Western's threat—"No, though I saw you expiring in the street, I would not relieve you with a morsel of bread"—as characteristic of the man either in diction or sentiment—it is hackneyed trope that belongs to any such situation in melodrama, not to a particular Squire who habitually speaks the most uncouth Somersetshire jargon, and whose childish intemperateness is not elsewhere shown capable of such an imaginative flight. To say that Sophia's and Western's speeches are grossly out of character would be an exaggeration; but they are undoubtedly directed entirely toward exploiting the comic *volte-face* and not toward making us witnesses of an actual interview between a father and daughter in real life.

It is probably an essential condition for the realization of Fielding's comic aim that the scene should not be rendered in all its physical and psychological detail; Fielding must temper our alarm for Sophia's fate by assuring us that we are witnessing, not real anguish, but that conventional kind of comic perplexity which serves to heighten our eventual pleasure at the happy ending, without in the meantime involving any unnecessary expenditure of tears on our part. Fielding's external and somewhat peremptory approach to his characters, in fact, would seem to be a necessary condition of the success of his main comic purpose: attention to the immediate counterpoint of misunderstanding and contradiction must not be dissipated by focussing interest on Sophia's feelings or on any other tangential issue.

A total contrast of purpose and method is offered by the way Richardson presents Clarissa's interview with Solmes, after her maid Hannah has warned her secretly that he is the husband that has been decided on for her. It is thus described in a letter to Anna Howe:

> I went down this morning when breakfast was ready with a very uneasy heart . . . wishing for an opportunity to appeal to my mother, in hopes to engage her interest in my behalf, and purposing to try to find one when she retired to her own apartment after breakfast; but, unluckily, there was the odious Solmes sitting asquat between my mother and sister, with *so much* assurance in his looks! But you know, my dear, that those we love not cannot do anything to please us.
>
> Had the wretch kept his seat, it might have been well enough: but the bent and broad-shouldered creature must needs rise and stalk towards a chair; which was just by that which was set for me.
>
> I removed it to a distance, as if to make way to my own: And down I sat, abruptly I believe; what I had heard all in my head.
>
> But this was not enough to daunt him. The man is a very confident, he is a very bold, staring man! Indeed, my dear, the man is very confident!
>
> He took the removed chair and drew it so near mine, squatting in it with his ugly weight, that he pressed upon my hoop. I was so offended (all I had

heard, as I said, in my head) that I removed to another chair. I own I had too little command of myself. It gave my brother and sister too much advantage. I dare say they took it. But I did it involuntarily, I think. I could not help it. I knew not what I did.

I saw that my father was excessively displeased. When angry, no man's countenance ever shows it so much as my father's. Clarissa Harlowe! said he with a big voice—and there he stopped. Sir! said I, trembling and curtsying (for I had not then sat down again): and put my chair nearer the wretch, and sat down—my face, as I could feel, all in a glow.

Make tea, child, said my kind mamma: sit by me, love, and make tea.

I removed with pleasure to the seat the man had quitted; and being thus indulgently put into employment, soon recovered myself; and in the course of the breakfasting officiously asked two or three questions of Mr. Solmes, which I would not have done, but to make up with my father. *Proud spirits may be brought to!* whisperingly spoke my sister to me over her shoulder, with an air of triumph and scorn: but I did not mind her.

My mother was all kindness and condescension. I asked her once if she were pleased with the tea. . . .

Small incidents these, my dear, to trouble you with; only as they lead to greater, as you shall hear.

Before the usual breakfast-time was over my father withdrew with my mother, telling her he wanted to speak to her. Then my sister and next my aunt (who was with us) dropped away.

My brother gave himself some airs of insult, which I understood well enough; but which Mr. Solmes could make nothing of: and at last he arose from *his* seat. Sister, says he, I have a curiosity to show you. I will fetch it. And away he went; shutting the door close after him.

I saw what all this was for. I arose; the man hemming up for a speech, rising and beginning to set his splay feet (indeed, my dear, the man in all his ways is hateful to me!) in an approaching posture. I will save my brother the trouble of bringing to me his curiosity, said I. I curtsied—your servant, sir. The man cried, madam, madam, twice, and looked like a fool. But away I went—to find my brother to save my word. But my brother, indifferent as the weather was, was gone to walk in the garden with my sister. A plain case that he had left his *curiosity* with me, and designed to show me no other.[9]

The passage is characteristic of Richardson's very different kind of realism. Clarissa is describing what happened "this morning," and is "as minute as" she knows Anna wishes her to be; only so can Richardson convey the physical reality of the scene—the party at breakfast, the jockeying for position over trifles, and all the ordinarily trivial domestic details which bear the main burden of the drama. The letter form gives Richardson access to thoughts and emotions of a kind that cannot issue in speech, and are hardly capable of rational analysis—the flux and reflux of Clarissa's lacerated sensibility as she struggles against parental tyranny on the battlefield of petty circumstance: as a result we have quite

⁹ Everyman ed., I, 68-70.

a different kind of participation from that which Fielding produces: not a lively but objective sense of the total comic pattern, but a complete identification with the consciousness of Clarissa while her nerves still quiver from the recollection of the scene, and her imagination recoils from the thought of her own strained alternation between involuntary revolt and paralyzed compliance.

Because Richardson's narrative sequence is based on an exploration in depth of the protagonist's reaction to experience, it encompasses many minor shades of emotion and character that are not found in the passages from *Tom Jones*. Fielding does not attempt to do more than to make us understand the rational grounds on which Sophia acts as she does—there is nothing which would not fit almost any sensible young girl's behavior in the circumstances: whereas Richardson's epistolary technique, and the intimacy of Clarissa with Anna, encourages him to go far beyond this, and communicate a host of things which deepen and particularize our picture of Clarissa's total moral being. Her shuddering ejaculation—"Indeed, my dear, the man is very confident," her scornful comment on her sister's intervention—"I did not mind her," and her admission of involvement in petty family rivalries—she regrets moving away from Solmes because "It gave my brother and sister too much advantage"—all these details of characterization must surely be overlooked by those who describe Richardson as a creator of "ideal" characters: there is, of course, great will and tenacity in Clarissa, but it is very definitely that of an inexperienced young woman, who has her fair share of sisterly vindictiveness and pert self-assertion, and who, far from being an idealized figure of virgin sainthood, is capable of the catty and sardonic emphasis on Mr. Solmes as a "curiosity." Nor is she by any means a disembodied being; we have no indications of any physical reaction on Sophia's part toward Blifil, but we are given Clarissa's very intense one to Solmes—an instinctive sexual revulsion from "his ugly weight."

The same setting of personal relationships in a minutely described physical, psychological and even physiological continuum is shown in the brief scene which is the counterpart of the second passage quoted from *Tom Jones*. After two private interviews with her mother, Clarissa has been faced with a family ultimatum, and her mother is with her to receive an answer:

> Just then, up came my father, with a sternness in his looks that made me tremble. He took two or three turns about my chamber, though pained by his gout. And then said to my mother, who was silent, as soon as she saw him:
> My dear, you are long absent. Dinner is near ready. What you had to say lay in a very little compass. Surely, you have nothing to do but to declare *your* will, and *my* will— but perhaps you may be talking of the preparations. Let us soon have you down—your daughter in your hand, if worthy of the name.

And down he went, casting his eye upon me with a look so stern that I was unable to say one word to him, or even for a few minutes to my mother.[10]

Richardson and Fielding portray the cruelty of the two fathers very differently; that of Squire Western has an involuntary and exaggerated quality, whereas Mr. Harlowe's is that of ordinary life; the latter's callous resolve seems all the more convincing because it is only manifested in his refusal to speak to Clarissa—our own emotional involvement in the inner world of Clarissa makes it possible for a father's silent look to have a resonance that is quite lacking in the physical and rhetorical hyperbole by which Fielding demonstrates the fury of Squire Western.

## II

On further analysis, then, it appears that Johnson's comparison between Richardson and Fielding does not directly raise the question of which was the better psychologist, but depends rather on their quite opposite literary intentions: those of Fielding allotted characterization a much less important place in his total literary structure, and precluded him even from attempting the effects which were suited to Richardson's very different aim. The full implications of the divergence can perhaps be most clearly and inclusively demonstrated in Fielding's handling of the plot in *Tom Jones*, for it reflects the whole of his social, moral, and literary outlook.

Fielding's conduct of the action, despite a few excrescences such as the interpolated story of the Man of the Hill, and some signs of haste and confusion in the concluding books,[11] exhibits a remarkably fine control over a very complicated structure, and abundantly justifies Coleridge's famous eulogy: "What a master of composition Fielding was! Upon my word, I think the *Oedipus Tyrannus*, the *Alchemist*, and *Tom Jones*, the three most perfect plots ever planned." [12]

Perfect for what? we must ask. Not, certainly, for the exploration of character and of personal relations, since in all three plots the emphasis falls on the author's skilfully contrived revelation of external and deterministic scheme: in *Oedipus* the hero's character is of minor importance compared with the consequences of his past actions, which were themselves the result of a prophecy made long before his birth; in the *Alchemist* the portrayal of Face and Subtle does not go far beyond the need for suitable instruments to carry out Jonson's complex series of chicaneries; while the plot of *Tom Jones* offers a combination of these

---

[10] I, 75-76.
[11] For a full account see F. H. Dudden, *Henry Fielding* (Oxford University Press, 1952), pp. 621-627.
[12] Blanchard, *op. cit.*, pp. 320-321.

features. As in Sophocles, the crucial secret, that of the hero's actual birth, is very elaborately prepared for and hinted at throughout the action, and its eventual disclosure brings about the final reordering of all the main issues of the story: while, as in Jonson, this final reordering is achieved through the unmasking of a complicated pattern of villainy and deception.

The three plots are alike in another respect: their basic direction is toward a return to the norm, and they therefore have a fundamentally static quality. In this they no doubt reflect the conservatism of their authors, a conservatism which in Fielding's case is probably connected with the fact that he belonged, not to the trading class like Defoe and Richardson, but to the gentry. The plots of the novels of Defoe and Richardson, as we have seen, mirrored certain dynamic tendencies in the outlook of their class: in *Moll Flanders*, for example, money has a certain autonomous force which determines the action at every turn. In *Tom Jones*, on the other hand, as in the *Alchemist*, money is something that the good characters either have or are given or momentarily lose: only bad actors devote any effort either to getting it or keeping it. Money, in fact, is a useful plot device but it has no controlling significance.

Birth, on the other hand, has a very different status in *Tom Jones*: as a determining factor in the plot it is almost the equivalent of money in Defoe or virtue in Richardson. In this emphasis, of course, Fielding reflects the general tenor of the social thought of his day: the basis of society is and should be a system of classes each with their own capacities and responsibilities. The vigor of Fielding's satire on the upper classes, for example, should not be interpreted as the expression of any egalitarian tendency: it is really a tribute to the firmness of his belief in the class premise. It is true that in *Amelia* he goes so far as to say that "of all kinds of pride, there is none so un-Christian as that of station." [13] But that, of course, is only a matter of *noblesse oblige*; and in *Tom Jones* Fielding also wrote that "liberality of spirits" was a quality which he had "scarce ever seen in men of low birth and education." [14]

This class fixity is an essential part of *Tom Jones*. Tom may think it unfortunate that, as a foundling of presumed low ancestry, he cannot marry Sophia; but he does not question the propriety of the asumption on which their separation is decreed. The ultimate task of Fielding's plot therefore is to unite the lovers without subverting the basis of the social order; and this can only be done by revealing that Mr. Jones, though illegitimate, is genteel. This, however, is not wholly a surprise to the perceptive reader, for whom Tom's eminent "liberality of spirit" has already suggested his superior pedigree; the recent Soviet critic, therefore, who

[13] Bk. VII, chap. x.
[14] Bk. IX, chap. i. See also A. O. Lovejoy, *The Great Chain of Being* (Cambridge: Harvard University Press, 1936), pp. 224, 245.

sees the story as the triumph of a proletarian hero[15] is neglecting, not only the facts of his birth, but its continuing implications for his character.

Fielding's conservatism accounts for another and much more general difference between the plots of *Tom Jones* and *Clarissa*: for whereas Richardson depicts the crucifixion of the individual by society, Fielding portrays the successful adaptation of the individual to society, and this entails a very different relation between plot and character.

In *Clarissa* the individual must be given priority in the total structure: Richardson merely brings together certain individuals, and their proximity is all that is necessary to set off an extended chain reaction which then proceeds under its own impetus and modifies all the characters and their mutual relationships. In *Tom Jones*, on the other hand, society and the larger order which it represents must have priority, and the plot's function, therefore, is to perform a physical rather than a chemical change: it acts as a kind of magnet that pulls every individual particle out of the random order brought about by temporal accident and human imperfection and puts them all back into their proper position. The constitution of the particles themselves—the characters—is not modified in the process, but the plot serves to reveal something much more important —the fact that all human particles are subject to an ultimate invisible force which exists in the universe whether they are there to show it or not.

Such a plot reflects the general literary strategy of neoclassicism; just as the creation of a field of force makes visible the universal laws of magnetism, so the supreme task of the writer was to make visible in the human scene the operations of universal order—to unveil the handiwork of Pope's "Unerring Nature, still divinely bright,/One clear, unchanged and universal light."

This much wider perspective on character obviously reduces the importance which will be attached to the nature and actions of any particular individual entity—they are mainly interesting as manifestations of the great pattern of Nature. This informs Fielding's treatment of every aspect of characterization—not only the extent to which his *dramatis personae* are individualized, but the degree of attention paid to their subjective lives, to their moral development, and to their personal relationships.

Fielding's primary objectives in the portrayal of character are clear but limited: to assign them to their proper category by giving as few diagnostic features as are necessary for the task. Such was his conception of "invention" or "creation": "a quick and sagacious penetration into the true essence of all the objects of our contemplation." [16] This meant in practice that once the individual had been appropriately labeled the author's only remaining duty was to see that he continued to speak and

---

[15] A. Elistratov, "Fielding's Realism," in *Iz Istorii Angliskogo Realizma* [On the History of English Realism] (Moscow, 1941), p. 63.

[16] *Tom Jones*, Bk. IX, chap. i.

act consistently. As Aristotle put it in the *Poetics*, "character" is "that which reveals the moral purpose," and consequently "speeches . . . which do not make this manifest . . . are not expressive of character." [17] Parson Supple must never cease to be supple.

So it is that Fielding does not make any attempt to individualize his characters. Allworthy is sufficiently categorized by his name, while that of Tom Jones, compounded as it is out of two of the commonest names in the language, tells us that we must regard him as the representative of manhood in general, in accordance with his creator's purpose to show "not men, but manners; not an individual, but a species." [18]

The scope of the word "manners" has dwindled so drastically in the last few centuries—no doubt as a result of the way individualism has reduced the areas in which identity of thought and action is generally expected—that the phrase "characters of manners" no longer means very much. It can perhaps be best explained in terms of the contrast with Richardson's "characters of nature." Richardson's literary objective, as B. W. Downs has pointed out,[19] is not so much character—the stable elements in the individual's mental and moral constitution—as personality: he does not analyze Clarissa, but presents a complete and detailed behavioral report on her whole being: she is defined by the fullness of our participation in her life. Fielding's purpose, on the other hand, is analytic: he is not interested in the exact configuration of motives in any particular person's mind at any particular time but only in those features of the individual which are necessary to assign him to his moral and social species. He therefore studies each character in the light of his general knowledge of human behavior, of "manners," and anything purely individual is of no taxonomic value. Nor is there any need to look inside: if, as Johnson said, Fielding gives us the husk, it is because the surface alone is usually quite sufficient to identify the specimen—the expert does not need to assay the kernel.

There are many other reasons for Fielding's predominantly external approach to character, reasons of a social and philosophical as well as of a literary order. To begin with, the opposite approach involved a breach of decorum: as Fielding's cousin Lady Mary Wortley Montagu pointed out, it was very bad manners for Richardson's heroines to "declare all they think," since "fig leaves are as necessary for our minds as our bodies." [20] It was also consistent with the classical tradition as a whole, as we have seen, to avoid the intimate and confessional approach to personality; and in any case the philosophical problems of self-consciousness had only begun to receive attention some six centuries after Aristotle in

---

[17] Chap. vi, No. 17.
[18] *Joseph Andrews*, Bk. III, chap. i.
[19] *Richardson* (London: Routledge & Kegan Paul, Ltd., 1928), pp. 125-126.
[20] *Letters and Works*, ed. Thomas (London, 1861), II, 291.

the works of Plotinus.[21] Lastly, as was evident in the treatment of Blifil and Sophia, Fielding's comic purpose itself required an external approach, and for a compelling reason. If we identify ourselves with the characters we shall not be in any mood to appreciate the humor of the larger comedy in which they are risible participants: life, we have been told, is a comedy only to the man who thinks, and the comic author must not make us feel every stroke of the lash as his characters squirm under his corrective rod.

At all events, Fielding avowedly and even ostentatiously refused to go too deep into the minds of his characters, on the general grounds that "it is our province to relate facts, and we shall leave causes to persons of much higher genius." We have noted how little was said about the feelings, as opposed to the rational determinations, of Blifil and Sophia. This was quite conscious on Fielding's part: he had already remarked ironically of Blifil that "it would be an ill office in us to pay a visit to the inmost recesses of his mind, as some scandalous people search into the most secret affairs of their friends, and often pry into their closets and cupboards, only to discover their poverty and meanness to the world"; similarly when Fielding came to present Sophia's feelings when she first learned of Tom's love, he excused himself in the words: "as to the present situation of her mind I shall adhere to the rule of Horace, by not attempting to describe it, from despair of success." [22]

Fielding's avoidance of the subjective dimension, then, is quite intentional: but that does not, of course, mean that it has no drawbacks, for it undoubtedly has, and they become very apparent whenever important emotional climaxes are reached. Coleridge, for all his love of Fielding, pointed out that in the soliloquies between Sophia and Tom Jones before their final reconciliation, nothing could be "more forced and unnatural: the language is without vivacity or spirit, the whole matter is incongruous, and totally devoid of psychological truth." [23] In fact, Fielding merely gave us a stock comic scene: elevated sentiments of penitent ardor on the hero's part were countered by wronged womanhood's equally elevated scorn of her faithless suitor. Soon after, of course, Sophia accepts Tom, and we are surprised by her very sudden and unexplained reversal: the denouement has been given a certain comic life, but at the expense of the reality of emotions involved.

This emotional artificiality is very general in *Tom Jones*. When the hero, for instance, is expelled from Allworthy's house we are told that "he presently fell into the most violent agonies, tearing his hair from his head, and using most other actions which generally accompany fits of madness, rage and despair"; and later that he read Sophia's parting letter

---

[21] See A. E. Taylor, *Aristotle* (London: Thomas Nelson & E. Jack Ltd., 1943), p. 108.
[22] Bk. II, chap. iv; Bk. IV, chaps. iii, xiv.
[23] Blanchard, *op. cit.*, p. 317.

"a hundred times over, and kissed it a hundred times as often." [24]
Fielding's use of these hackneyed hyperboles to vouch for the intensity of
the emotions of his characters underlines the price that he pays for his
comic approach: it denies him a convincing and continuous access to the
inner life of his characters, so that whenever he has to exhibit their
emotional life, he can only do it externally by making them have exaggerated physical reactions.

The fact that Fielding's characters do not have a convincing inner life
means that their possibilities of psychological development are very
limited. Tom Jones's character, for example, exhibits some development,
but it is of a very general kind. Tom's early imprudences, his youthful
lack of worldly wisdom, and his healthy animality, for example, lead to
his disgrace, his expulsion from the Allworthy household, his subsequent
difficulties on the road and in London, and his apparently irrecoverable
loss of Sophia's love. At the same time his good qualities, his courage,
honor, and benevolence, all of which have been glimpsed at the beginning, eventually combine to extricate him from the nadir of his misfortunes, and restore him to the love and respect of those who surround
him. But although different qualities come to the fore at different times
they have all been present from the beginning, and we have not been
taken close enough to Tom's mind to be able to do anything but take
on trust Fielding's implication, which is that his hero will be able to control his weaknesses by the wisdom he has learned of experience.

In taking this essentially static view of human nature Fielding was
following the time-hallowed Aristotelian view, which was actually held
with much greater rigidity by most of the philosophers and literary critics
of his time.[25] It is, of course, an a-historical view of character, as Fielding
showed in *Joseph Andrews*, when he asserted that his characters were
"taken from the life," but added that the particular lawyer in question
was "not only alive, but hath been so this four thousand years." [26] It
follows logically that if human nature is essentially stable, there is no
need to detail the processes whereby any one example of it has reached
its full development; such processes are but temporary and superficial
modifications of a moral constitution which is unalterably fixed from
birth. Such, for example, is the premise of the way that although Tom
and Blifil share the same mother and are brought up in the same household by the same tutors, their respective courses are unalterably set in
different directions from the very beginning.

Once again the contrast with Richardson is complete. Much of our
sense of Clarissa's psychological development arises from the way that

---

[24] Bk. VI, chap. xii.
[25] See Leslie Stephen, *History of English Thought in the Eighteenth Century* (2d ed.,
London, 1902), II, 73-74; R. Hubert, *Les Sciences sociales dans l'Encyclopédie* (Paris,
1923), pp. 167 ff.
[26] Bk. II, chap. i.

her experience brings a continual deepening of her understanding of her own past: as a result character and plot are indivisible. Tom Jones, on the other hand, is not in touch with his own past at all: we feel a certain unreality in his actions because they always seem to be spontaneous reactions to stimuli that the plot has been manipulated to provide; we have no sense that they are manifestations of a developing moral life. We cannot but feel surprise, for instance, when, immediately after accepting 50 pounds from Lady Bellaston, Tom gives his famous lecture to Nightingale on sexual ethics.[27] It is not that the two actions are inherently contradictory—Tom's ethics have throughout been based on the much greater heinousness of harming others than of failing to live up to one's moral code oneself; but if we had been given some indication that Tom was aware of the apparent contradictions between his speech and his own past practice he might have sounded less priggish and more convincing. Actually, of course, separate parts of Tom's nature can hold very little converse with each other, because there is only one agency for such converse—the individual consciousness through which the whole repertoire of past actions operates—and Fielding does not take us into this consciousness because he believes that individual character is a specific combination of stable and separate predispositions to action, rather than the product of its own past.

For the same reasons personal relationships are also relatively unimportant in *Tom Jones*. If there is a controlling force independent of the individual actors and their positions with respect to each other, and if their own characters are innate and unchanging, there is no reason why Fielding should give close attention to their mutual feelings, since they cannot play a decisive role. Here, again, the scene between Sophia and Blifil was typical in that it reflected the extent to which the structure of *Tom Jones* as a whole depends on the lack of any effective communication between the characters: just as Blifil must misunderstand Sophia, so Allworthy must fail to see Blifil in his true light, and Tom must be unable either to understand Blifil's true nature or to explain himself properly either to Allworthy or Sophia until the closing scenes. For, since Fielding's view of human life and his general literary purpose did not permit him to subordinate his plot to the deepening exploration of personal relationships, he needed a structure based on an elaborate counterpoint of deception and surprise, and this would be impossible if the characters could share each other's minds and take their fates into their own hands.

There is, then, an absolute connection in *Tom Jones* between the treatment of plot and of character. Plot has priority, and it is therefore plot which must contain the elements of complication and development.

[27] Bk. XIV, chap. vii.

Fielding achieves this by superimposing on a central action, that is in essentials as simple as that in *Clarissa*, a very complex series of relatively autonomous subplots and episodes which are in the nature of dramatic variations on the main theme. These relatively independent narrative units are combined in a concatenation whose elaboration and symmetry is suggested in the most obvious outward aspect of the book's formal order: unlike the novels of Defoe and Richardson, *Tom Jones* is carefully divided into compositional units of different sizes—some two hundred chapters which are themselves grouped into eighteen books disposed into three groups of six, dealing respectively with the early lives, the journeys to London, and the activities on arrival, of the main characters.

This extreme diversification of the narrative texture reinforces, of course, Fielding's tendency not to dwell for long on any one scene or character. In the passages quoted, for example, there was none of the intensive treatment which Richardson gave to Clarissa's interview with Solmes; most of Fielding's time was spent on making clear the initial misunderstanding, and the scale of the scene allowed no more in the way of characterization than a designing hypocrite, a trapped maiden, and a heavy father. But even if there had been any full absorption in the feelings of Sophia, for example, it would soon have been terminated by the management of the ensuing scenes: for, just as we left Sophia immediately after Squire Western had stormed out of the room, and were thus spared any prolonged awareness of her sufferings, so in the next chapter our attention was soon switched away from her parting interview with Tom Jones by Fielding's announcement that "the scene, which I believe some of my readers will think had lasted long enough, was interrupted by one of so different a nature, that we shall reserve the relation of it for a different chapter." [28]

This is typical of the narrative mode of *Tom Jones*: the author's commentary makes no secret of the fact that his aim is not to immerse us wholly in his fictional world, but rather to show the ingenuity of his own inventive resources by contriving an amusing counterpoint of scenes and characters; quick changes are the essence of Fielding's comic manner, and a new chapter will always bring a new situation for the characters, or present different characters in a similar scene for ironical contrast. In addition, by a great variety of devices, of which the chapter headings are usually significant pointers, our attention is continually drawn to the fact that the ultimate cohesive force of the book resides not in the characters and their relationships, but in an intellectual and literary structure which has a considerable degree of autonomy.

The effects of this procedure and its relationship to Fielding's treatment of character can be summarized in relation to a brief scene which occurs after Tom has heard that Allworthy is to recover from his illness.

[28] Bk. VI, chap. viii.

He takes a walk "in a most delicious grove," and contemplates the cruelty of fortune which separates him from his beloved Sophia:

> Was I but possessed of thee, one only suit of rags thy whole estate, is there a man on earth whom I would envy! How contemptible would the brightest Circassian beauty, dressed in all the jewels of the Indies, appear to my eyes! But why do I mention another woman? Could I think my eyes capable of looking at any other with tenderness, these hands should tear them from my head. No, my Sophia, if cruel fortune separates us for ever, my soul shall dote on thee alone. The chastest constancy will I ever preserve to thy image. . . .
>
> At these words he started up and beheld—not his Sophia—no, nor a Circassian maid richly and elegantly attired for the grand Signior's seraglio . . .

but Molly Seagrim, with whom, "after a parley" which Fielding omits, Tom retires to "the thickest part of the grove." [29]

The least convincing aspect of the episode is the diction: the speech habits manifested here obviously bear little relation to those we expect of Tom Jones. But, of course, they are a stylistic necessity for Fielding's immediate purpose—the comic deflation of the heroic and romantic pretenses of the human word by the unheroic and unromantic eloquence of the human deed. Tom Jones is no more than a vehicle for the expression of Fielding's skepticism about lovers' vows; and he must be made to speak in terms that parody the high-flown rhetoric of the pastoral romance to give point to the succeeding wayside encounter which belongs to the very different world of the *pastourelle*. Nor can Fielding pause to detail the psychological processes whereby Tom is metamorphosed from Sophia's romantic lover to Molly's prompt gallant: to illustrate the commonplace that "actions speak louder than words," the actions must be very silent and they must follow very hard upon very loud words.

The relation of this episode to the larger structure of the novel is typical. One of Fielding's general organizing themes is the proper place of sex in human life; this encounter neatly illustrates the conflicting tendencies of headstrong youth, and shows that Tom has not yet reached the continence of moral adulthood. The scene, therefore, plays its part in the general moral and intellectual scheme; and it is also significantly connected with the workings of the plot, since Tom's lapse eventually becomes a factor in his dismissal by Allworthy, and therefore leads to the ordeals which eventually make him a worthier mate for Sophia.

At the same time Fielding's treatment of the scene is also typical in avoiding any detailed presentation of Tom's feelings either at the time or later—to take his hero's faithlessness too seriously would jeopardize Fielding's primarily comic intention in the episode, and he therefore manip-

[29] Bk. V, chap. x.

ulates it in such a way as to discourage us from giving it a significance
which it might have in ordinary life. Comedy, and especially comedy on
an elaborate scale, often involves this kind of limited liability to psychological interpretation: it applies to Blifil's malice and to Sophia's sufferings in the scenes quoted earlier, and Allworthy's sudden illness and recovery, which have led to Tom's lapse, must be placed in the same perspective. We must not dwell on the apparent fact that Allworthy is incapable of distinguishing between a cold and a mortal illness, since we are
not intended to draw the implications for his character that he is either
an outrageous hypochondriac or lamentably unskilled in choosing phy-
sicians: Allworthy's illness is only a diplomatic chill, and we must not
infer anything from it except a shift in Fielding's narrative policy.

*Tom Jones*, then, would seem to exemplify a principle of considerable
significance for the novel form in general: namely, that the importance
of the plot is in inverse proportion to that of character. This principle has
an interesting corollary: the organization of the narrative into an extended
and complex formal structure will tend to turn the protagonists into its
passive agents, but it will offer compensatingly greater opportunities for
the introduction of a variety of minor characters, whose treatment will
not be hampered in the same way by the roles which they are allotted
by the complications of the narrative design.

The principle and its corollary would seem to lie behind Coleridge's
contrast of the "forced and unnatural quality" of the scenes between the
protagonists in *Tom Jones* and Fielding's treatment of the "characters of
postilions, landlords, landladies, waiters" where "nothing can be more
true, more happy or more humorous." [30] These minor characters figure
only in scenes which require exactly the amount of psychological indi-
viduality which they are possessed of; relieved of any responsibility for
carrying out the major narrative design, Mrs. Honour can get herself
dismissed from the Western household by methods which are at once
triumphantly comic, sociologically perceptive, and eminently characteristic;[31] nor is there any question of the violence to character and probability which colors the ways whereby Tom Jones, for example, or
Sophia leaves home.

Such is the pattern of most comic novels with elaborate plots, from
Fielding and Smollett to Dickens: the creative emphasis is on characters
who are minor at least in the sense that they are not deeply involved in
the working out of the plot: whereas the Tom Joneses, the Roderick
Randoms and the David Copperfields are less convincing as characters
because their personalities bear little direct relation to the part they
must play, and some of the actions in which the plot involves them

[30] Blanchard, *op. cit.*, p. 317.
[31] Bk. VII, chap. vii.

suggest a weakness or folly which is probably at variance with the actual intentions of their author toward them.

On the other hand, the type of novel which is perhaps most typical of the genre, and which achieves effects which have not been duplicated in any other literary form, has used a very different kind of plot. From Sterne and Jane Austen to Proust and Joyce the Aristotelian priority of plot over character has been wholly reversed, and a new type of formal structure has been evolved in which the plot attempts only to embody the ordinary processes of life and in so doing becomes wholly dependent on the characters and the development of their relationships. It is Defoe and above all Richardson who provide this tradition with its archetypes, just as it is Fielding who provides that for the opposite tradition.

### III

Johnson's most famous criticism of Fielding's novels is concerned with their basic technique, but from his own point of view it was probably their moral shortcomings which were the decisive factor. It is certainly this with which he was concerned in his only published reference to Fielding, although even here it is only by implication. In the *Rambler* (1750) Johnson attacked the effects of "familiar histories" whose wicked heroes were made so attractive that "we lose abhorrence of their faults," apparently with *Roderick Random* (1748) and *Tom Jones* (1749) chiefly in mind.[32] He certainly later told Hannah More that he "scarcely knew a more corrupt work" than *Tom Jones*,[33] and, on the other hand, praised *Clarissa* on the significant grounds that "it was in the power of Richardson alone to teach us at once esteem and detestation; to make virtuous resentment overpower all the benevolence which wit, elegance, and courage naturally excite, and to lose at last the hero in the villain." [34]

We find it difficult today to share much of Johnson's abhorrence of the morality of *Tom Jones* and are, indeed, more likely to be unjust to Richardson, and to assume without question that his concern, and that of his heroines, for feminine chastity, can only be explained by prurience on his part or hypocrisy on theirs. But this may not be so, and, conversely, we must in fairness recognize that there are many moral offences in *Tom Jones* which receive a much more tolerant treatment than any Puritan moralist would have accorded them. Defoe and Richardson, for example, are unsparing in their denunciation of drunkenness; but when Tom Jones gets drunk in his joy at Allworthy's recovery, Fielding shows no reprobation: it is admittedly an imprudence which later contributes to the

---

[32] *Rambler*, No. 4.
[33] *Johnsonian Miscellanies*, II, 190.
[34] "Rowe," *Lives of the Poets*, ed. Hill (Oxford University Press, 1905), II, 67.

hero's expulsion, but Fielding's only direct comment is a humorous editorial development of the *in vino veritas* commonplace.[35]

It is the sexual issue, however, which is crucial, both in the moral scheme of *Tom Jones*, and in the objections of its critics. Fielding certainly does not endorse his hero's incontinence, and Tom himself admits that he has been "faulty" in this respect; but the general tendency throughout the novel is surely to qualify the condemnation and make unchastity appear a venial sin—even the good Mrs. Miller, for example, seems to think she has put a fairly good face on matters by pleading to Sophia that Tom has "never been guilty of a single instance of infidelity to her since . . . seeing her in town." [36]

Fielding's plot obviously does not punish the sexual transgressions either of Tom Jones or of the many other characters who are guilty in this respect so severely as Richardson, for example, would have wished. Even in *Amelia*, where Booth's adultery is both more serious in itself than anything that can be charged against Tom Jones, and is treated much more severely by Fielding, the plot eventually rescues Booth from the consequences of his acts. There is therefore considerable justification for Ford Madox Ford's denunciation of "fellows like Fielding, and to some extent Thackeray, who pretend that if you are a gay drunkard, lecher, squanderer of your goods, and fumbler in placket holes you will eventually find a benevolent uncle, concealed father, or benefactor who will shower on you bags of ten thousands of guineas, estates, and the hands of adorable mistresses—these fellows are dangers to the body politic and horribly bad constructors of plots." [37]

Ford, of course, chooses to disregard both Fielding's positive moral intentions and the tendency of comic plots in general to achieve a happy ending at the cost of certain lenity in the administration of justice. For —although Fielding was long regarded as something of a debauchee himself and did not indeed have full justice done to his literary greatness until scholarship had cleared him of the charges made by contemporary gossip and repeated by his first biographer, Murphy—Fielding was in fact as much of a moralist as Richardson, although of a different kind. He believed that virtue, far from being the result of the suppression of instinct at the behest of public opinion, was itself a natural tendency to goodness or benevolence. In Tom Jones he tried to show a hero possessed of a virtuous heart, but also of the lustiness and lack of deliberation to which natural goodness was particularly prone, and which easily led to error and even to vice. To realize his moral aim, therefore, Fielding had to show how the good heart was threatened by many dangers in its hazardous course to maturity and knowledge of the world;

[35] Bk. V, chap. ix.

[36] Bk. XVIII, ch. 10.

[37] *The English Novel from the Earliest Days to the Death of Conrad* (London: Constable & Co., Ltd., 1930), p. 93.

yet, at the same time and without exculpating his hero, he had also
to show that although Tom's moral transgressions were a likely and perhaps even a necessary stage in the process of moral growth, they did not
betoken a vicious disposition; even Tom Jones's carefree animality has a
generous quality that is lacking in Clarissa's self-centered and frigid
virtue. The happy conclusion of the story, therefore, is very far from
representing the kind of moral and literary confusion which Ford alleges,
and is actually the culmination of Fielding's moral and literary logic.

The contrast between Fielding and Richardson as moralists is
heightened by the effects of their very different narrative points of view.
Richardson focuses attention on the individual, and whatever virtue or
vice he is dealing with will loom very large, and have all its implications
reflected in the action: Fielding, on the other hand, deals with too many
characters and too complicated a plot to give the single individual virtue
or vice quite this importance.

Besides this tendency of the plot, it is also part of Fielding's intention
as a moralist to put every phenomenon into its larger perspective. Sexual
virtue and sexual vice, for example, are placed in a broad moral perspective, and the results do not always produce the kind of emphasis that
the sexual reformer would wish. Fielding knows, for example, and wishes
to show, that some marriage designs may be more vicious than the most
abandoned profligacy: witness Blifil whose "designs were strictly honourable as the phrase is, that is to rob a lady of her fortune by marriage."
He knows, too, that moral indignation against promiscuity is not necessarily the result of a real love of virtue: witness the passage in which we
are told that "to exclude all vulgar concubinage, and to drive all whores
in rags from within the walls is within the power of everyone. This my
landlady very strictly adhered to, and this her virtuous guests, who did
not travel in rags, would very reasonably have expected from her." [38]
Here Fielding's Swiftian suavity reminds us of the cruelty and injustice
with which complacent virtue is too often associated; but a narrow-
minded moralist might see behind the irony a shocking failure to condemn "whores in rags," and even, perhaps, an implicit sympathy for
them.

Fielding, then, attempts to broaden our moral sense rather than to
intensify its punitive operations against licentiousness. But, at the same
time, his function as the voice of traditional social morality means that
his attitude to sexual ethics is inevitably normative; it certainly does not,
as Boswell said, "encourage a strained and rarely possible virtue," [39] but
rather reflects, as Leslie Stephen put it, "the code by which men of sense
generally govern their conduct, as distinguished from that by which they
affect to be governed in language." [40] Aristotle's Golden Mean is often,

[38] Bk. XI, chap. iv; Bk. IX, chap. iii.
[39] *Life of Johnson*, ed. Hill-Powell, II, 49.
[40] *History of English Thought in the Eighteenth Century*, II, 377.

perhaps, capable of a certain subversion of rigid ethical principles: and it is perhaps as a good Aristotelian that Fielding comes very close to suggesting that too much chastity in Blifil is as bad as Tom's too little.

There is a further reason why Johnson, who was, after all, an ethical rigorist in his own way, should have found *Tom Jones* a corrupt work. Comedy—if only to maintain an atmosphere of good humor between audience and participants—often involves a certain complicity in acts and sentiments which we might not treat so tolerantly in ordinary life. Perhaps the most insistent note in *Tom Jones* is Fielding's worldly-wise good humor, and it often persuades us to regard sexual irregularities as ludicrous rather than wicked.

Mrs. Fitzpatrick, for instance, is dismissed with the words: "she lives in reputation at the polite end of town, and is so good an economist that she spends three times the income of her fortune without running into debt." [41] Mrs. Fitzpatrick must remain true to character, and yet be included in the happy ending; nor can Fielding upset the conviviality of his final meeting with his readers to express his abhorrence at the lamentable source of income which we must surmise for his character.

On other occasions, of course, Fielding's humor on that perennial comic resource, sex, is much more overt: in *Jonathan Wild,* for example, when the captain of the ship asks the hero "if he had no more Christianity in him than to ravish a woman in a storm?" [42] or in *Tom Jones* when Mrs. Honour gives her celebrated retort to Sophia's "Would you not, Honour, fire a pistol at any one who should attack your virtue?"—"To be sure, ma'am, . . . one's virtue is a dear thing, especially to us poor servants; for it is our livelihood, as a body may say: yet I mortally hate firearms." [43] There is, of course, the same broadening tendency in Fielding's humor here as in his treatment of moral issues in general: we must not forget that even the most virtuous indignation is capable of elementary logical fallacies, or that humankind's allegiance to virtue is capable of cautious afterthoughts. But the tacit assumption of much of Fielding's humor is surely one which suggests that "broad-mindedness" in its modern sense, which typically tends to have a sexual reference, is part of the expansion of sympathy to which his novels as a whole invite us: a relish for wholesome bawdy, in fact, is a necessary part of the moral education of a sex-bedeviled humanity: such, at least, was the classical role of comedy, and Fielding was perhaps the last great writer who continued that tradition.

[41] Bk. XVIII, chap. xiii.
[42] Bk. II, chap. x.
[43] Bk. VII, chap. vii.

## IV

As far as most modern readers are concerned it is not Fielding's moral but his literary point of view which is open to objection. For his conception of his role is that of a guide who, not content with taking us "behind the scenes of this great theatre of nature," [44] feels that he must explain everything which is to be found there; and such authorial intrusion, of course, tends to diminish the authenticity of his narrative.

Fielding's personal intrusion into *Tom Jones* begins with his dedication to the Honourable George Lyttleton, a dedication, it must be admitted, which goes far to justify Johnson's definition of this form of writing—"a servile address to a patron." There are numerous further references in the body of his work to others among Fielding's patrons, notably Ralph Allen and Lord Chancellor Hardwicke, not to mention other acquaintances whom Fielding wished to compliment, including one of his surgeons, Mr. John Ranby, and various innkeepers.

The effect of these references is certainly to break the spell of the imaginary world represented in the novel: but the main interference with the autonomy of this world comes from Fielding's introductory chapters, containing literary and moral essays, and even more from his frequent discussions and asides to the reader within the narrative itself. There is no doubt that Fielding's practice here leads him in completely the opposite direction from Richardson, and converts the novel into a social and indeed into a sociable literary form. Fielding brings us into a charmed circle composed, not only of the fictional characters, but also of Fielding's friends and of his favorites among the poets and moralists of the past. He is, indeed, almost as attentive to his audience as to his characters, and his narrative, far from being an intimate drama which we peep at through a keyhole, is a series of reminiscences told by a genial raconteur in some wayside inn—the favored and public locus of his tale.

This approach to the novel is quite consistent with Fielding's major intention—it promotes a distancing effect which prevents us from being so fully immersed in the lives of the characters that we lose our alertness to the larger implications of their actions—implications which Fielding brings out in his capacity of omniscient chorus. On the other hand, Fielding's interventions obviously interfere with any sense of narrative illusion, and break with almost every narrative precedent, beginning with that set by Homer, whom Aristotle praised for saying "very little *in propria persona*," and for maintaining elsewhere the attitude either of a dispassionate narrator, or of an impersonator of one of the characters. [45]

[44] Bk. VII, chap. i.
[45] *Poetics*, chaps. xxiv, iii.

Few readers would like to be without the prefatory chapters, or Field-ing's diverting asides, but they undoubtedly derogate from the reality of the narrative: as Richardson's friend, Thomas Edwards, wrote, "we see every moment" that it is Fielding who "does *personam gerere*," whereas Richardson is "the thing itself." [46] So, although Fielding's gar-rulity about his characters and his conduct of the action initiated a popular practice in the English novel, it is not surprising that it has been condemned by most modern critics, and on these grounds. Ford Madox Ford, for instance, complained that the "trouble with the Eng-lish novelist from Fielding to Meredith, is that not one of them cares whether you believe in their characters or not";[47] and Henry James was shocked by the way Trollope, and other "accomplished novelists," con-cede "in a digression, a parenthesis or an aside" that their fiction is "only make-believe." James went on to lay down the central principle of the novelist's attitude to his creation, which is very similar to that described above as inherent in formal realism: Trollope, and any nov-elist who shares his attitude, James says,

> admits that the events he narrates have not really happened, and that he can give the narrative any turn the reader may like best. Such a betrayal of a sacred office seems to me, I confess, a terrible crime; it is what I mean by the attitude of apology, and it shocks me every whit as much in Trollope as it would have shocked me in Gibbon or Macaulay. It implies that the novel-ist is less occupied in looking for the truth (the truth of course I mean, that he assumes, the premises that we must grant him, whatever they may be) than the historian, and in so doing it deprives him at a stroke of all his standing room.[48]

There is not, of course, any doubt as to Fielding's intention of "look-ing for the truth"—he tells us indeed in *Tom Jones* that "we determined to guide our pen throughout by the directions of truth." But he perhaps underestimated the connection between truth and the maintenance of the reader's "historical faith." This, at least, is the suggestion of a passage toward the end of *Tom Jones* when he proclaims that he will let his hero be hanged rather than extricate him from his troubles by unnatural means "for we had rather relate that he was hanged at Tyburn (which may very probably be the case) than forfeit our integrity, or shock the faith of our reader." [49]

This ironical attitude toward the reality of his creation was probably responsible in part for the main critical doubt which *Tom Jones* sug-

---

[46] A. D. McKillop, *Samuel Richardson: Printer and Novelist* (Chapel Hill: University of North Carolina Press, 1936), p. 175.

[47] *English Novel*, p. 89.

[48] "The Art of Fiction" (1888); cited from *The Art of Fiction*, ed. Morris Roberts (New York: Oxford University Press, 1948), p. 5.

[49] Bk. III, chap. i; Bk. XVII, chap. i.

gests. It is, in the main, a very true book, but it is by no means so clear that its truth has, to quote R. S. Crane, been "rendered" in terms of the novel.[50] We do not get the impressive sense of Fielding's own moral qualities from his characters or their actions that we do from the heroic struggles for human betterment which he conducted as a magistrate under the most adverse personal circumstances, or even from the *Journal of a Voyage to Lisbon*; and if we analyze our impression from the novels alone it surely is evident that our residual impression of dignity and generosity comes mainly from the passages where Fielding is speaking in his own person. And this, surely, is the result of a technique which was deficient at least in the sense that it was unable to convey this larger moral significance through character and action alone, and could only supply it by means of a somewhat intrusive patterning of the plot and by direct editorial commentary. As Henry James put it: Tom Jones "has so much 'life' that it amounts, for the effect of comedy and application of satire, almost to his having a mind"; almost, but not quite, and so it was necessary that "his author—*he* handsomely possessed of a mind—[should have] such an amplitude of reflection for him and round him that we see him through the mellow air of Fielding's fine old moralism. . . ." [51]

All this, of course, is not to say Fielding does not succeed: *Tom Jones* is surely entitled to the praise of an anonymous early admirer who called it "on the whole . . . the most lively book ever published." [52] But it is a very personal and unrepeatable kind of success: Fielding's technique was too eclectic to become a permanent element in the tradition of the novel—*Tom Jones* is only part novel, and there is much else—picaresque tale, comic drama, occasional essay.

On the other hand, Fielding's departure from the canons of formal realism indicated very clearly the nature of the supreme problem which the new genre had to face. The tedious asseveration of literal authenticity in Defoe and to some extent in Richardson, tended to obscure the fact that, if the novel was to achieve equality of status with other genres it had to be brought into contact with the whole tradition of civilized values, and supplement its realism of presentation with a realism of assessment. To the excellent Mrs. Barbauld's query as to the grounds on which he considered Richardson to be a lesser writer than Shakespeare, Coleridge answered that "Richardson is *only* interesting." [53] This is no doubt unfair as a total judgment on the author of *Clarissa*, but it indicates the likely limits of a realism of presentation: we shall be wholly

---

[50] "The Concept of Plot and the Plot of Tom Jones," *Critics and Criticism: Ancient and Modern* (Chicago: University of Chicago Press, 1952), p. 639.
[51] Preface, *The Princess Casamassima* (1886).
[52] *Essay on the New Species of Writing Founded by Mr. Fielding* (1751), p. 43.
[53] Blanchard, *op. cit.*, p. 316.

immersed in the reality of the characters and their actions, but whether we shall be any wiser as a result is open to question.

Fielding brought to the genre something that is ultimately even more important than narrative technique—a responsible wisdom about human affairs which plays upon the deeds and the characters of his novels. His wisdom is not, perhaps, of the highest order; it is, like that of his be-loved Lucian, a little inclined to be easygoing and on occasion opportun-ist. Nevertheless, at the end of *Tom Jones* we feel we have been exposed, not merely to an interesting narrative about imaginary persons, but to a stimulating wealth of suggestion and challenge on almost every topic of human interest. Not only so: the stimulation has come from a mind with a true grasp of human reality, never deceived or deceiving about him-self, his characters or the human lot in general. In his effort to infuse the new genre with something of the Shakespearean virtues Fielding departed too far from formal realism to initiate a viable tradition, but his work serves as a perpetual reminder that if the new genre was to challenge older literary forms it had to find a way of conveying not only a convincing impression but a wise assessment of life, an assessment that could only come from taking a much wider view than Defoe or Richard-son of the affairs of mankind.

So, although we must agree with the tenor of Johnson's watch simile, we must also add that it is unfair and misleading. Richardson, no doubt, takes us deeper into the inner workings of the human machine; but Fielding is surely entitled to retort that there are many other machines in nature besides the individual consciousness, and perhaps to express his surprised chagrin that Johnson should apparently have overlooked the fact that he was engaged in the exploration of a vaster and equally intricate mechanism, that of human society as a whole, a literary subject which was, incidentally, much more consonant than Richardson's with the classical outlook which he and Johnson shared.

# Tom Jones

## by William Empson

I had been meaning to write about *Tom Jones* before, but this essay bears the marks of shock at what I found said about the book by recent literary critics, and my students at Sheffield; I had to consider why I find the book so much better than they do. Middleton Murry was working from the same impulse of defense in the chief of the *Unprofessional Essays* (1956) written shortly before he died; I agree with him so much that we chose a lot of the same quotations, but he was still thinking of Fielding as just "essentially healthy" or something like that, and I think the defense should be larger. Of American critics, I remember a detailed treatment of the plot by a Chicago Aristotelian, who praised what may be called the calculations behind the structure; I thought this was just and sensible, but assumed the basic impulse behind the book to be pretty trivial. English critics tend to bother about *Tom Jones* more than American ones and also to wince away from it more, because it is supposed to be so frightfully English, and they are rightly uneasy about national self-praise; besides, he is hearty and they tend to be anti-hearty. What nobody will recognize, I feel, is that Fielding set out to preach a doctrine in *Tom Jones* (1749), and said so, a high-minded though perhaps abstruse one. As he said after the attacks on *Joseph Andrews* (1742) that he would not write another novel, we may suppose that he wouldn't have written *Tom Jones* without at least finding for himself the excuse that he had this important further thing to say. Modern critics tend to assume both (a) that it isn't artistic to preach any doctrine and (b) that the only high-minded doctrine to preach is despair and contempt for the world; I think the combination produces a critical blind spot, so I hope there is some general interest in this attempt to defend *Tom Jones*, even for those who would not mark the book high anyhow.

"*Tom Jones*." From *The Kenyon Review*, XX (Spring, 1958), 217-249. Copyright 1958 by *The Kenyon Review*. Reprinted by permission of the author and *The Kenyon Review*; and revised by the author. For an interesting reply, see C. J. Rawson, "Professor Empson's *Tom Jones*," *Notes and Queries*, N. S., VI (November, 1959), 400-404.

Fielding, then, is regarded with a mixture of acceptance and contempt, as a worthy old boy who did the basic engineering for the novel because he invented the clockwork plot, but tiresomely boisterous, "broad" to the point of being insensitive to fine shades, lacking in any of the higher aspirations, and hampered by a style which keeps his prosy common-sense temperament always to the fore. Looking for a way out of this clump of prejudices, I think the style is the best place to start. If you take an interest in Fielding's opinions, which he seems to be expressing with bluff directness, you can get to the point of reading *Tom Jones* with fascinated curiosity, baffled to make out what he really does think about the filial duties of a daughter, or the inherent virtues of a gentle-man, or the Christian command of chastity. To leap to ambiguity for a solution may seem Empson's routine paradox, particularly absurd in the case of Fielding; but in a way, which means for a special kind of ambiguity, it has always been recognized about him. His readers have always felt sure that he is somehow recommending the behavior of Tom Jones, whether they called the result healthy or immoral; whereas the book makes plenty of firm assertions that Tom is doing wrong. The reason why this situation can arise is that the style of Fielding is a habitual double irony; or rather, he moves the gears of his car up to that as soon as the road lets it use its strength. This form, though logically rather complicated, needs a show of lightness and carelessness whether it is being used to cheat or not; for that matter, some speakers convey it all the time by a curl of the tongue in their tone of voice. Indeed, I understand that some Americans regard every upper-class English voice as doing that, however unintentionally; to divide the national honors, I should think the reason for the suspicion is that every tough American voice is doing it, too. Single irony presumes a censor; the ironist (A) is fooling a tyrant (B) while appealing to the judgment of a person ad-dressed (C). For double irony A shows both B and C that he understands both their positions; B can no longer forbid direct utterance, but I think can always be picked out as holding the more official or straight-faced belief. In real life this is easier than single irony (because people aren't such fools as you think), so that we do not always notice its logical structure. Presumably A hopes that each of B and C will think "He is secretly on my side, and only pretends to sympathize with the other"; but A may hold some wise balanced position between them, or con-trariwise may be feeling "a plague on both your houses." The trick is liable to be unpopular, and perhaps literary critics despise its evasiveness, so that when they talk about irony they generally seem to mean some-thing else; but a moderate amount of it is felt to be balanced and un-fussy. The definition may **seem** too narrow, but if you generalize the term to cover almost any complex state of mind it ceases to be useful. I do not want to make large claims for "double irony," but rather to narrow it down enough to show why it is peculiarly fitted for *Tom Jones*.

There it serves a purpose so fundamental that it can come to seem as massive as the style of Gibbon, who seems to have realized this in his sentence of praise. He had already, in Chapter xxxii of the *Decline and Fall*, describing a Byzantine palace intrigue, compared it in a footnote to a passage of *Tom Jones*, "the romance of a great master, which may be considered the history of human nature." This would be about 1780; in 1789, discussing ancestors at the beginning of his *Autobiography*, for example the claim of Fielding's family to be related to the Hapsburgs, he said, "But the romance of *Tom Jones*, that exquisite picture of human manners, will outlive the palace of the Escurial and the imperial eagle of the House of Austria." This has more to do with Fielding than one might think, especially with his repeated claim, admitted to be rather comic but a major source of his nerve, that he was capable of making a broad survey because he was an aristocrat and had known high life from within. I take it that Gibbon meant his own irony not merely to attack the Christians (in that use it is "single") but to rise to a grand survey of the strangeness of human affairs. Of course both use it for protection against rival moralists, but its major use is to express the balance of their judgment. Fielding is already doing this in *Joseph Andrews*, but there the process seems genuinely casual. In *Tom Jones* he is expressing a theory about ethics, and the ironies are made to interlock with the progress of the demonstration. The titanic plot, which has been praised or found tiresome taken alone, was devised to illustrate the theory, and the screws of the engine of his style are engaging the sea. That is, the feeling that he is proving a case is what gives *Tom Jones* its radiance, making it immensely better, I think, than the other two novels (though perhaps there is merely less discovery about proving the sad truths of *Amelia*); it builds up like Euclid. Modern critics seem unable to feel this, apparently because it is forbidden by their aesthetic principles, even when Fielding tells them he is doing it; whereas Dr. Johnson and Sir John Hawkins, for example, took it seriously at once, and complained bitterly that the book had an immoral purpose. It certainly becomes much more interesting if you attend to its thesis; even if the thesis retains the shimmering mystery of a mirage.

Consider for example what Fielding says (XII, viii) when he is reflecting over what happened when Sophia caught Tom in bed with Mrs. Waters at the Upton Inn, and incidentally telling us that that wasn't the decisive reason why Sophia rode away in anger, never likely to meet him again:

> I am not obliged to reconcile every matter to the received notions concerning truth and nature. But if this was never so easy to do, perhaps it

might be more prudent in me to avoid it. For instance, as the fact before us now stands, without any comment of mine upon it, though it may at first sight offend some readers, yet, upon more mature consideration, it must please all; for wise and good men may consider what happened to Jones at Upton as a just punishment for his wickedness in regard to women, of which it was indeed the immediate consequence; and silly and bad persons may comfort themselves in their vices by flattering their own hearts that the characters of men are owing rather to accident than to virtue. Now, perhaps the reflections which we should be here inclined to draw would alike contradict both these conclusions, and would show that these incidents contribute only to confirm the great, useful, and uncommon doctrine which it is the whole purpose of this work to inculcate, and which we must not fill up our pages by frequently repeating, as an ordinary parson fills up his sermon by repeating his text at the end of every paragraph.

He does, as I understand, partly tell us the doctrine elsewhere, but never defines it as his central thesis; perhaps he chooses to put the claim here because XII is a rather desultory book, fitting in various incidents which the plot or the thesis will require later, and conveying the slowness of travel before the rush of London begins in XIII. To say "the fact before us" makes Fielding the judge, and his readers the jury. He rather frequently warns them that they may not be able to understand him, and I think this leaves the modern critic, who assumes he meant nothing, looking rather comical. Perhaps this critic would say it is Empson who fails to see the joke of Fielding's self-deprecating irony; I answer that the irony of the book is double, here as elsewhere. Fielding realizes that any man who puts forward a general ethical theory implies a claim to have very wide ethical experience, therefore should be ready to laugh at his own pretensions; but also he isn't likely to mean nothing when he jeers at you for failing to see his point. Actually, the modern critic does know what kind of thing the secret is; but he has been badgered by neoclassicism and neo-Christianity and what not, whereas the secret is humanist, liberal, materialist, recommending happiness on earth and so forth, so he assumes it is dull, or the worldly advice of a flippant libertine.

Nobody would want to argue such points who had felt the tone of the book; it is glowing with the noble beauty of its gospel, which Fielding indeed would be prepared to claim as the original Gospel. The prose of generalized moral argument may strike us as formal, but it was also used by Shelley, who would also appeal to the Gospels to defend a moral novelty, as would Blake; an idea that the Romantics were original there seems to confuse people nowadays very much. When Fielding goes really high in *Tom Jones* his prose is like an archangel brooding over mankind, and I suppose is actually imitating similar effects in Handel; one might think it was like Bach, and that Handel would be too earthbound, but we know Fielding admired Handel. I admit that the effect is

sometimes forced, and strikes us as the theatrical rhetoric of the Age of
Sentiment; but you do not assume he is insincere there if you recognize
that at other times the effect is very real.

A moderate case of this high language comes early in the book when
Squire Allworthy is discussing charity with Captain Blifil (II, v). The
captain is trying to ruin young Tom so as to get all the estate for himself, and has just remarked that Christian charity is an ideal, so ought not
to be held to mean giving anything material; Allworthy falls into a glow
at this, and readily agrees that there can be no merit in merely dis-
charging a duty, especially such a pleasant one; but goes on:

> To confess the truth, there is one degree of generosity (of charity I would
> have called it), which seems to have some show of merit, and that is where,
> from a principle of benevolence and Christian love, we bestow on another
> what we really want ourselves; where, in order to lessen the distresses of
> another, we condescend to share some part of them, by giving what even
> our necessities cannot well spare. This is, I think, meritorious; but to relieve
> our brethren only with our superfluities—

—to do one thing and another, go the balanced clauses, "this seems to
be only being rational creatures." Another theme then crosses his mind
for the same grand treatment:

> As to the apprehension of bestowing bounty on such as may hereafter prove
> unworthy objects, merely because many have proved such, surely it can never
> deter a good man from generosity.

This, too, is argued with noble rhetoric, and then the captain inserts his
poisoned barb. Now, the passage cannot be single irony, meant to show
Allworthy as a pompous fool; he is viewed with wonder as a kind of
saint (e.g., he is twice said to smile like an angel, and he is introduced
as the most glorious creature under the sun); also he stood for the real
benefactor Allen whom Fielding would be ashamed to laugh at. Fielding
shows a Proust-like delicacy in regularly marking a reservation about
Allworthy without ever letting us laugh at him (whereas critics usually
complain he is an all-white character). Allworthy is something less than
all-wise; the plot itself requires him to believe the villains and throw
Tom out of Paradise Hall, and the plot is designed to carry larger meanings. The reason why he agrees so eagerly with the captain here, I take
it, apart from his evidently not having experienced what he is talking
about, is a point of spiritual delicacy or gentlemanly politeness—he
cannot appear to claim credit for looking after his own cottagers, in
talking to a guest who is poor; that was hardly more than looking after
his own property, and the reflection distracts him from gauging the
captain's motives. What is more important, he speaks as usual of doing

good on principle, and here the central mystery is being touched upon.

One might think the answer is: "Good actions come only from good impulses, that is, those of a good heart, not from good principles"; the two bad tutors of Jones make this idea obvious at the beginning (especially III, v). Dr. Johnson and Sir John Hawkins denounced the book as meaning this, and hence implying that morality is no use (by the way, in my *Complex Words*, p. 173, I ascribed a sentence of Hawkins to Johnson, but they make the same points). Fielding might well protest that he deserved to escape this reproach; he had twice stepped out of his frame in the novel to explain that he was not recommending Tom's imprudence, and that he did not mean to imply that religion and philosophy are bad because bad men can interpret them wrongly. But he seems to have started from this idea in his first revolt against the *ethos* of Richardson which made him write *Shamela* and *Joseph Andrews*; I think it was mixed with a class belief, that well-brought-up persons (with the natural ease of gentlemen) do not need to keep prying into their own motives as these hypocritical nonconformist types do. As a novelist he never actually asserts the idea, which one can see is open to misuse, and in *Tom Jones* (1749) he has made it only part of a more interesting idea; but, after he had been attacked for using it there, he arranged an ingenious reply in the self-defensive *Amelia* (1751). He gave the opinion outright to the silly Booth, a freethinker who disbelieves in free will (III, v); you are rather encouraged to regard Booth as a confession of the errors of the author when young. When he is converted at the end of the novel (XII, v) the good parson laughs at him for having thought this a heresy, saying it is why Christianity provides the motives of Heaven and Hell. This was all right as an escape into the recesses of theology; but it was the Calvinists who had really given up free will, and Fielding could hardly want to agree with them; at any rate Parson Adams, in *Joseph Andrews*, had passionately disapproved of Salvation by Faith. Fielding was a rather special kind of Christian, but evidently sincere in protesting that he was one. Adams is now usually regarded as sweetly Anglican, but his brother parson (in I, xvii) suspects he is the devil, after he has sternly rejected a series of such doctrines as give a magical importance to the clergy. I take it Fielding set himself up as a moral theorist, later than *Joseph Andrews*, because he decided he could refute the view of Hobbes, and of various thinkers prominent at the time who derived from Hobbes, that incessant egotism is logically inevitable or a condition of our being. We lack the moral treatise in the form of answers to Bolingbroke which he set out to write when dying, but can gather an answer from *Tom Jones*, perhaps from the firm treatment of the reader in VI, i, which introduces the troubles of the lovers and tells him that no author can tell him what love means unless he is capable of experiencing it. The doctrine is thus: "If good by nature, you can imagine other people's feelings so directly that you have an impulse to act on

them as if they were your own; and this is the source of your greatest
pleasures as well as of your only genuinely unselfish actions." A modern
philosopher might answer that this makes no logical difference, but it
clearly brings a large practical difference into the suasive effect of the
argument of Hobbes, which was what people had thought worth discussing in the first place. The most striking illustration is in the sexual
behavior of Jones, where he is most scandalous; one might, instead, find
him holy, because he never makes love to a woman unless she first makes
love to him. Later on (XIII, vii) we find he thinks it a point of honor
to accept such a challenge from a woman, no less than a challenge to
fight from a man (and that is the absolute of honor, the duel itself); but
in his first two cases, Molly Seagrim and Sophia, he is unconscious that
their advances have aroused him, and very grateful when they respond.
Fielding reveres the moral beauty of this, but is quite hard-headed
enough to see that such a man is too easily fooled by women; he regards
Tom as dreadfully in need of good luck, and feels like a family lawyer
when he makes the plot give it to him. He is thus entirely sincere in
repeating that Tom needed to learn prudence; but how this relates to
the chastity enjoined by religion he does not explain. We may however
observe that nobody in the novel takes this prohibition quite seriously
all the time; even Allworthy, when he is friends again, speaks only of
the imprudence of Tom's relations with Lady Bellaston (XVIII, x). In
any case, the sexual affairs are only one of the many applications of the
doctrine about mutuality of impulse; I think this was evidently the
secret message which Fielding boasts of in *Tom Jones*, a book which
at the time was believed to be so wicked that it had caused earth-
quakes.

We need not suppose he was well up in the long history of the question, but I would like to know more about his relations to Calvin; Professor C. S. Lewis, in his *Survey of Sixteenth-Century Literature*, brings
out what unexpected connections Calvin can have. He maintained that
no action could deserve heaven which was done in order to get to heaven;
hence we can only attain good, that is nonegotist, motives by the sheer
grace of God. In its early years the doctrine was by no means always
regarded as grim; and it has an eerie likeness to the basic position of
Fielding, that the well-born soul has good impulses of its own accord,
which only need directing. At least, a humble adherent of either doctrine
may feel baffled to know how to get into the condition recommended.
However, I take it this likeness arises merely because both men had
seriously puzzled their heads over the Gospel, and tried to give its paradoxes their full weight. Fielding never made a stronger direct copy of a
Gospel parable than in *Joseph Andrews* (I, xii) when Joseph is dying
naked in the snow and an entire coach-load finds worldly reasons for
letting him die except for the postboy freezing on the outside, who
gives Joseph his overcoat and is soon after transported for robbing a

hen-roost. But I think he felt the paradoxes of Jesus more as a direct challenge after he had trained and practiced as a lawyer, and had come into line for a job as magistrate; that is, when he decided to write *Tom Jones*. He first wrote seriously in favor of the Government on the 1745 Rebellion, in a stream of indignant pamphlets, and this was what made him possible as a magistrate; he was horrified at the public indifference to the prospect of a Catholic conquest, from which he expected rack and fire. He must then also be shocked at the indifference, or the moon-eyed preference for the invader, shown by all the characters in *Tom Jones*; nor can he approve the reaction of the Old Man of the Hill, who thanks God he has renounced so lunatic a world. To realize that Fielding himself is not indifferent here, I think, gives a further range to the vistas of the book, because all the characters are being as imprudent about it as Tom Jones about his own affairs; and this at least encourages one to suppose that there was a fair amount going on in Fielding's mind.

Tom Jones is a hero because he is born with good impulses; indeed, as the boy had no friend but the thieving gamekeeper Black George, among the lethal hatreds of Paradise Hall, he emerges as a kind of Noble Savage. This is first shown when, keen to shoot a bird, he follows it across the boundary and is caught on Squire Western's land; two guns were heard, but he insists he was alone. The keeper had yielded to his request and come, too; if Tom says so, the keeper will be sacked, and his wife and children will starve, but Tom as a little gentleman at the great house can only be beaten. "Tom passed a very melancholy night" because he was afraid the beating might make him lose his honor by confessing, says Fielding, who adds that it was as severe as the tortures used in some foreign countries to induce confessions. The reader first learns to suspect the wisdom of Allworthy by hearing him say (III, ii) that Tom acted here on a *mistaken* point of honor; though he only says it to defend Tom from further assaults by the bad tutors, who discuss the point with splendid absurdity. Whether it was mistaken one would think, depended on whether the child thought Allworthy himself could be trusted not to behave unjustly. I have no respect for the critics who find the moralizing of the book too obvious; the child's honor really is all right after that; he is a fit judge of other ideas of honor elsewhere. Modern readers would perhaps like him better if they realized his basic likeness to Huck Finn; Mark Twain and Fielding were making much the same protest, even to the details about dueling. But Mark Twain somehow could not bear to have Huck grow up, whereas the chief idea about Tom Jones, though for various reasons it has not been recognized, is that he is planned to become awestrikingly better during his brief experience of the world. You are first meant to realize this is happening halfway through the book, when the Old Man of the Hill is recounting his life, and Tom is found smiling quietly to himself at a slight error in the ethical position of that mystical recluse (VIII, xiii). Old Man is a saint, and Fielding can provide him with some grand devotional prose, but he is too much of a stoic to be a real Gospel Christian, which is what Tom is turning into as we watch him.

All critics call the recital of Old Man irrelevant, though Saintsbury labors to excuse it; but Fielding meant to give a survey of all human experience (that is what he meant by calling the book an epic) and Old Man provides the extremes of degradation and divine ecstasy which Tom has no time for; as part of the structure of ethical thought he is essential to the book, the keystone at the middle of the arch. The critics could not have missed understanding this if they hadn't imagined themselves forbidden to have intellectual interests, as Fielding had. For that matter, the whole setting of the book in the 1745 Rebellion gets its point when it interlocks with the theory and practice of Old Man. So far from being "episodic," the incident is meant to be such an obvious pulling together of the threads that it warns us to keep an eye on the subsequent moral development of Tom. As he approaches London unarmed, he is challenged by a highwayman; removing the man's pistol, and inquiring about the motives, he gives half of all he has to the starving family—rather more than half, to avoid calculation. Fielding of course knew very well that this was making him carry out one of the paradoxes of Jesus, though neither Fielding nor Tom must ever say so. The first time he earns money by selling his body to Lady Bellaston, a physically unpleasant duty which he enters upon believing at each step that his honor requires it (and without which, as the plot goes, he could probably not have won through to marrying Sophia), he tosses the whole fifty to his landlady, Mrs. Miller, for a hard luck case who turns out to be the same highwayman, though she will only take ten; when the man turns up to thank him, with mutual recognition, Tom congratulates him for having enough honor to fight for the lives of his children, and proceeds to Lady Bellaston "greatly exulting in the happiness he has procured," also reflecting on the evils that "strict justice" would have caused here (XIII, x). His next heroic action is to secure marriage for his landlady's daughter, pregnant by his fellow lodger Nightingale, thus "saving the whole family from destruction"; it required a certain moral depth, because the basic difficulty was to convince Nightingale that this marriage, which he greatly desired, was not forbidden to him by his honor. We tend now to feel that Tom makes a grossly obvious moral harangue, but Nightingale feels it has pooh-poohed what he regards as the moral side of the matter, removing his "foolish scruples of honor" so that he can do what he prefers (XIV, vii). Indeed the whole interest of the survey of ideas of honor is that different characters hold such different ones; no wonder critics who do not realize this find the repetition of the word tedious. These chapters in which the harangues of Tom are found obvious are interwoven with others in which his peculiar duty as regards Lady Bellaston has to be explained, and we pass on to the crimes which poor Lord

Fellamar could be made to think his honor required. Critics would not grumble in the same way at Euclid, for being didactic in the propositions they have been taught already and immoral in the ones they refuse to learn. The threats of rape for Sophia and enslavement for Tom, as the plot works out, are simply further specimens of the code of honor; that danger for Tom is settled when Lord Fellamar gathers, still from hearsay, that the bastard is really a gentleman and therefore ought not to be treated as a kind of stray animal—he is "much concerned" at having been misled (XVIII, xi). There is a less familiar point about codes of honor, indeed it struck the Tory critic Saintsbury as a libel on squires, when we find that Squire Western regards dueling as a Whig townee corruption, and proposes wrestling or single-stick with Lord Fellamar's second (XVI, ii); but Fielding means Western to be right for once, not to prove that the old brute is a coward, and had said so in his picture of country life (V, xii). When you consider what a tyrant Western is on his estate, it really does seem rather impressive that he carries no weapon.

Fielding meant all this as part of something much larger than a picture of the ruling-class code of honor; having taken into his head that he is a moral theorist, he has enough intelligence to be interested by the variety of moral codes in the society around him. A tribe, unlike a man, can exist by itself, and when found has always a code of honor (though not police, prisons, and so forth) without which it could not have survived till found; such is the basis upon which any further moral ideas must be built. That is why Fielding makes Tom meet the King of the Gypsies, who can rule with no other force but shame because his people have no false honors among them (XII, xii)—the incident is rather forced, because he is obviously not a gypsy but a Red Indian, just as Old Man, with his annuity and his housekeeper, has obviously no need to be dressed in skins like Robinson Crusoe; but they make you generalize the question. By contrast to this, the society which Fielding describes is one in which many different codes of honor, indeed almost different tribes, exist concurrently. The central governing class acts by only one of these codes and is too proud to look at the others (even Western's); but they would be better magistrates, and also happier and more sensible in their private lives, if they would recognize that these other codes surround them. It is to make this central point that Fielding needs the technique of double irony, without which one cannot express imaginative sympathy for two codes at once.

It strikes me that modern critics, whether as a result of the neo-Christian movement or not, have become oddly resistant to admitting that there is more than one code of morals in the world, whereas the central purpose of reading imaginative literature is to accustom yourself to this basic fact. I do not at all mean that a literary critic ought to avoid making moral judgments; that is useless as well as tiresome, because the reader has enough sense to start guessing round it at once. A critic had better say what his own opinions are, which can be done quite briefly, while recognizing that the person in view held different ones. (As for myself here, I agree with Fielding and wish I were as good.) The reason why Fielding could put a relativistic idea across on his first readers (though apparently not on modern critics) was that to them the word "honor" chiefly suggested the problem whether a gentleman had to duel whenever he was huffed; one can presume they were already bothered by it, because it was stopped a generation or two later—in England, though not in the America of Huckleberry Finn. But Fielding used this, as he used the Nightingale marriage, merely as firm ground from which he could be allowed to generalize; and he does not find relativism alarming, because he feels that to understand codes other than your own is likely to make your judgments better. Surely a "plot" of this magnitude is bound to seem tiresome unless it is frankly used as a means by which, while machining the happy ending, the author can present all sides of the question under consideration and show that his attitude to it is consistent. The professional Victorian novelists understood very well that Fielding had set a grand example there, and Dickens sometimes came near it, but it is a hard thing to plan for.

All the actions of Tom Jones are reported to Allworthy and Sophia, and that is why they reinstate him; they are his judges, like the reader. Some readers at the time said it was wilful nastiness of Fielding to make Tom a bastard, instead of discovering a secret marriage at the end; and indeed he does not explain (XVIII, vii) why Tom's mother indignantly refused to marry his father when her brother suggested it (Fielding probably knew a reason, liking to leave us problems which we can answer if we try, as Dr. Dudden's book shows, but I cannot guess it). But there is a moral point in leaving him a bastard; he is to inherit Paradise Hall because he is held to deserve it, not because the plot has been dragged round to make him the legal heir. Lady Mary Wortley Montagu, a grand second cousin of Fielding who thought him low, said that *Amelia* seemed to her just as immoral as his previous books, and she could not understand why Dr. Johnson forgave it, because it, too, encouraged young people to marry for love and expect a happy ending. She had enjoyed the books, and thought that Richardson's were just as immoral. I take it that, after a rather uncomfortable marriage for money, she found herself expected to give a lot of it away to her poor relations, so she thought they all ought to have married for money. Wrong though she may have been, the eighteenth century assumption that a novel has a moral seems to me sensible; *Tom Jones* really was likely to make young people marry for love, not only because that is presented as almost a point of honor but because the plot does not make the gamble seem hopeless. The machinery of the happy ending derives from the fairy tale, as Fielding perhaps recognized, as well as wanting to sound like Bunyan, when he called the house Paradise Hall. The third son seeking his fortune gives his crust to the withered crone and thus becomes a prince because she is Queen of the Fairies; the moral is that this was the right thing to do, even if she hadn't been, but the tale also suggests to the child that maybe this isn't such a bad bet as you might think, either. The mind of Fielding, as he gets near in the actual writing to the end of a plot which he is clearly following from a complete dated skeleton, begins to play round what it means when an author, as it were, tosses up to see whether to give his characters joy or sorrow; he is the creator here, he remarks, but he will promise not to work miracles, and so forth. Rather earlier, he positively asserts that generous behavior like Tom's is not rewarded with happiness on earth, indeed that it would probably be un-Christian to suppose so. This is in one of the introductory chapters of literary prattle (XV, i); it is answered in XV, vii, after a joke about whether Tom has selfish motives for a good action (and the reader who remembers IV, xi may well brace himself to hear a new scandal about Tom), by a firm assertion that the immediate results of such behavior are among the greatest happinesses that earth can provide. However, this play of mind does not arrive at telling us what the happy ending means, and indeed could not, as its chief function is to make the suspense real even for a thoughtful reader. I take it that the childish magic of the fairy tale, and its elder brother, the belief that good actions ought to be done because they will be rewarded in heaven, are reinforced in this novel by a practical idea which would not always apply; the outstanding moral of *Tom Jones*, if you look at it as Lady Mary did but less sourly, is that when a young man leaves home he is much more in a goldfish bowl than he thinks. The reader is to be influenced in favor of Tom's behavior by seeing it through the eyes of Allworthy and Sophia, whom one might think sufficiently high-class and severe. But the end conveys something much more impressive than that these examiners give him a pass degree; he has become so much of a Gospel Christian that he cannot help but cast a shadow even on them. Against all reason and principle, and therefore to the consternation of Allworthy, he forgives Black George.

George robbed him, just after he was cast out, of the money Allworthy had given him to save him from degradation, for example, being pressed to sea as a vagabond, which nearly occurred. The gamekeeper was an old friend rather than a remote peasant, had become comfortable solely through the efforts of Tom to get him a job, and one would also think, as Tom's supposed natural-father-in-law, must have had an interest in letting him even now have a sporting chance. Fielding rated friendship specially highly, and always speaks of this betrayal in the tone of sad wonder he keeps for desperate cases. He says nothing himself about Tom forgiving George, but makes Allworthy give a harangue calling it wicked because harmful to society. We are accustomed in Fielding to hear characters wriggle out of the absolute command by Jesus to forgive, comically bad ones as a rule, and now the ideal landlord is saddled with it. The time must clearly come, if a man carries through a consistent program about double irony, when he himself does not know the answer; and here, as it should do, it comes at the end of the novel. The practical lawyer and prospective magistrate would have to find the Gospel puzzling on this point; it is quite fair for Fielding still to refuse to admit that All-worthy is in the wrong, because he may well suspect that the command of Jesus would bring anarchy. To be sure, this is not one of the im-pressive tests of Tom; he is merely behaving nicely, just when everything is falling into his hands, and would lose our sympathy if he didn't; it comes to him naturally, which not all the previous cases did. But still, we have been moving through a landscape of the ethic of human im-pulses, and when Tom rises above Allworthy he is like a mountain.

There is already a mystery or weird pathos about George when he is first worked back into the plot (XV, xii). Partridge is overjoyed, after all their troubles in London, to meet someone who loves Tom so much:

> Betray you indeed! why I question whether you have a better friend than George upon earth, except myself, or one that would go further to serve you.

The reader is bound to take this as single irony at first, but Fielding is soon cheerfully explaining that George really did wish Tom well, as much as a man could who loved money more than anything else; and then we get him offering money to Tom in prison. Though not allowed to be decisive for the plot, he is useful in smuggling a letter to Sophia and trustworthy in hiding it from his employer. As to his love of money, we should remember that we have seen his family starving (III, ix) after a bad bit of eighteenth century administration by Allworthy. I think Fielding means to play a trick, just after the theft, when he claims to put us fully inside the mind of George; acting as go-between, George wonders whether to steal also the bit of money sent by Sophia to the exile, and decides that would be unsafe (VI, xiii). No doubt we are to believe the details, but Fielding still feels free, in his Proust-like way, to give a different picture of the man's character at the other end of the novel; I take it he refused to believe that the "inside" of a person's mind (as given by Richardson in a letter, perhaps) is much use for telling you the real source of his motives. You learn that from what he does, and therefore a novelist ought to devise an illustrative plot. George of course has not reformed at the end; he has arranged to come to London with his new employer, Western, the more safely to cash the bill he stole, though, as he chooses the lawyer who is the father of Nightingale, the precaution happens to be fatal. I think the mind of Fielding held in reserve a partial justification for George, though he was careful with it and would only express it in the introductory prattle to Book XII, where both the case of George and its country setting are particularly far from our minds; indeed, I had to read the book again to find where this comment is put. While pretending to discuss literary plagiarism, Fielding lets drop that the villagers on these great estates consider it neither sin nor shame to rob their great neighbors, and a point of honor to protect any other villagers who have done so. George might assume, one can well imagine, that Tom was going to remain a grandee somehow whatever quarrels he had; in fact, Tom at the time is so much wrapped up in his unhappy love affair that he seems hardly to realize himself how much he will need money. On this view, it would be shameful for George to miss a chance of robbing Tom; for one thing, it would be robbing his own family, as the soldier reflects in VII, xiv. I agree that, so far from advancing this argument, Fielding never weakens the tone of moral shock with which he regards the behavior of George (who was right to be so ashamed that he ran away); but I think he means you to gather that the confusion between different moral codes made it intelligible. This background I think adds to the rather thrilling coolness with which Tom does not reply to the harangue of Allworthy denouncing his forgiveness; it is in any case time for him to go and dress to meet Sophia.

Sophia has the same kind of briefing as a modern Appointments Board; thus she does not waste time over his offer of marriage to Lady Bellaston; Sophia holds the document, but understands that this was merely the way to get rid of Lady Bellaston, so it joins the list of points already cleared. The decisive question in her mind is whether he has become a libertine, that is, whether his impulses have become corrupted; if they have, she is quite prepared again to refuse to unite by marriage the two largest estates in Somersetshire. Fielding has been blamed for making the forgiveness of Tom too easy, but I think his training as a bad playwright served him well here, by teaching him what he could throw away. A reader does not need to hear the case again, and Fielding disapproved of women who argue, indeed makes Allworthy praise Sophia for never doing it; and he himself has a certain shyness about expressing his doctrine, or perhaps thought it dangerous to express clearly. Beastly old Western comes yelling in to say for the average reader that we can't be bothered with further discussion of the matter, and Sophia decides that she can allow it to have settled itself. The fit reader, interested in the doctrine, is perhaps meant to feel rather disappointed that it is not expounded, but also that this is good taste in a way, because after all the man's impulses have evidently not been corrupted. Even so, it is nothing like the view of Flaubert, Conrad, and so forth, that a novelist is positively not allowed to discuss the point of his novel.

I want now, though there is so much else to choose from in this rich book, to say something about the thought of incest which terrifies Jones in prison; both because it affects the judgment of Sophia and because it has been a major bone of contention among other critics. Dr. F. H. Dudden, in his treatise *Henry Fielding* (1952), though concerned to do justice to an author whose morals have been maligned, admits that he had a rather nasty habit of dragging fear of incest into his plots (it also comes into *Joseph Andrews*); but decides that he means no harm by it, and that it was probably just an effect of having to write bad plays when he was young. On the other hand a *Times Literary Supplement* reviewer, quoted with indignation by Middleton Murry in *Unprofessional Essays*, had thought this frightening of Jones a specially moral part of the plot. When he goes to bed with Mrs. Waters at Upton, says the reviewer, Fielding

> seems to be making light of it, or even conniving at it. Yet it is the first step in a moral progress downhill. . . . And then, much later in the book, evidence comes to light which suggests [that she was his mother] . . Field ing's connivance was a pretence. He has sprung a trap on Tom and us; he has made us realize—as a serious novelist always makes us realize, and a frivolous novelist often makes us forget—that actions have their con-sequences. . . . It is this sense of the moral structure of life that makes Fielding important.

I could have quoted more sanctimonious bits, but this was the part which Middleton Murry found perverse:

> What to a more normal sensibility constitutes the one doubtful moment in the book—the one moment at which we feel that Fielding *may* have sounded a wrong note, by suggesting an awful possibility outside the range of the ex-perience he invites us to partake—becomes in this vision the one thing which makes the book considerable.

The reviewer of course was trying to speak up for Fielding, and make him something better than a flippant libertine; and it is in favor of his view that the Upton incident is the one place where Fielding says in person that casual sex is forbidden by Christianity as expressly as murder (IX, iii). Dr. Dudden might be expected to agree with the reviewer; he maintains you have only to attend to the text to find that Fielding always not only denounces sin but arranges to have it punished "inexorably and terribly." This indeed is one half of what Fielding intended, though the adverbs hardly describe the purring tone of the eventual forgiveness of Tom, as when we are told that he has, "by reflection on his past follies, acquired a discretion and prudence very uncommon in one of his lively parts." Instead, we find that Dr. Dudden agrees with Middleton Murry; they are more in sympathy with Fielding than the reviewer, but feel they have to confess that the incest trick is rather bad; chiefly, I think, because they like him for being healthy, and that seems clearly not.

I think the basic reason why Fielding twice uses this fear is that he had a philosophical cast of mind, and found it curious that those who laugh at ordinary illicit sex take incest very seriously. As to *Joseph Andrews*, the starting point is that Fielding is to parody Richardson's Pamela, a servant who made her master marry her by refusing to be seduced. He had already done this briefly and fiercely in *Shamela*, where an ex-prostitute acts like Pamela out of conscious calculation—the moral is that Pamela is *un*consciously calculating, and that girls ought not to be encouraged to imitate this minx. He is now to do it by swapping the sexes; a footman would be cowardly, or have some other low motive, if he refused a lady, and a lady would be lacking in the delicacy of her caste if she even wanted a footman. Thus the snobbish Fielding, in opposition to the democratic Richardson, can prove that the class structure ought not to be disturbed. Or rather, he did not actually have to write this stuff, because he could rely on his readers to imagine he had, as they still do. It is false to say, as is regularly said, that Fielding started on his parody and then wrote something else because he found he was a novelist; he did not start on it at all. From the first words, he treats his story with an almost over-refined, a breathless delicacy; and by the time Lady Booby has offered marriage, and Joseph, though attracted by her, still refuses her because he wants to marry his humble sweetheart, most of the laughing readers should be pretty well outfaced. No doubt Fielding himself, if the story had been outlined at his club, would have laughed as heartily as the others; but he is concerned in this novel, where he is rather oddly safe from being thought a hypocrite, to show that his sympathy is so broad that he can see the question all around, like a judge. I think he did discover something in writing it, but not what is usually said; he discovered how much work he could leave the public to do for him. One type of reader would be jeering at Joseph, and another admiring him, and feeling indignant with the first type; and both of them would hardly notice what the author was writing down. You can understand that he might want to take some rather firm step, toward the end, to recover their attention. What he is really describing is the chastity of the innocent Joseph, adding of course the piercing simplicity of his criticisms of the great world; Parson Adams, whom Fielding certainly does not intend us to think contemptible, preaches to him a rather overstrained doctrine of chastity all along. Just as all seems ready for the happy ending with his humble sweetheart, a twist of the plot makes them apparently brother and sister; they decide to live together chastely, as Parson Adams had always said they should be able to do. Here the clubmen who form Type A of the intended readers no longer dare to jeer at Joseph for believing he has a duty of chastity; the opposed groups are forced to combine. I thus think that this turn of the plot is entirely justified; for that matter, I think that modern critics are rather too fond of the strategic device of claiming to be embarrassed.

In *Tom Jones*, I can't deny, the trick is chiefly used to heighten the excitement at the end of the plot—Tom must go either right up or right down. I agree with the *Times Literary Supplement* reviewer that it marks a change in the attitude of the hero, but it comes only as an extra at the end of a gradual development. Saintsbury defended Tom's relations with Lady Bellaston by saying that the rule against a gentleman taking money from a mistress had not yet been formulated; certainly it doesn't seem to have hampered the first Duke of Marlborough, but Tom comes to suspect of his own accord that some such rule has been formulated. He felt it when he first met Sophia in London (XIII, ii); "the ignominious circumstance of his having been kept" rose in his mind when she began to scold him, and stopped his mouth; the effect of this was good, because her actual accusations came as a relief and were the more easy to argue off convincingly. It is not till XV, ix that Nightingale, as a fair return for the teaching of basic morals, warns him that he is liable to become despised by the world, and explains that the way to break with Lady Bellaston is to offer her marriage. Learning that he is one of a series makes Tom feel free to break with her, which he thought before would be ungrateful. By the way, I take it Fielding admired her firmness about marriage, as a protest against unjust laws on women's property; her criminal plot against the lovers is chiefly meant as a satire against the worldly code—she can be taken as sincere in telling Lord Fellamar that the intention is to save her ward Sophia from ruin, and Fielding only means to describe her Unconsciousness when he adds in XVI, viii that women support this code out of jealousy. Tom refuses to marry a rich widow immediately afterwards (XV, ii); this is the sternest of his tests, and he is "put into a violent flutter," because he suspects it is a duty of honor to accept this fortune so as to release Sophia from misery. He seems like Galahad when he rejects the point of honor for love, and it does prove that in learning "prudence," which is how Fielding and Allworthy describe his moral reform, he is not falling into the opposite error of becoming a calculating type. We next have him refusing to make love to Mrs. Fitzpatrick, while easily rejecting her spiteful advice to make love to Sophia's aunt (XVI, ix). Both she and Lady Bellaston are affronted by his frank preference for Sophia and yet find their passions excited by its generosity—"strange as it may seem, I have seen many instances." The last of the series is his refusal to go to bed with Mrs. Waters when she visits him in jail with the news that her supposed husband is not dying, so that he is safe from execution (XVII, ix); this might seem ungenerous rather than reformed, but he has just heard from Mrs. Miller that Sophia has become determined to refuse him because of his incontinency. The next and final book opens with the supposed discovery that Mrs. Waters is his mother, so that he committed incest with her at Upton. This throws him into a state of shaking horror which serves to illustrate his courage; we realize how undisturbed he was before at the prospect of being hanged for an act of self-defense. It is thus not the case that Tom was shocked into disapproving of his previous looseness by the thought that it might cause accidental incest, because this fear came after he had become pru-

dent; still less that the fear of death and the horror of incest were needed
together to crack such a hard nut as the conscience of Tom, because he
has been freed from the fear of death just before the other alarm arrives.
(I understand he was technically in danger under ecclesiastical law, but
prosecution was very unlikely; in any case the question never occurs to
him.) Fielding as a magistrate, surely, would think it contemptible to cheat
a prisoner into reform by this trick, whereas the *Times Literary Supplement* reviewer seems to assume it would be moral. What one can say is
that the shock puts Tom into a grave frame of mind, suitable for meeting
Sophia; and Sophia really does need winning over, with some extra
moral solemnity however acquired, because she is quite pig-headed
enough to fly in the face of the world all over again, and start refusing
Tom just because he has become the heir.

My own objection to this bit about incest has long been something
quite different, which I should think occurs oftener to a modern reader;
and I think the book feels much better when it is cleared up. I thought
the author was cheating in a way that whodunit authors often do, that
is, he put in a twist to make the end more exciting though the characters would not really have acted so. Those who dislike Fielding generally
say that he makes his characters so obvious, especially from making them
so selfish, that they become tiresome like performing toys; but the reason
why Mrs. Waters gets misunderstood here is that here as always she is
unusually generous-minded. A penniless but clever girl, she learned Latin
under Partridge when he was a village schoolmaster and did so well that
he kept her on as an assistant, but she learned too much Latin; a fatal
day came (II, iii) when he jovially used Latin to ask her to pass a dish
at dinner, and, "the poor girl smiled, perhaps at the badness of the Latin,
and, when her mistress cast eyes upon her, blushed, possibly with a consciousness of having laughed at her master." This at once made Mrs.
Partridge certain not only that they were lovers but that they were jeering
at her by using this code in her presence; and such is the way most of
us fail to understand her final letter. A ruinous amount of fuss goes
on, and it becomes convenient for her to work with Allworthy's sister
in the secret birth of Jones, acting as her personal servant at the great
house and paid extra to take the scandal of being his mother before
leaving the district. The story is improbable, but as Fielding arranges it
you can call it credible. Allworthy gives her a grand sermon against illicit
love when she confesses to the bastard, but is impressed by the honor and
generosity of her replies; he sends her an allowance, but stops it when
he hears she has run off with a sergeant. We next see her when Jones
saves her life (IX, ii); the villain Northerton is trying to murder her for
what money she carries, and it is startling for the reader to be told, what
Jones is too delicate to ask her (IX, vii), that she was only wandering
about with this man to save him from being hanged, and only carrying
the money to give it to him. She had expected to rejoin Captain Waters

after his winter campaign against the rebels, but meanwhile Lieutenant Northerton was afraid of being hanged for murdering Jones (whereas it had been very lucky for Jones that the drunken assault removed him from the army), and needed to be led across hill country to a Welsh port. Fielding always admires women who can walk, instead of being tight-laced and townee, and though he tends to grumble at learned women he had evidently met a variety of them; he can forgive Mrs. Waters her Latin. She need not be more than thirty-six when she meets Tom, and the struggle has exposed her breasts, which it appears have lasted better than her face. She stops Tom from hunting for Northerton,

> earnestly entreating that he would accompany her to the town whither they had been directed. "As to the fellow's escape," said she, "it gives me no uneasiness; for philosophy and Christianity both preach up forgiveness of injuries. But for you, sir, I am concerned at the trouble I give you; nay, indeed, my nakedness may well make you ashamed to look me in the face; and if it were not for the sake of your protection, I would wish to go alone."
>
> Jones offered her his coat; but, I know not for what reason, she absolutely refused the most earnest solicitation to accept it. He then begged her to forget both the causes of her confusion.

He walks before her all the way so as not to see her breasts, but she frequently asks him to turn and help her. The seduction is entirely free from any further designs on him; she is as foot-loose as a character in the *Faerie Queene*, though perhaps her happening to fall in with Fitzpatrick next morning at the Upton Inn is what saves Jones from finding her even a momentary responsibility. Even so, her capacity to handle Fitzpatrick is rather impressive; the only occupation of this gentleman is to hunt for the woman he cheated into marriage in the hope of bullying her out of what little of her money is secured from him by the law, after wasting the rest; one would hardly think he was worth milking, let alone the unpleasantness of his company, so that she had better have gone back to her officer. Perhaps she wanted to get to London; the only story about her is that she is independent. We are told at the end that she eventually married Parson Shuffle.

When Fielding says he doesn't know the reason he always means it is too complicated to explain. Walking with her lifesaver Jones she liked to appear pathetic, and she wanted to show him her breasts, but also she really could not bear to let him take his coat off, not on such a cold day. The decision becomes a nuisance when they get to the inn because it makes her almost unacceptable, but this is got over; and she gathers from the landlady that Jones is in love with a younger woman.

> The awkward behavior of Mr. Jones on this occasion convinced her of the truth, without his giving a direct answer to any of her questions; but she was not nice enough in her amours to be particularly concerned at the dis-

covery. The beauty of Jones highly charmed her eye; but as she could not see his heart she gave herself no concern about it. She could feast heartily at the table of love, without reflecting that some other had been, or hereafter might be, feasted with the same repast. A sentiment which, if it deals but little in refinement, deals, however, much in substance; and is less capricious, and perhaps less ill-natured and selfish, than the desires of those females who can be contented enough to abstain from the possession of their lovers, provided that they are sufficiently satisfied that nobody else possesses them.

This seems to me a particularly massive bit of double irony, worthy to outlast the imperial eagles of the House of Austria, though I take it Fielding just believed what he said, and only knew at the back of his mind that the kind of man who would otherwise complain about it would presume it was irony.

Such is our main background information about Mrs. Waters when she visits him in prison, assures him that her supposed husband is recovering fast so that there is no question of murder, and is rather cross with him for refusing to make love to her. Then her entirely unexpected letter arrives, which I must give in full (XVIII, ii):

> Sir—Since I left you I have seen a gentleman, from whom I have learned something concerning you which greatly surprises and affects me; but as I have not at present leisure to communicate a matter of such high importance, you must suspend your curiosity till our next meeting, which shall be the first moment I am able to see you. Oh, Mr. Jones, little did I think, when I passed that happy day at Upton, the reflection upon which is like to embitter all my future life, who it was to whom I owed such perfect happiness.— Believe me to be ever sincerely your unfortunate
>
> J. Waters.
>
> P.S.—I would have you comfort yourself as much as possible, for Mr. Fitzpatrick is in no manner of danger; so that, whatever other grievous crimes you may have to repent of, the guilt of blood is not among the number.

Partridge, who happened not to see Mrs. Waters at Upton, has seen her visit the prison and eavesdropped on her talk with Jones, so he has just horrified Jones by telling him she is his mother; they think this letter confirms the belief, and certainly it is hard to invent any other meaning. We are not told who the gentleman was till XVIII, viii, when she tells Allworthy that the lawyer Dowling had visited her, and told her that

> if Mr. Jones had murdered my husband, I should be assisted with any money I wanted to carry on the prosecution, by a very worthy gentleman, who, he said, was well apprised what a villain I had to deal with. It was by this man I discovered who Mr. Jones was. . . . I discovered his name by a very odd accident; for he himself refused to tell it to me; but Partridge, who met him at my lodgings the second time he came, knew him formerly at Salisbury.

On discovery from Dowling that Jones had been the baby she once helped to plant on Allworthy, she assumed it must be Allworthy who was persecuting him in this relentless manner; whereas Allworthy knew it must be Blifil, already driven on by blackmail from Dowling. Since she greatly revered Allworthy, though herself some kind of freethinker, she assumed that Jones had done something to deserve it—this explains the postscript "whatever other grievous crimes." "The second time" is an important detail; the second time Dowling came was when Partridge was there and recognized him, and this was after he had written the letter to Jones. As soon as Partridge saw her he would tell her Jones's fear of incest and she would dispel it; but Partridge has to come, to meet Dowling and tell her his name (otherwise the plot of Blifil could not be exposed). We have next to consider how she knew, when she wrote the letter, about the anger of Sophia; but Jones would tell her this himself, when she visited him in prison, because he would feel he had to offer a decent reason for refusing to go to bed with her. A deep generosity, when she has thought things over after the unpleasant talk with Dowling, is what makes her write down that if Sophia refuses to marry Tom it will embitter all the rest of her life. The delusion about incest is the kind of mistake which is always likely if you interpret in selfish terms the remarks of a very unselfish character. Certainly, the coincidences of the plot are rigged almost to the point where we reject them unless we take them as ordained by God; Fielding would be accustomed to hearing pious characters call any bit of luck a wonderful proof of Providence, and might hope they would feel so about his plot—as Partridge encourages them to do (e.g., XII, viii). But the reaction of the character to the plot is not rigged; she behaves as she always does.

I ought finally to say something about his attitude to the English class system, because opinions about what he meant there seem often to be decisive for the modern reader. What people found so entertaining at the time, when Fielding attacked Richardson in a rather explosive class situation (the eager readers of Richardson in French were presumably heading toward the French Revolution) was that the classes seemed to have swapped over. The printer's apprentice was the gentlemanly expert on manners, indeed the first English writer to be accepted as one by the polite French; whereas if you went to see Fielding, they liked to say at the time, you would find him drunk in bed with his cook still boasting he was related to the Hapsburgs. His answer to Richardson was thus: "But I know what a gentleman is; I am one." The real difference was about the meaning of the term; Fielding thought it should mean a man fit to belong to the class which actually rules in his society, especially by being a just judge. His behavior eventually made a lot of people feel he had won the argument, though not till some time after his death. To die poor and despised while attempting to build up the obviously needed

London police force, with obvious courage and humanity, creating astonishment by his refusal to accept the usual bribes for such dirty work, and leaving the job in hands which continued it—this became too hard to laugh off; he had done in the heart of London what empire builders were being revered for doing far away. He provided a new idea of the aristocrat, with the added claim that it was an older tradition; and he did seem to clear the subject up rather—you could hardly deny that he was a better idea than Lord Chesterfield. An impression continued that, if you are very rude and rough, that may mean you are particularly aristocratic, and good in an emergency; I doubt whether, without Fielding, the Victorian novelists (however much they forbade their daughters to read his books) would have retained their trust in the rather hidden virtues of the aristocracy.

Much of this was wished onto Fielding later, but we have a series of jokes against the current idea of a gentleman during Tom's journey to London. The remarks in favor of the status are perhaps what need picking out. Tom leaves Old Man because he hears cries for help; he thus saves the life of Mrs. Waters from the villain Northerton, who might seem to justify the contempt for mankind of Old Man. This is at the beginning of Book IX; at the very end of it, after the reader has learned how bad the case is, Fielding urges him not to think he means to blame army officers in general:

> Thou wilt be pleased to consider that this fellow, as we have already informed thee, had neither the birth nor the education of a gentleman, nor was a proper person to be enrolled among the number of such. If, therefore, his baseness can justly reflect on any besides himself, it must be only on those who gave him his commission.

We learn incidentally, from this typical rounding on an administrator, that Fielding presumed men ought to be promoted to the ruling class, as a regular thing; the point is merely that the system of promotion should be adequate to save it from contempt. The exalted cynicism of Old Man (who by the way did not try to help Mrs. Waters, though he and not Tom had a gun) might make one suspect that adequate members of such a class cannot be found, and Fielding has kept in mind the social question of how you should do it. I have known readers think Fielding wanted to abolish gentlemen, and indeed the jokes against them are pretty fierce; but he had planted another remark at the beginning of Book IX, in the chapter of introductory prattle, which is clearly meant to fit the last words of that Book. An author needs to have experienced both low life and high life, he is saying; low life for honesty and sincerity; high life, dull and absurd though it is, for

> elegance, and a liberality of spirit; which last quality I have myself scarce ever seen in men of low birth and education.

The assertion seems moderate, perhaps hardly more than that most men don't feel free to look all round a question, unless their position is comfortable enough; but "liberality of spirit" feels rather near to the basic virtue of having good impulses. Of course, he does not mean that all gentlemen have it; the total egotism of young Blifil, a theoretically interesting case, with a breakdown into sadism, which critics have chosen to call unlifelike, is chiefly meant to make clear that they do not. But it seems mere fact that Fielding's society needed a governing class, however things may work out under universal education; so it is reasonable of him to take a reformist view, as the communists would say, and merely recommend a better selection.

Indeed, it is perhaps flat to end this essay with an example which yields so placid a solution to a build-up of "double irony"; nor is it a prominent example, because after we get to London the ironies are about honor rather than gentility. But I suspect that today both halves of the puzzle about gentlemen are liable to work against him; he gets regarded as a coarse snob, whose jovial humor is intended to relax the laws only in favor of the privileged. This at least is unjust; no one attacked the injustices of privilege more fiercely. His position was not found placid at the time, and there is one class paradox which he repeatedly labored to drive home; though to judge from a survey of opinions on him (*Fielding the Novelist*, F. H. Blanchard, 1926) this line of defense never gave him any protection in his lifetime. "Only low people are afraid of having the low described to them, because only they are afraid of being exposed as themselves low." The paradox gives him a lot of powerful jokes, but so far from being far-fetched it follows directly from his conception of a gentleman, which was if anything a literal-minded one. He means by it a person fit to sit on the bench as a magistrate, and naturally such a man needs to know all about the people he is to judge; indeed, the unusual thing about Fielding as a novelist is that he is always ready to consider what he would do if one of his characters came before him when he was on the bench. He is quite ready to hang a man, but also to reject the technical reasons for doing so if he decides that the man's impulses are not hopelessly corrupted. As to the reader of a novel, Fielding cannot be bothered with him unless he, too, is fit to sit on a magistrate's bench, prepared, in literature as in life, to handle and judge any situation. That is why the reader gets teased so frankly. The same kind of firmness, I think, is what makes the forgiveness by Tom at the end feel startling and yet sensible enough to be able to stand up to Allworthy. I think the chief reason why recent critics have belittled Fielding is that they find him intimidating.

# Fielding's *Amelia:*
# An Interpretation

## *by George Sherburn*

Fielding is a novelist of many intentions. On the original titlepage of his *Amelia* he placed two lines from Horace and two from Simonides of Amorgos[1] that perhaps sufficiently indicated (to those who could translate) that the novel was by its author intended to present a picture of durable matrimony and of the beauty of virtue in woman. But if his readers thought *Amelia* a police-court tract, he could hardly deny that he had shown concern over the failure of the courts to dispense true justice. Other readers have liked to regard the story as one of an exposed and neglected wife. The book, again, is plausibly regarded as a sort of monument to the author's lasting love for his first wife, Charlotte. It is not my present purpose to deny any of these interpretations, but it does seem possible that to restudy the novel may serve to emphasize certain important shaping ideas in the domestic drama that Fielding wished to unfold.

If an author of established reputation changes his tone or technique, his public is apt to be surprised and even disappointed. Hence, in general, the unfavorable reception of *Amelia* in 1751. There are so many reasons for the relative failure of this novel that critics have tended to attack or defend its reputation rather than to search out just what Fielding was trying to do in it.

*Amelia* is not necessarily duller than his earlier stories, but obviously it is more serious and less high-spirited. This seriousness is not accidental; it is intentional. It is not that ill health has robbed Fielding of his facetious humours. Parts of *Amelia*—the History of Captain Trent (Bk. XI, chap. iii), for example—abound in brilliant and caustic facetiousness,

"Fielding's *Amelia*: An Interpretation." From *ELH (Journal of English Literary History)*, III (1936), 1-14. Copyright 1936 by the Johns Hopkins Press. Reprinted by permission of the author and publisher, the Johns Hopkins Press.

[1]
Felices ter et amplius
Quas irrupta tenet Copula.           Horace, *Carm.* 1. 13. 18.
γυναικὸς οὐδὲν χρῆμ᾽ ἀνὴρ ληΐζεται
ἐσθλῆς ἄμεινον, ᾽οὐδὲ ῥίγιον κακῆς.      Simonides, *Iamb.* 6.

and so does much of the later *Covent-Garden Journal.* Fielding had not lost that tone: he had simply changed it for another. A bit of superficial evidence will show the consciously serious and "high-class" intention here dominant, and that evidence is his quotation of the classics. Fielding knew his classics far better than did most of his contemporaries, and he quotes them in all his works; but the quotation in *Amelia* is much more frequent, comes from a wider range of reading, and at least a score of passages of Latin and Greek are given without translation. Some of these (notably one from Claudian) are essential to the motivation of his characters or situations, and the failure to translate them obviously limited appreciation of the story to readers who were not, to use Fielding's word, "illiterate." Amelia herself knew neither Latin nor Greek, and most of Fielding's readers were probably in the same state.

Similar evidence of Fielding's "high-brow" seriousness is seen in the imitation of the classical epic that marks the structure of the novel. *Joseph Andrews* and *Tom Jones* had been described by Fielding as comic prose epics. The phrase in variant forms caught on, and has since obsessed critics of the novels. In spite of the comic-epic label placed on these works by Fielding, there is less of epic tradition in them than in the more serious *Amelia*. But in *Amelia* he follows, not the tradition of the comic epic—really that of Cervantes and Scarron, among others—but rather a newer tradition of the epic in prose. The epic in prose, in its turn, is not so much the tradition of *Telemachus* as it is a tradition of private history done with fidelity to the facts of everyday life. Fielding has left us various accounts of this tradition, the best of which perhaps is the last—found in the *Journal of a Voyage to Lisbon.* Here a passage contrasts Fielding's own plodding, prosaic Voyage with the marvels to be found in the *Odyssey* and in *Telemachus;* thus pointing the favorite antithesis between "romance and true history, the former being the confounder and corrupter of the latter."

I am far [he says] from supposing, that Homer, Hesiod, and the other antient poets and mythologists, had any settled design to pervert and confuse the records of antiquity; but it is certain they have effected it; and, for my part, I must confess I should have honoured and loved Homer more had he written a true history of his own times in humble prose, than those noble poems that have so justly collected the praise of all ages; for though I read these with more admiration and astonishment, I still read Herodotus, Thucydides, and Xenophon, with more amusement and more satisfaction.[2]

In this spirit Fielding undertook in *Amelia* to write a sober, faithful history of his own times in humble prose—a history that yet should, in its structure, its organizing themes, and in its pictures of domesticity, re-

[2] *The Journal of a Voyage to Lisbon* ("Oxford World's Classics" [Oxford University Press, 1907]), p. 8.

call at least remotely the masterpiece of Vergil. Soon after the book was published, its author had to defend it, and in so doing he asserts its epic pattern unmistakably in the *Covent-Garden Journal* for 28 January, 1752:

> I . . . avow, that of all my Offspring she is my favourite Child. I can truly say that I bestowed a more than ordinary Pains in her Education; in which I will venture to affirm, I followed the Rules of all those who are acknowledged to have writ best on the Subject; and if her Conduct be fairly examined, she will be found to deviate very little from the strictest Observation of all those Rules; neither Homer nor Virgil pursued them with greater Care than myself, and the candid and learned Reader will see that the latter was the noble model, which I made use of on this Occasion.

It would be possible to take this statement too seriously, but *Amelia* does have serious and semiserious relations to the Vergilian epic. These certainly include the epic "cut-back" in which Booth narrates his past fortunes to Miss Matthews, as Æneas does his to Dido. A touch worthy of James Joyce is the using of Newgate Prison to parallel the palace of the Carthaginian queen and the cave where was consummated the fateful *furtivum amorem*. More serious[3] is the preoccupation of Fielding with an organizing theme—held in his day to be a prime essential in epics. This epic proposition, the *arma virumque* of the novel, is stated in the first sentence in a style consciously suited to the idea of an epic in prose. It reads:

> The various accidents which befel a very worthy couple after their uniting in the state of matrimony will be the subject of the following history.

The utmost malice of Fortune, he continues, might seem to have been working against this couple, except that (as he avows) it is doubtless a mistake to blame Fortune when we involve ourselves in misfortune "by quitting the directions of Prudence, and following the blind guidance of a predominant passion." "To retrieve the ill consequences of a foolish conduct, and by struggling manfully with distress to subdue it, is one of the noblest efforts of wisdom and virtue."

This then is the theme that the novel attempts to dramatize. There is

---

[3] One respect should be noted in which the seriousness of *Amelia* is no innovation. Fielding had always been grimly severe when portraying London high society. His early comedies—*The Temple Beau, The Modern Husband, The Universal Gallant*— are as censorious of the upper classes, are as completely lacking in comic playfulness, as anything he ever wrote, though their picture is not, like that in *Amelia*, pointed by the presence of definitely rationalized social themes. Fielding drops his high spirits whenever he writes about London. Even in *Tom Jones* the London episodes are all somber, and Lady Bellaston and Lord Fellamar belong as much to the atmosphere of *Amelia* as they do to that of *Tom Jones*.

nothing new in it. The idea of a predominant or ruling passion doubtless developed out of the physiology and psychology of the four humours. It was well established long before Pope popularized it for the eighteenth century in his *Essay on Man*. Fielding seems to agree that only the passions stimulate to action; and he asserts, as do most of his contemporaries, a dualism of passion: the good passions headed by benevolence or love of man; the bad by self-love (in the selfish sense) or pride. Booth's error is variously stated: sometimes we are told that men's actions are ruled by a single predominant passion; at others, that men act from whichever passion happens to be uppermost.[4]

It is necessary to consider the relation of these ideas to the characters of Fielding's "worthy couple"—and first of all necessary to insist that they are a worthy couple. Amelia doubtless is far the worthier of the two; for she is a devout Christian with no doubts or beliefs in a ruling passion. Born of a gentle family and reared as a considerable heiress, she nevertheless more than once suggests eagerly that she be allowed to work with her own hands to help support the family. Such "low-mindedness" on her part was disgusting to lady novel-readers of the period, but it seemed heroic to the man who had been Charlotte Fielding's husband. Amelia is not merely the idealization of the *Ewig-Weibliche*; she is an embodiment of moral courage—precisely what her husband lacks.

Booth's sins live after him more vigorously than his virtues; but Fielding tries always to insist on his essential nobility of character. Booth acts almost always from benevolent instincts—not like most of his friends from self-interest only; he is, all told, a devoted husband; and all his faults (which are not so many) are those of the eighteenth-century gentleman. No man of his station (except Sir Charles Grandison) could have refused the overtures of Miss Matthews in Newgate. The lady, furthermore, plies him with rack-punch before he yields; and once out of Newgate he forsakes her as promptly as Æneas does Dido. He is arrested three times; but once it is through the malice of his Wiltshire neighbors who have lied about him to Dr. Harrison; another time illegally through the trickery of Captain Trent (for debts of honor were not actionable in law); and the first time he is arrested, he is sent to Newgate through the grossest miscarriage of justice when actually he deserved the thanks of the court. He sets up a coach before he can afford one, and that snobbishness on his part brings distress: he once gambles at cards (again through the machination of Captain Trent); and when his wife pawns all her trinkets to pay the debt, Booth unwisely gives the money to a great man in the war office, who (he has reason to believe) thus will be led to get Booth back his commission at once. We naturally blame Booth for bribery; but Field-

---

[4] Bk. III, chap. iv, v; Bk. IV, chap. vi; Bk. X, chap. ix. Booth is nowhere depicted as the victim of one ruling passion; he is rather the victim of a belief that men act from their passions, whether permanently predominant or only temporarily so. As a result of this belief he lacks moral courage to struggle against misfortune.

ing's comment indicates that such presents were probably quite the normal thing in 1750. He says:

> The great man received the money, not as a gudgeon doth a bait, but as a pike receives a poor gudgeon into his maw. To say the truth, such fellows as these may well be likened to that voracious fish, who fattens himself by devouring all the little inhabitants of the river.[5]

This sort of thing, however, is not the worst of Booth: the worst is that his moral courage is weak because he believes men act from their natural and not from their rational appetites—to use the jargon of his day. His "chief doubt" in matters moral or religious was, he said, "that, as men appeared . . . to act entirely from their passions, their actions could have neither merit nor demerit." [6] Booth, to be sure, despises Mandeville's perverse account of the passions, and believes heartily in benevolence; but he says of his friend Colonel James:

> The behaviour of this man alone is a sufficient proof of the truth of my doctrine, that all men act entirely from their passions; for Bob James can never be supposed to act from any motive of virtue or religion, since he constantly laughs at both; and yet his conduct towards me alone demonstrates a degree of goodness which, perhaps few of the votaries of either virtue or religion can equal.[7]

Doubtless this idea (that goodness asks no sanction from religion) is what at times led the pious Amelia to fear that her husband "was little better than an atheist." Of this last error, however, he was not guilty. At the beginning of the story Fielding tells us:

> . . . as to Mr. Booth, though he was in his heart an extreme well-wisher to religion (for he was an honest man), yet his notions of it were very slight and uncertain. To say truth, he was in the wavering condition so finely described by Claudian:
>
> 
>
> labefacta cadebat
> Religio, causaeque viam *non sponte* sequebar
> Alterius; vacuo quae currere semina motu
> Affirmat; magnumque novas per inane figuras
> Fortuna, non arte, regi; quae numina sensu
> Ambiguo, vel nulla putat, vel nescia nostri.[8]
>
> 

[5] Bk. XI, chap. v.
[6] Bk. XII, chap. v.
[7] Bk. III, chap. v.
[8] *In Rufinum*, I, 14-19. Fielding does not translate this passage for his readers. For the Loeb Classical Library Platnauer has translated it as follows: "then in turn my belief in God was weakened and failed, and even against mine own will I embraced the tenets of that other philosophy [Epicureanism] which teaches that atoms drift in

This way of thinking, or rather of doubting, he had contracted from the same reasons which Claudian assigns, and which had induced Brutus in his latter days to doubt the existence of that virtue which he had all his life cultivated. In short, poor Booth imagined that a larger share of misfortunes had fallen to his lot than he had merited . . . (Bk I, chap. iii).

It was the psychological and moral task of the novel to rescue Booth from this mental state. Obviously a change of character is necessary, but neither Fielding nor his contemporaries had any modern technique for such portrayal. In *Tom Jones* there is some improvement in Tom's prudence alleged at the end of the novel as due to the ripening effects of experience and age. Booth, however, is no boy, and supernatural intervention seems almost essential. And so, during Booth's last incarceration he reads Dr. Barrow's sermons in proof of the Christian religion, and is quite suddenly convinced of his errors. Little is done by way of direct preparation for this conversion, which, however, seems requisite to the plot from the very beginning—from the moment, in fact, when the parallel to Claudian's state is given.

Any possible milestones on the road to this conversion are more apparent to the reader than they were to Booth: after all, for moral effectiveness, it was more essential that readers should be convinced than that Booth should be; and so Fielding's views, expressed for the reader rather than to Booth frequently concern Booth's problems and the problems involved in reconciling pagan ethics (that is, Stoicism) with Christian principles. Dr. Harrison is the usual mouthpiece; his thinking is scarcely novel, but Fielding clothes it with tactful eloquence, and at times it is effectively dramatized. One exposition of the superiority of the Christian system is as follows:

If the poor wretch, who is trudging on to his miserable cottage, can laugh at the storms and tempests, the rain and whirlwinds, which surround him, while his richest hope is only that of rest; how much more cheerfully must a man pass through such transient evils, whose spirits are buoyed up with the certain expectation of finding a noble palace and the most sumptuous entertainment ready to receive him! [9]

The best discussion of these matters is that between Harrison and a young cleric, destined obviously to become a second Thwackum. Here, to be discouraged, Harrison says: "A true Christian can never be disappointed, if he doth not receive his reward in this world; the labourer might as well complain that he is not paid his hire in the middle of the day." [10]

purposeless motion and that new forms throughout the vast void are shaped by chance and not design—that philosophy which believes in God in an ambiguous sense, or holds that there be no gods, or that they are careless of our doings."

[9] Bk. III, chap. x.
[10] Bk. IX, chap. viii.

The discussion then turns to philanthropy, charity, and universal benevolence—which Harrison holds to be essentially Christian. The unchari-
table young cleric protests:

"Pardon me . . . that is rather a heathenish than a Christian doctrine.
Homer, I remember, introduces in his Iliad one Axylus, of whom he says,—

—φίλος δ'ἦν ἀνθρώποισι
πάντας γὰρ φιλέεσκεν

But Plato, who, of all the heathens, came nearest to the Christian philosophy,
condemned this as impious doctrine; so Eustathius tells us, folio 474."
   "I know he doth," cries the doctor, "and so Barnes tells us, in his note
upon the place."

And the doctor proceeds to heap up counter authorities on the point
(not to be found in Barnes) and concludes triumphantly, "Whom is it,
therefore, we imitate by such extensive benevolence?" The impressed but
unsympathetic response from the father of the young man is: "What a
prodigious memory you have!"
   Then the argument turns to the forgiveness of enemies—one of Fielding's favorite topics—on which we get expressions of opinion from many
persons in *Amelia*—even from Billy Booth, jr., aged six. Harrison
throughout the story embodies the recognition, held by Fielding, of the
superiority of Christian thinking over ancient philosophy. His last pro-
nouncement to Booth on the passions is central in his thinking and in
the thought of Fielding's day:

. . . if men act, as I believe they do, from their passions, it would be fair
to conclude that religion to be true which applies immediately to the
strongest of these passions, hope and fear; choosing rather to rely on its rewards and punishments than on the native beauty of virtue which some of
the ancient philosophers thought proper to recommend to their disciples.[11]

In converting Booth, Fielding does not stress process, but it is nevertheless curious that he should not have used Booth's selfish and false
friend, Colonel James, to bring about disillusionment with freethinking
and to arouse an impulse toward religion. James seems a good friend,
though he laughs at virtue and religion. Either through selfish policy or
through casual impulse he is often generous in an undiscriminating
fashion;[12] but he is quite without emotions of benevolence. His mind,
Fielding tells us,

was formed of those firm materials, of which nature formerly hammered out
the Stoic, and upon which the sorrows of no man living could make an im-

[11] Bk. XII, chap. v.
[12] Bk. VIII, chap. vi.

pression. A man of this temper, who doth not much value danger, will fight for the person he calls his friend, and the man that hath but little value for his money will give it him; but such friendship is never to be absolutely depended on; for, whenever the favourite passion interposes with it, it is sure to subside and to vanish into air. Whereas the man whose tender disposition really feels the miseries of another, will endeavor to relieve them for his own sake; and, in such a mind, friendship will often get the superiority over every other passion.

But, from whatever motive it sprung, the colonel's behaviour to Booth seemed truly amiable. . . .[13]

Later on when it is perfectly evident to the reader that James is trying to win Amelia as a mistress, Booth might well have been made aware of his friend's true character, and the disillusionment might have been used to strengthen religious inclinations in Booth. Fielding, however, strangely enough never makes Booth really conscious of James's designs, and the day after Booth is finally released from the bailiff's house the worthy couple, at the instance of Dr. Harrison, dine with the Jameses. Whether this is by implication forgiveness of one's enemies, or whether Fielding is ironically indicating that life goes on as usual even after conversion, or whether it is simply the outburst of exuberant good nature that frequently affects English authors (even Shakespeare) at a joyful conclusion, it is hard to say. Certainly Colonel James is typical of the callous sort of aristocrat that causes most of Booth's troubles.

It will be remembered that Booth's religious and moral doubts were ascribed vaguely to the same causes as those of Claudian and Brutus—that is, to the prosperity of the wicked in high places. *Diu floruere nocentes*, complains Claudian, whose Rufinus is remotely paralleled by Fielding's colonels and noble lords.

The nature of man [Dr. Harrison tells Amelia] is far from being in itself evil; it abounds with benevolence, charity, and pity, coveting praise and honour, and shunning shame and disgrace. Bad education, bad habits, and bad customs, debauch our nature, and drive it headlong as it were into vice. The governors of the world, and I am afraid the priesthood, are answerable for the badness of it. Instead of discouraging wickedness to the utmost of their power, both are too apt to connive at it.[14]

Booth's personal problem is a private concern—like the wrath of Achilles; but the corruption of the aristocracy and their failure to distinguish and reward merit is as public a theme as the fall of Troy. It is clear from many passages in Fielding's works that he had an interesting philosophical class consciousness. Its basis is a belief in the necessity of "allegiance to the whole" on the part of the individual. In the *Essay on*

[13] Bk. VIII, chap. v.
[14] Bk. IX, chap. v.

*Man* this idea received perhaps its most popular statement in Fielding's day. There the universe, socially considered, is a "vast chain of being," an ordered *continuum*, kept cohesive by the mutual dependence of all the parts.

> Nothing is foreign: Parts relate to whole;
> One all-extending, all-preserving Soul
> Connects each being, greatest with the least;
> Made Beast in aid of Man, and Man of Beast;
> All served, all serving: nothing stands alone;
> The chain holds on, and where it ends, unknown.

In a pamphlet published less than two years after *Amelia* Fielding (addressing the governing classes in behalf of the unemployed) makes the following observations on the duties of the extremes in the social scale:

> Those duties . . . which fall to the higher Ranks of Men, even in this Commonwealth, are by no Means of the lightest or easiest Kind. . . . It is true, indeed, that in every Society where Property is established and secured by Law, there will be some among the Rich whose Indolence is superior to the Love of Wealth and Honour, and who will therefore avoid these Public Duties, for which Avarice and Ambition will always furnish out a sufficient Number of Candidates; yet however idle the Lives of such may be, it must be observed, First, That they are by no Means burthensome to the Public, but do support themselves on what the Law calls their own; a Property acquired by the Labour of their Ancestors, and often the Rewards, or Fruits at least of Public Services. 2dly, That while they dispose what is their own for the Purposes of Idleness, (and more especially, perhaps, if for the Purposes of Luxury,) they may be well called useful Members of trading Commonwealths, and truly said to contribute to the Good of the Public.
>
> But with the Poor (and such must be in any Nation where Property is, that is to say, where there are any Rich) this is not the Case: For having but their Labour to bestow on the Society, if they withhold this from it, they become useless Members; and having nothing but their Labour to procure a Support for themselves, they must of Necessity become burthensome.[15]

This is Fielding's typical view, but in *Amelia* he is less tolerant of the idle rich, or the governing classes. In the earlier parts of the story he illustrates most vividly the miscarriages of justice in the established courts of law, and in the later books he repeatedly exclaims over the callousness of the upper classes, over their selfishness and lack of benevolence. Hearing the story of honest Bob Bound, a half-pay officer of the same regiment as Booth, Amelia cries:

---

[15] *A Proposal for making an Effectual Provision for the Poor*, 1753, pp. 5-6.

"Good Heavens! . . . what are our great men made of? are they in reality a distinct species from the rest of mankind? are they born without hearts?"

"One would, indeed, sometimes," cries Booth, "be inclined to think so. In truth, they have no perfect idea of those common distresses of mankind which are far removed from their own sphere. Compassion, if thoroughly examined, will, I believe, appear to be the fellow-feeling only of men of the same rank and degree of life for one another, on account of the evils to which they themselves are liable. Our sensations are, I am afraid, very cold towards those who are at a great distance from us, and whose calamities can consequently never reach us." [16]

Their fault seems to be that they act either carelessly or only from motives of self-interest. Repeatedly this idea is dramatized by Fielding. The colonel at Gibraltar is willing to lend money to Booth while he thinks Booth has married a fortune; but when he is really in need, the colonel will not help.[17] Tom Bennet's noble friend of college days has forgotten him, and does not wish to renew an acquaintance with a needy clergyman (Bk. VIII, chap. v). Mrs. James implies that her class grants preferments according to policy, not merit, when, coyly starting a movement for bigger and better guardsmen, she insists that her husband (acting out of interest only) shall *not* get Booth a commission in an American regiment but shall place him nearer home: "Are we resolved [she exclaims] never to encourage merit, but throw away all our preferments on those who do not deserve them? What a set of contemptible wretches do we see strutting about the town in scarlet?" The central plot problem of getting Booth back into the commission he so richly deserves is the most glaring case of this callousness. Colonel James could get him back in a moment, but, as he says, he has just secured "two places of a hundred a year each for two of" his "footmen, within this fortnight" (Bk. XI, chap. i), and feels unable to ask further favors at the moment. The noble lord (of amorous propensities) could, if he liked, get the coveted commission within twenty-four hours—he did it for Atkinson, and he had lavishly provided for such a creature as Captain Trent. But this peer is perhaps not quite an average sort, and so Fielding introduces (Bk. XI, chap. ii) another peer, made expressly to enforce the point of this phase of the plot. This is the lord whom Dr. Harrison approaches in behalf of Booth. His lordship is perfectly willing to be of service, not as he frankly avows, because of Booth's obvious merits, but purely out of regard for the worthy Doctor—though it immediately appears that his regard for the Doctor depends entirely on whether that clergyman will use his influence in favor of an inferior candidate who wants to be mayor. Dr. Harrison will not. Whatever the office at stake, this peer does not scrutinize the qualifications of his candidate. "With

[16] Bk. X, chap. ix.
[17] Bk. III, chap. vii.

regard to the personal merit of these inferior officers, I believe I need not tell you that it is very little regarded." Later Doctor Harrison comes doggedly back to this point:

> "Is his own merit, then, my lord, no recommendation?" cries the doctor.
> "My dear, dear sir," cries the other, "what is the merit of a subaltern officer?"
> "Surely, my lord," cries the doctor, "it is the merit which should recommend him to the post of a subaltern officer. And it is a merit which will hereafter qualify him to serve his country in a higher capacity. And I do assure you of this young man, that he hath not only a good heart but a good head too. And I have been told by those who are judges that he is, for his age, an excellent officer."
> "Very probably!" cries my lord. "And there are abundance with the same merit and the same qualifications who want a morsel of bread for themselves and their families."
> "It is an infamous scandal on the nation," cries the doctor; "and I am heartily sorry it can be said even with a colour of truth."
> "How can it be otherwise?" says the peer. "Do you think it is possible to provide for all men of merit?"
> "Yes, surely do I," said the doctor; "and very easily too."
> "How, pray?" cries the lord. "Upon my word, I shall be glad to know."
> "Only by not providing for those who have none. The men of merit in any capacity are not, I am afraid, so extremely numerous that we need starve any of them, unless we wickedly suffer a set of worthless fellows to eat their bread."
> "This is all mere Utopia," cries his lordship; "the chimerical system of Plato's commonwealth, with which we amused ourselves at the university; politics which are inconsistent with the state of human affairs." . . . "Do you not know, doctor, that this is as corrupt a nation as ever existed under the sun? And would you think of governing such a people by the strict principles of honesty and morality?"

Harrison is quite conscious of the dangers of political degeneracy, and hotly urges:

> "Wherever true merit is liable to be superseded by favour and partiality, and men are intrusted with offices without any regard to capacity or integrity, the affairs of that state will always be in a deplorable situation. . . . But, my lord, there is another mischief which attends this kind of injustice, and that is, it hath a manifest tendency to destroy all virtue and all ability among the people, by taking away all that encouragement and incentive which should promote emulation and raise men to aim at excelling in any art, science, or profession." [18]

At this point the two themes[19] that Fielding uses in depicting Booth's

---

[18] Bk. XI, chap. ii.

[19] For analysis of epic structure into a remotely similar dual motivation see Bossu's *Treatise of the Epick Poem* (2d. English ed., 1719), Bk. I, chap. viii (the *Iliad*), chap. x (the *Odyssey*), chap. xi (the *Aeneid*).

lot most nearly meet: his belief in a dominant passion has sapped his zest for life as a moral struggle, and the lack of recognition of his undisputed merit has destroyed incentive that might lead him to excellence as a servant of his country.

Many critics have thought that the happy ending of *Amelia* to a certain extent contradicts the narrative premises of the story. Such an idea is partly based on a lower conception of the character of Booth than Fielding intended; and Booth's conversion, whether through argument with Harrison or through Barrow's sermons, is more than once foreshadowed in the book—though hardly more than foreshadowed. The recovery of Amelia's fortune through the confession of Robinson is certainly an artificial, though time-honored device. It saves Booth from the army, and Henry Fielding was enough of a pacifist to be pleased with that result. But could Henry Fielding the political and social reformer—or as the consistent artist, for that matter—regard this result as a proper "happy ending"? Obviously, if the fears of political and social degeneracy were not to be justified, what was really needed was the conversion, not of Booth, but of some noble lord, who acting from pure desire to secure an able officer for the guards would get the long-coveted commission for Booth. No such person appeared; no Rufinus fell: *diu floruere nocentes.* Fielding simply turns his back on his larger theme, and content to make his worthy couple happy, lets them retire to Wiltshire and an untroubled country life.

*Amelia* was published in December, 1751. Its attack on the aristocracy for callousness and lack of recognition of merit was, of course, nothing new. About two months before the death of Alexander Pope, much of whose writing decries the bad taste and corruption of the aristocracy, Dr. Johnson had published his *Life of Richard Savage,* which told a story motivated much as Booth's was to be. In 1748 in *Roderick Random* Smollett had displayed the acidity of his heart in the story of the difficulties of Melopoyn in securing a patron for his tragedy—transparently the story of Smollett's own difficulties over his *Regicide.* Four years after *Amelia,* Dr. Johnson penned his famous letter to the Earl of Chesterfield about patronage, and in 1759 Goldsmith's *Enquiry* reiterated this tale of the lack of recognition of merit. In brief, this sort of thing, always evident in literary circles, was in the eighteenth century by way of becoming an agent to dissipate respect and regard for noble lords. It consequently is wise to realize that none of these authors was an intentional or conscious revolutionary: they were practically all of them thorough conservatives of the best sort, who wrote with a desire to reform the aristocracy and thus to make the world safe for what we now call the *ancien regime.*

# Fielding and "Conservation of Character"

## by John S. Coolidge

Fielding's *Amelia* differs in form and technique from his other novels to such an extent that it is no longer a "comic romance" or "comic epic poem in prose" but a different kind of novel.[1] Always an artist supremely aware of what he is doing, Fielding may be assumed to have reasons for altering his methods between *Tom Jones* and *Amelia*, especially since in terms of theme and intellectual interest *Amelia* is, as Sir Walter Scott observed, "a continuation of 'Tom Jones.' "[2] But, whatever those reasons are, he is as reticent about them in *Amelia* as he was loquacious on the subject of his art in his earlier books. In fact, the very absence of those typically Fieldingesque critical discussions is an important clue to the nature of the difference between this last novel and the others.

Characteristic of Fielding's first three novels is the sense that the author is creating, not only the work immediately under his pen, but the art itself in which he is working. He is consciously producing the *défense et illustration* of a literary form, establishing criteria for it and defining its

---

[1] George Sherburn observes that *Amelia* does not belong to the tradition of the comic epic but rather to "a newer tradition," which, however, he does not discuss further than to characterize it briefly (see below, n. 22). A recent article by Willi Erzgräber, "Das Menschenbild in Henry Fieldings Roman *Amelia*," *Die neueren Sprachen*, III (1957), 105-116, well states the question to which the present study is addressed: "Die besondere Aufgabe, die sich bei der Interpretation von Fieldings Gesamtwerk ergibt, ist folgende: es ist zu klären, weshalb Fielding, der mit dem so sicher bewältigten *Tom Jones* in seiner harmonischen Ausgeglichenheit und gerundeten Fülle ein episches Meisterwerk der Weltliteratur schuf, von der einmal erreichten Formkunst abwich." Erzgräber concludes very justly that Fielding was "eher bereit, ästhetische Prinzipien aufzugeben als seinen Glauben an das Gute im Menschen und die Macht des Guten in der Welt," but his discussion does not attempt to show why such an alternative should impose itself—unless the general remark that Fielding now found the world no laughing matter be sufficient explanation—or what changes in form and technique constitute Fielding's departure from his "einmal erreichten Formkunst."

[2] Quoted by Wilbur Cross, *The History of Henry Fielding* (New Haven: Yale University Press, 1918), II, 323.

conventions even as he writes in it. In this preoccupation with the rules of his art Fielding is typical of his age, which was above all a prefatory one. But he is more than typical; his way, like that of the great epic poets before him, is to assimilate the common elements of his culture, so subjecting them to his own distinctive genius that what emerges is something quite original. Those introductory chapters in *Tom Jones*— somewhat uneasily defended even by so sympathetic a modern reader as George Sherburn[3]—have a function in the work which sets them apart from the common run of critical prefaces. They are analogous to those passages in *Paradise Lost* in which "God the Father turns a school divine" to explain the great design of creation.

"This work," Fielding says, "may, indeed, be considered as a great creation of our own." [4] However, unlike "those persons of surprising genius, the authors of immense romances," [5] he is not free to follow his creative fantasy at will. True, he asserts that he is not "accountable to any court of critical jurisdiction whatever," being "at liberty to make what laws I please" for this "new province of writing";[6] but, if that liberty has any meaning, it can only be that his commitment to follow an essential, rational order in his creation is itself voluntary. As regards literary creation, that controlling order is formulated in terms of critical principles. It follows that *Tom Jones* would be inconceivable without "those initial essays which we have prefixed to the historical matter contained in every book; and which we have determined to be essentially necessary to this kind of writing." [7] Fielding's introductory commentaries on the rules of his art are not simply a writer's notes on his trade gratuitously added to the narration of a story; to fix the formal principles of this art is an integral part of this creation. Indeed, this art is the "Nature" of the book.

It is in its literary principles that the world of the novel finds its coherence: they are its necessities. They are loyally derived from the apparent necessities of the world we live in, and hence the book is in a special sense "realistic" rather than fantastic or falsely systematic; but they are known from the beginning of this creation and hence are not, like the laws of nature as we mortal creatures apprehend them, subject to modification or enlargement in the course of experience. Thus there is a kind of finality about *Tom Jones*. Creating this book and inventing—

---

[3] "Practically everything except the introductory essays to the eighteen books is organic; and since these essays are as brilliantly written as any essays in this essay-writing century, only harassed undergraduates wish them away" (*A Literary History of England*, ed. Albert C. Baugh [New York: Appleton-Century-Crofts, Inc., 1948], p. 958).

[4] *Tom Jones*, X, i, p. 446. Page references are made to the most readily available editions: the "Modern Library" editions of *Joseph Andrews* and *Tom Jones* and the "Everyman's Library" edition of *Amelia*. Except where otherwise indicated these texts have been used.

[5] *Joseph Andrews*, III, i, p. 217.

[6] *Tom Jones*, II, i, p. 41.

[7] V, i, p. 159.

that is, as Fielding is careful to define it, "finding out" [8]—this art are one and the same process. Once that creation is complete, there seems nothing left to do but to contemplate it. As Aurélien Digeon observes, after *Jonathan Wild* and *Joseph Andrews* "we no longer expect a literary revelation" from Fielding;[9] it only remains for him to carry out the great design more fully. *Tom Jones* stands as the complete work of neo-classical art.

This fixity of nature is particularly significant as regards the individual creatures. Fielding's principle of the "conservation of character" [10] is the classical one most concisely expressed in Horace's *Ars poetica*.[11] It is part of the equipment which Fielding brings with him from the theater; it underlies the method of the English comedy of humours, in which each person is defined by a "character" of him, frequently delivered explicitly at some point in the conversation of the other dramatis personae Writing a novel, Fielding can supply the "character" of each person from his omniscient point of view, and he almost invariably does so on the person's first appearance.[12] From that point on his task is to keep each person acting in a way which can be deduced from that original idea of him. The "characters" are to the individual creatures of this world of the novel what the introductory essays are to that world as a whole.

This literary principle of character presentation corresponds to the philosophical conviction that the essential reality of a person is a certain idea which is his nature and to which he has a kind of duty to conform.[13]

---

[8] IX, i, p. 415.

[9] *The Novels of Fielding* (London, 1925), p. 129.

[10] VIII, i, p. 337; in the "Modern Library" edition the phrase appears erroneously as "conversation of character."

[11] Lines 119-127, concluding: "si quid inexpertum scaenae committis et audes / personam formare novam, servetur ad imum, / qualis ab incepto processerit, et sibi constet."

[12] Where the author does not give us such a "character" in full, it is nonetheless clear that he is working from one, as he tells us in effect at one point: "He [Partridge] had a great many other particularities in his character, which I shall not mention, as the reader will himself very easily perceive them on his farther acquaintance with this extraordinary person" (VIII, iv, p. 346).

[13] "Sed tum servare illud poetas, quod deceat, dicimus, cum id quod quaque persona dignum est, et fit et dicitur, ut si Aeacus aut Minos diceret *'oderint dum metuant'* aut *'natis sepulchro ipse est parens'* indecorum videretur, quod eos fuisse iustos accepimus; at Atreo dicente plausus excitantur, est enim digna persona oratio. Sed poetae quid quemque deceat, ex persona iudicabunt, nobis autem personam imposuit ipsa natura magna cum excellentia praestantiaque animantium reliquarum; quocirca poetae in magna varietate personarum etiam vitiosis quid conveniat et quid deceat videbunt, nobis autem cum a natura constantiae, moderationis, temperantiae, verecundiae partes datae sint cumque eadem natura doceat non neglegere, quemadmodum nos adversus homines geramus, efficitur ut et illud, quod ad omnem honestatem pertinet, decorum quam late fusum sit appareat et hoc, quod spectatur in uno quoque genere virtutis" (Cicero *De officiis* i. 28. 97-98). By "us" Cicero means those who have the most perfect human character to sustain. From there it is only a short step—especially to a mind instructed in what Lovejoy has labeled "the principle of plenitude"—to the conclusion

On the stage this philosophical assumption is kept from being particularly apparent by the unity of time, since, if people do change in real life—otherwise, that is, than by simply coming to know their own essential natures better—it does not seem likely that they should do so within a few hours or a day. But when the convention is transferred to the novel, whose time span may be greater, the limitation it imposes becomes significant. In this respect as in others, the world of *Tom Jones* is, for all its meticulous chronology, a timeless one.

In this comic epic, then, the great questions of "Fixt Fate, Free will, Foreknowledge absolute" appear as questions of literary procedure. When Fielding assures his reader that, "notwithstanding any affection which we may be supposed to have for this rogue, whom we have unfortunately made our hero, we will lend him none of that supernatural assistance with which we are entrusted, upon condition that we use it only on very important occasions," [14] he is thinking of the classical injunction against recourse to supernatural agencies "nisi dignus vindice nodus inciderit"; but the remark also reflects the restricted place of miracles in the plan of the universe as envisaged by the Enlightenment. However, the creator's affection for his "rogue" is not quite so inconsequential as this declaration might make it seem, for the limits of probability leave a certain margin within which Fortune is free to operate. That goddess is custodian of such mystery as persists in this comic cosmos. Both irrational and somehow purposive, she seems perversely bent on persecuting those persons with whom we sympathize; but in the end the prayer "ut redeat miseris, abeat fortuna superbis" is answered, and one has a sense that she intended from the beginning that it should be. Tom Jones's salvation can be materially assisted by this obscure agency, but only, it would seem, if he shows himself able to effect it without her. That is up to him, as his creator says, but his problem is not simply the external one of finding "some natural means of fairly extricating himself from all his distresses." It is a far more perplexing one, not so much for Tom as for his creator: how can a person whose nature it is to run into generous but dangerous faults become prudent in the course of the work? The very principles upon which the world of *Tom Jones* is created appear to preclude any such change in character.[15]

---

that it is likewise fitting that less admirable "natures" such as Atreus' should exist and that those who embody them should remain constant to them, in life as on the stage. Recall Fielding's remark that his "mean selfish" lawyer in *Joseph Andrews* "is not only alive, but hath been so these four thousand years; and I hope G—— will indulge his life as many yet to come" (III, i, p. 218). The pertinence of this and other passages in the *De officiis* to Horace's *Ars poetica* has been noted by G. C. Fiske, *Cicero's "De oratore" and Horace's "Ars poetica"* ("Studies in Language and Literature," No. 27 [Madison: University of Wisconsin Press, 1929]), pp. 45-51.

[14] XVII, i, pp. 780-781.

[15] The deterministic implications of the method of character presentation that Fielding employs in *Tom Jones* have been referred to here in terms of the theory of ideas

The closest that Fielding comes in *Tom Jones* to dealing with this problem in theoretical terms is to propose a solution whereby the acquisition of prudence would not really constitute an alteration in character. The solution implies a kind of benign Machiavellianism of private life. Fielding admits that Blifil's schemes to discredit Tom with Mr. Allworthy were assisted by Tom's "own wantonness, wildness, and want of caution"; wherefore he admonishes

> those well-disposed youths who shall hereafter be our readers . . . that goodness of heart and openness of temper . . . will by no means, alas! do their business in the world. Prudence and circumspection are necessary even to the best of men. They are indeed, as it were, a guard to Virtue, without which she can never be safe. It is not enough that your designs, nay, that your actions, are intrinsically good; you must take care they shall appear so.[16]

The good man will calculate in defense of his own simplicity, wear a mask to match his face. Prudence and good nature will not really combine in him; prudence will be kept external to the real character of the person, serving as a regrettably necessary "guard" for the immaculate ingenuousness within. But this solution encounters a difficulty which the very words by which Fielding leads up to it make clear. "Wantonness and wildness" are of the very nature of that "openness of temper" which prudence is to protect without changing. The inconsistency is obvious. Prudence cannot really guard the fort without being admitted to the inner councils.

In terms of the plot, the solution of the problems centering on the character of Tom Jones is to be signalized by Sophia's acceptance of him.[17] It would not be in keeping with the clear-eyed intelligence of her character for her to be convinced by a solution which was not really convincing, and her insistence on a further probationary period for Tom may be taken as a kind of acknowledgment that those problems have still not been dealt with. The difficulty is got over in a scene of masterful comic consistency: Squire Western could hardly be imagined acting otherwise than to turn immediately from bullheaded persecution of the lovers to bullheaded insistence that they be made happy at once, and Sophia would not be Sophia without the good, womanly passion that makes her

---

from which the critical precepts of Cicero and Horace derive (see R. K. Hack, *The Doctrine of Literary Forms* ["Harvard Studies in Classical Philology," Vol. XXVII (Cambridge: Harvard University Press, 1916)]). They might also be discussed, of course, in terms of the psychology of the humours which served to give physical underpinning to the idea of *decorum personae* in the Renaissance or in terms of "the doctrine of the passions" in which Booth was so interested.

[16] III, vii, pp. 97-98.

[17] His reconciliation to Allworthy is less significant in effect, because Allworthy has in the main simply been duped, whereas Sophia's reasons for hesitating correspond to the real difficulties involved in Tom's character and have been carefully developed in the course of the book.

amenable to parental wisdom on this occasion. The scene is no less a triumph in terms of the book's formal principles for being indicative of failure in terms of its substantial concerns. It epitomizes the triumph and the failure of *Tom Jones*.

The case that Tom makes for himself to Sophia rests heavily on the argument that he could never have been guilty of his lapses with other women had he not been in despair of ever possessing her.[18] It may occur to the reader that this explanation was not advanced at the time of the transgressions themselves. However, now that Sophia is his, Tom will have a lifetime to demonstrate the immunity to such temptations which that happiness provides. But that would be another story—and another kind of story.

After *Tom Jones*, then, there follows a novel which takes up its story after the beatific marriage with which a romance—comic or otherwise— naturally brings its story to an end. The "comic romance" had run its course without bringing Fielding to a convincing resolution of the moral and psychological dilemma with which he was preoccupied, and so he set out again where that kind of novel left off. His literary career had been a long, thoughtful process of constructing a complex artistic form out of the literary resources of his age; yet he was willing to put that triumph behind him, to go beyond the formal conclusion of his art in an effort to master the substantial problems with which he felt himself confronted in life. His audacity in beginning at the conventional terminus of the romance typifies at the very outset the nature of his artistic undertaking in *Amelia*.

The opening sentence of the book announces this new departure and further indicates its nature:

> The various accidents which befel a very worthy couple after their uniting in the state of matrimony will be the subject of the following history.

Compare this with the opening sentence of *Tom Jones*:

> An author ought to consider himself, not as a gentleman who gives a private or eleemosynary treat, but rather as one who keeps a public ordinary, at which all persons are welcome for their money.

In the beginning of *Tom Jones* was the author. By the end of the first sentence both his relation to the story and our attitude toward him were already well on the way to being established: the story was his performance. We were inclined to take his side as against other possible authors in general and to agree that he had the right approach. But in *Amelia* the story's the thing. It is not presented as the author's performance but as something which did happen and which the speaker is simply in a position to report. As "the exordium" proceeds, the speaker presents himself, but instead of the exuberant creator of *Tom Jones* there is simply a decent sort of "man of sense" who is telling the story because he thinks it deserves telling and will venture to offer his own comments only as the story seems to call for them:

> The distresses which they waded through were some of them so exquisite, and the incidents which produced these so extraordinary, that they seemed to require not only the utmost malice, but the utmost invention, which superstition hath ever attributed to Fortune: though whether any such being interfered in the case, or, indeed, whether there be any such being in the universe, is a matter which I by no means presume to determine in the affirmative. To speak a bold truth, I am, after much mature deliberation, inclined to suspect that the public voice hath, in all ages, done much injustice to Fortune, and hath convicted her of many facts in which she had not the least concern.

The familiar Fieldingesque irony is still here, but it is subdued, and its function is not quite what it was in *Tom Jones*. There it was a standing assertion of the author's presence and easy authority; it served to divide the readers hypothetically into two parties: those dullards or ill-natured ones whom the author's irony banished and "the happy few" who joined the author in knowing scorn of all those others. Here the irony arises from the speaker's almost naïve diffidence about opposing his own good sense to "the public voice." The speaker in *Amelia* does claim a competent knowledge of the ways of the world in which the story takes place, but it is a world he never made.

Fielding renounces the aid of Fortune. To have recourse to Fortune, even within the limits assigned her in *Tom Jones*, in accounting for the failure or success of human projects in the world of *Amelia* would be objectionable as it was not in the world of *Tom Jones*. Rather than representing a reservation of mystery and voluntary caprice on the part of the rational creator, it would now be simply a human evasion. Booth— who, unlike Tom Jones in this respect, combines with his moral incompetence a set of theories to match—is "in the wavering condition so finely described by Claudian" of believing that events are ruled "by Fortune, not by art." [19] The world of *Tom Jones* was simply declared— on the best authority, that of its maker—to be a work of "art," that is, of rational design. *Amelia* sets out to "prove" that its world is so. The test will be whether that world reveals a rational order in its workings by responding satisfactorily in the end to a rational way of life on the part of individuals. In *Amelia*, no less than in *Tom Jones*, we are following the "finding-out" of an art, but we are not to do so by means of intro-

[19] I, iii, Vol. I, p. 14.

ductory chapters on literary principles, for now it is not the art of creating a novel that concerns us but "this most useful of all arts, which I call the ART OF LIFE." [20]

The realism of *Amelia* is thus different from that of *Tom Jones*. For the reasons which have been discussed, *Tom Jones* may be called a deductive presentation of reality; *Amelia* sets out to follow a process of observation and discovery. That is, where *Tom Jones* presents a reality which is essentially known as the outset, *Amelia* ostensibly follows the process by which mortal human intelligences build up such knowledge of the world as they can. Booth appears at the beginning of the second chapter, and we follow him through four chapters, learning what he is learning about the workings of English justice and the prison house, before we learn much about him. There is what we might call today a "documentary interest." This aspect of *Amelia* recalls Defoe or Le Sage or, especially, Smollett, whose *Roderick Random* appeared as *Tom Jones* was approaching completion.[21] It is in this exploratory approach to reality that *Amelia* is most significantly akin to the "newer tradition" of which Sherburn speaks.[22]

This exploratory approach is reflected in the method by which the major characters of *Amelia* are presented. Instead of being supplied from the beginning with the essential idea of each person, we receive only what might be described as an "idea" in the Lockean sense, an impression which will be combined with others in the course of our developing experience of the person. These people come into the story in the same way that people come into our lives. In Roderick Random's phrase, the characters of people "open upon" us.[23] Our knowledge of a person's character is always provisory, pending further discovery. A new word or act may bring a new revelation, causing a shift in our interpretation and evaluation of a person's character. The kind of interest which we take in the character may alter as a new turn in the story presents a new danger or promise centering on him; or he may reveal, under new conditions and in new human relations, aspects of his character which had existed only in hidden potentiality; or his character may undergo a real change.

*Amelia* would seem, then, to represent a well-considered effort on

[20] I, i, Vol. I, p. 4.

[21] For a discussion of the probable dating of Fielding's reading of *Roderick Random* see F. Homes Dudden, *Henry Fielding, His Life, Works, and Times* (Oxford University Press, 1952), II, 654.

[22] "But in *Amelia* he follows, not the tradition of the comic epic—really that of Cervantes and Scarron, among others,—but rather a newer tradition of the epic in prose. The epic in prose, in its turn, is not so much the tradition of *Telemachus* as it is a tradition of private history done with fidelity to the facts of every-day life" ("Fielding's *Amelia*: An Interpretation," *ELH*, III [March, 1936], 2).

[23] "Having taken possession of a room, called for French wine, and bespoke supper, the glass went about pretty freely, and the characters of my associates opened upon me more and more" (chap. xlvi).

Fielding's part to escape the limitations of the "comic epic poem in prose." If this is so, the failure of *Amelia* should at least be re-examined. Far from showing that the author's energy was declining or that his duties as a magistrate were distracting him from his literary efforts, the book might well be given the youthful designation of "experimental." However, Fielding appears to waver in his design. Early in the second chapter, for example, he suddenly reverts both to the tone and to the method of *Tom Jones*:

> But here, reader, before we proceed to the trials of these offenders, we shall, after our usual manner, premise some things which it may be necessary for thee to know.[24]

There follows a short essay on the constitution and its administration, a brilliantly arch performance in the "usual manner" of *Tom Jones*, leading to a "character" of Justice Thrasher. We are for a moment back in the world of Fielding's earlier novels, but then the sober tone returns, relieved by only a muted strain of the old irony, as we witness the desolate little procession of the victims of Thrasher's capricious "justice." This procession includes Booth, but all we are told about him is what brought him there, and the only indication that he is to be any more important than the others is that his name is given: "A young fellow, whose name was Booth." [25] This vacillation between the two tones and the two methods characterizes the book throughout. It seems a real inconsistency of kind, and it is in these terms that the real artistic failure of *Amelia*, to the extent that it is a failure, may best be described.

More damaging still, even where it would appear by the obvious signs —the absence of the preliminary "character," notably—that Fielding intends to be working by the new method, his conceptions may nevertheless turn out to be formed in the manner of *Tom Jones*. Unfortunately, this appears to be the case with Booth himself. The incident of the supposed beating of the watchman which provides our first impression of him is in effect an implicit "character," at least to any reader familiar with *Tom Jones*. Booth's having gone immediately to the assistance of a man whom he saw being attacked in the street by two others supplies us with the essential idea of his generous imprudence, and his actions thereafter derive from that initial idea of him with exasperating consistency. Since the whole enterprise of *Amelia* was undertaken in Booth's interest, as it were, it may seem devoted to failure from the start if his character turns out to belong to the artistic world of *Tom Jones* after all.

However, a remarkable thing appears to happen in the course of the novel. The important concerns involved in the character of Booth, remaining unresolved in terms of the development of his character, seem to be re-expressed in the form of a confrontation between his Amelia and another kind of woman.

Fielding's good men, from Heartfree to Booth, show a persistent tendency to fall back gratefully but helplessly on the moral, and frequently material, support of their good women. Perhaps Joseph Andrews is an exception, and the scene in which he carries Fanny safely down the hill which Parson Adams has just tumbled down headlong in the night is an emblematic one:

> Learn hence, my fair countrywomen, to consider your own weakness, and the many occasions on which the strength of a man may be useful to you; and duly weighing this, take care that you match not yourselves with the spindle-shanked beaux and *petit-maîtres* of the age, who, instead of being able, like Joseph Andrews, to carry you in lusty arms through the rugged ways and downhill steeps of life, will rather want to support their feeble limbs with your strength and assistance.[26]

But Joseph is never really put to the big test of city life. The new order, or disorder, of things that is encountered in London would destroy any of Fielding's good men, it appears, but for the succor of those good creatures whom he once bid consider their own weakness. As *Amelia* is Fielding's first novel to plunge directly into the depths of the city and stay there, so this tendency of the Fielding male to sink into moral dependency on his woman reaches its extreme in Booth.

Sherburn has pointed out that the seduction of Booth by Miss Matthews in the prison designedly parallels the episode of Dido in the *Aeneid*.[27] Like Dido, Miss Matthews presents the hero with the possibility of a different basis of value in life from that to which he is dedicated. As Booth tells his story, she seizes on every opportunity to inject remarks tending to build up a contrast between Amelia's value as a woman and her own. It is Cleopatra against Octavia, the "woman of spirit" against the insipid paragon. "Our lives resembled a calm sea," recalls Booth. " 'The dullest of all ideas,' cries the lady." [28]

However, Booth himself hardly seems to sense the significance of this temptation. He seems to succumb to it automatically, almost mechanically. Perhaps his moral simplicity serves him well in this juncture by preventing the full implications of this lapse from registering with him. He feels his guilt—and, what is more, the speaker of the book can only speak equivocally in his favor—but there is no question of his responding deeply to the dark appeal of a tragic passion as against the bland warmth of his Amelia. Miss Matthews may have involved Booth in serious guilt, but

---

[26] III, ii, pp. 224-225.
[27] See n. 22 above. See also Lyall H. Powers, "The Influence of the *Aeneid* on Fielding's *Amelia*," *MLN*, LXXI (May, 1956), 330-336.
[28] III, xii, Vol. I, p. 151.

she has not really succeeded in lodging her claim against Amelia, and Fielding apparently finds himself at a loss what to do with her. Every indication through the first quarter of the novel is that she is to be a central figure in it, and yet she is shortly "drawn off" by Colonel James and—except for Booth's lingering sense of guilt and the edifying revelation later that all has been known and forgiven—she simply fades from the book. Nevertheless, the possibility of a challenge to Amelia has been suggested, if not to Booth's mind, to the reader's—and perhaps to the writer's.

The story gropes forward and it soon develops that Amelia herself is to be exposed to a skilful attempt at seduction. The scene in which she asks Booth to explain his refusal to let her go to the masquerade makes an ironic counterpart to that in which Milton's Eve obtains Adam's consent to leave his side on that fatal morning. "What is it you fear?" she asks—

> you mention not force, but snares. Is not this to confess, at least, that you have some doubt of my understanding? do you then really imagine me so weak as to be cheated of my virtue?—am I to be deceived into an affection for a man before I perceive the least inward hint of my danger? [29]

This Adam, however, has already fallen, and, to complete his disgrace, his Eve knows it and has already forgiven him. Booth's best hope is to be uxorious. Yet Amelia is, in fact, mistaken, for the man who sent that masquerade ticket does have designs upon her which she does not perceive.

The temptation of Amelia presents the same kind of difficulty as that of Eve.[30] Precisely because she is innocent, she should not perceive "the least inward hint" of any evil. The theme is one which keeps turning up in Fielding. Heartfree, Parson Adams, Allworthy, Sophia, and Amelia play the changes on the idea that innocence and suspicion are incompatible.[31] It is a companion theme to that of the incompatibility between good nature and prudence. If both themes seem psychologically unconvincing —curiously arbitrary problems to form the main focus of a major writer's work—it is because it is not in strictly psychological terms that their real significance is to be understood. They are redactions in Augustan terms

---

[29] VI, vi, Vol. I, pp. 284-285.

[30] For an excellent discussion of this problem in *Paradise Lost* see Millicent Bell, "The Fallacy of the Fall in *Paradise Lost*," *PMLA*, LXVIII, (September, 1953), 863-883, and her exchange with Wayne Shumaker in "Notes, Documents, and Critical Comment," *PMLA*, LXX (December, 1955), 1185-1203.

[31] Compare Milton's explanation of how Satan could deceive the high intelligence of an angel: "And oft though wisdom wake, suspicion sleeps / At wisdom's Gate, and to simplicity / Resigns her charge, while goodness thinks no ill / Where no ill seems: Which now for once beguil'd / *Uriel*, though Regent of the Sun, and held / The sharpest-sighted Spirit of all in Heav'n . . ." (*Paradise Lost*, III, 686-691).

of the great, recurrent question of the relation of evil to good. For Tom Jones to acquire prudence, or for Amelia to see through the designs of a tempter who diabolically couches his appeal in terms of all that is good —generosity and justice, affection for children, and so forth—would imply knowledge of evil in themselves. Can such knowledge be part of essential goodness? Can good admit the participation of evil without ceasing to be essentially itself? But in a world where evil exists, can good preserve itself without that participation of evil?

The invitation to the masquerade is finally accepted, once again the novel seems to be shaping toward its crisis, and again the test is averted. Another woman interposes her experience between Amelia's innocence and the danger. But this evasion, even assuming that is what it is at the outset, develops into something else. Mrs. Bennet, later Atkinson, emerges to dominate the central portion of the book, superseding Miss Matthews as the "other woman" of the novel—though not of Booth, and perhaps it is the very fact that her character is in no way involved with his that enables it to develop as it does. In the character of Mrs. Bennet the possibilities of Fielding's new method are brilliantly demonstrated, and "the lore of good and evil" is explored in a manner which nothing in Fielding's earlier work would prepare us to expect.[32]

Her first appearance in the novel is reported in the same matter-of-fact manner as was that of Booth.[33] We learn little about her, but an aura of sorrow and mystery invests her; she is the young woman with a tragic story. This idea of her seems to be confirmed later when her friend Mrs. Ellison suddenly darts at her a malicious jibe: "Oh! to be sure, . . . *All for Love, or the World well Lost,* is a motto very proper for some folks to wear in their coat of arms." [34] Apparently we are in the presence of a second Cleopatra-figure—but a chastened one, for she replies mildly, even meekly, to Mrs. Ellison's cruel allusion to her tragedy. Mrs. Ellison at this point is coming to be distinctly suspect. The reader surely sympathizes with Mrs. Bennet's expression of preference for "the honest serjeant" Atkinson over his lordship, which is what brought on Mrs. Ellison's rejoinder; this is the first hint that Mrs. Bennet may help to frustrate any scheme that may be behind his lordship's obliging behavior to Amelia. This exchange of words takes place, moreover, at a time when it seems to be Mrs. Ellison who is shaping up as the woman likely to marry the good Sergeant. Amelia and Booth regard this potential match complacently, but the reader may catch hopefully at the hint of a different marital possibility for Atkinson. As our suspicions darken about Mrs. Ellison, our hopes, both for the Sergeant's happiness and for Amelia's

---

[32] "The history of Mrs. Fitzpatrick" in *Tom Jones* foreshadows that of Mrs. Bennet in several ways, but its potential significance is not developed and only becomes apparent in retrospect from Mrs. Bennet's story.

[33] IV, ix, Vol. I, pp. 203-204.

[34] V, iii, Vol. I, p. 223.

safety, come to center on this mysterious young woman. Yet in the next moment the author intervenes to suggest his opinion that Mrs. Bennet spoke out of jealousy at the attentions which his lordship had shown to Amelia.

A new situation several chapters later gives us a new impression of Mrs. Bennet, lowering her from her tragic status and complicating our idea of her with a new question, that of the propriety of learning in women. In the "chapter in which there is much learning" Mrs. Bennet behaves "with more than ordinary gaiety," which converts Booth to a favorable opinion of her, and holds forth with much force and astonishing erudition against second marriages—obviously protesting a bit too much, like Dido, whose similar declaration she takes for her text. If we suspect that she has got herself a man, we no longer find ourselves looking on her precisely as a tragic person; this unwonted gaiety in her is the price the character pays for a sturdy determination to proceed with life: it lapses from its tragic elevation. As a *femme savante*, however, she is in danger of descending further in the scale of kinds and becoming a subject of satire. She suddenly appears as Amelia's opposite in an important respect, and perhaps the satirical strain that now appears in the treatment of her character is, likewise, a price the character pays for departing from the kind of woman's role to which it had been complacently assigned.

In the following chapter the suggestion of hidden animosity between Mrs. Ellison and Mrs. Bennet becomes unmistakable. Mrs. Ellison's conduct toward Mrs. Bennet "appeared utterly unaccountable to Amelia, and, upon the whole, she knew not whether to conclude Mrs. Ellison to be a friend or enemy to Mrs. Bennet." [35] Mrs. Ellison has been our principal source of information about Mrs. Bennet. This perplexing relationship between the two women casts a shadow of uncertainty over Mrs. Bennet's character as we know it. The time is ripe for the revelation of character that begins with the mysterious warning note which Amelia recognizes to be in Mrs. Bennet's hand and which leads to her hearing Mrs. Bennet's story.

Mrs. Bennet begins dramatically:

> "O Mrs. Booth! . . . I find I have undertaken what I am not able to perform. You would not wonder at my emotion if you knew you had an adulteress and a murderer now standing before you."

The tragic theme comes suddenly to the fore again in Mrs. Bennet's character. In the next instant it is again compromised, but in a new way, as she attempts to excuse her actions in the very words in which she says she never can:

[35] VI, viii, Vol. I, p. 292.

"I believe, indeed, your candour . . . will be readier to acquit me than I am to acquit myself. Indiscretion, at least, the highest, most unpardonable indiscretion, I shall always lay to my own charge: and, when I reflect on the fatal consequences, I can never, never forgive myself." [36]

She is suggesting the same argument by which the author of *Tom Jones* extenuated the blame for the actions of his rogue—that indiscretion is a venial fault and indicative of a certain saving generosity of temper. However, it makes a great deal of difference that now it is not the author-creator who states the case. What Mrs. Bennet says is open to question. In the world of *Amelia* there is a real possibility that indiscretion may have consequences involving the imprudent person in guilt—unintentional, in a sense undeserved, but serious guilt.

All through the story that Mrs. Bennet goes on to tell it is possible to suspect her of evasion or equivocation. An alternative story can be constructed by reinterpreting the events she relates. Was she, for instance, really the pitiable victim of the machinations of the young widow who became her stepmother? Or was she the perhaps equally pitiable "only darling" of her father, fighting desperately and even viciously to drive out a rival for his love? And, again, in telling of Mr. Bennet's courtship and his final declaration of his passion, she says:

"He did this in so forcible though gentle a manner, with such a profusion of fervency and tenderness at once, that his love, like a torrent, bore everything before it; and I am almost ashamed to own to you how very soon he prevailed upon me to— to— in short, to be an honest woman, and to confess to him the plain truth." [37]

Her sentence seems pretty obviously to be leading up to an event upon which, in Fielding's customary phrase, it might be best to draw a curtain —is Mrs. Bennet, in the way she ends the sentence, drawing a curtain? If not, the sentence is constructed as a kind of trick, in the manner of a certain genre of ribald songs, to lead the listener to expect a guilty outcome and then disappoint that expectation with a perfectly innocent conclusion. Note, too, the possible play on the words "honest woman": an "honest woman" is one who confesses "the plain truth" of her desires, not a hypocrite obsessed with her "honesty." If Mrs. Bennet is indeed drawing a curtain here, she may at the same time be thinking of a justification of her behavior. If we should put this interpretation on her words, we would surely be led to suspect also that the conversation which her aunt overheard on a later occasion "in a very thick arbour in the garden" [38] gave her a more substantial reason than merely her own in-

[36] VII, i, Vol. II, p. 3.
[37] VII, v, Vol. II, p. 24.
[38] VII, v, Vol. II, p. 25.

jured vanity for turning them both out of doors immediately—that
there was a strong reason for his marrying the young lady within two
days. We may, if we are perhaps ill-natured readers, form for ourselves
a very natural but unlovely picture: a high-spirited, intensely vain young
woman, alienated from her father by her jealousy, driven from his household when she was on the point of wrecking it, cooped up with a boring
and equally vain maiden aunt in the country, faced with the imminent
necessity of going "into service"; she sees her escape in a poor young
clergyman, plays her eyes upon him successfully, and soon makes sure of
him; by her inability to get on with his superior she makes his curacy
untenable, and *la voilà* in London at last, going to plays night after night
until their meager capital is exhausted, slipping finally into the trap
which a libertine lord has contrived for her kind, betraying and polluting
the poor young man who so desperately loves her. When she has told
the story of her "unpardonable indiscretion" and relates that, afterward,
she was afraid to look her husband in the face, there is an unconscious
irony in her words:

> "I was conscious of I knew not what—guilt I hope it cannot be called."
> "I hope not, nay, I think not," cries Amelia.[39]

Even Amelia's candor cannot prevent a momentary hesitation in declaring
this imprudent woman guiltless.

Yet even putting the worst construction on her story, her motives at
every point must elicit sympathy. A good number of them, at least, come
down to nothing more wicked than the desire of a high-spirited nature
to escape what must have been intolerably bleak circumstances. If we
are not uncritical of her account, neither can we condemn her. Whatever
evasions her confession may contain, she is rendering Amelia a truly noble
service—and a difficult one—in making it. Our idea of her by this time
is complex, as is the judgment on the nature of guilt which it involves.
Then, at the most horrible moment of her story—as she is recounting
the young clergyman's discovery of his pollution—her visible distress
causes Amelia to cry out, Atkinson comes running at the sound, and we
learn, or are reminded if we had already surmised, that this is the woman
that the loyal, open-hearted Sergeant has married.

It is a moment of very human drama, and the drama is also one of
ideas. The reader can hardly subscribe to Amelia's simple verdict:

> "Indeed, madam," says she, "you are much too severe a judge on yourself;
> for they must have very little candour, in my opinion, who look upon your
> case with any severe eye. To me, I assure you, you appear highly the object
> of compassion; and I shall always esteem you as an innocent and an un-
> fortunate woman." [40]

[39] VII, viii, Vol. II, p. 41.
[40] VII, x, Vol. II, p. 49.

But perhaps it is to be read less as a verdict than as an absolution. "To retrieve the ill consequences of a foolish conduct," as "the exordium" said, with Booth in mind, "and by struggling manfully with distress to subdue it, is one of the noblest efforts of wisdom and virtue." [41] Is that not the effort that Mrs. Bennet, now Mrs. Atkinson, is making?

Amelia's innocence, then, is preserved by another's experience; goodness is guarded by a knowledge of evil not its own. The pattern is like that by which Fielding had proposed to put prudence into the service of good nature while still keeping the two distinct. It is acted out graphically in what follows, for Mrs. Atkinson goes in Amelia's mask to the place of temptation, the masquerade, while Amelia herself remains safe at home. But the solution is disturbed by what Mrs. Atkinson does at the masquerade.

One of the great themes of *Amelia*, as Sherburn has shown,[42] is that of protest against the failure of contemporary English society to reward merit. To be honest and deserving, like Booth or Atkinson, is to be put on half-pay or kept in the ranks. That is to say that one of the forms which the problem of the preservation of goodness assumes in the book is the question of how virtue is to be rewarded in an evil world without resort to unvirtuous means. Mrs. Atkinson at the masquerade hits on a way of putting his lordship's viciousness to use to get a commission for Atkinson. Giving some encouragement to the advances he makes to the supposed Amelia, she stipulates that, as evidence of good faith, he procure a commission for the husband of a lady who, she has recently heard, once suffered a great deal by according his lordship her favors.

Two days later a letter comes for Amelia. Mrs. Atkinson is with her and, we can be sure, watches attentively as Amelia reads. Amelia nearly faints, and Mrs. Atkinson, hastening to hold her up, betrays her own agitation by an unexpectedly sharp remark: "But don't be so affected," she says—and it is not certain in which of its senses the word is meant— "the letter cannot eat you or run away with you." [43] She quickly ascertains the contents of the letter and explains them to Amelia, whose distress is not allayed by the explanation. "Indeed, I am very glad of any good fortune that can attend poor Atkinson," is her reaction, "but I wish it had been obtained some other way." She will not listen to Mrs. Atkinson's argument that there is no real danger of her reputation's being "blown up," since Mrs. Atkinson can now make an appointment in her name to see his lordship and reveal the whole trick. Apparently, no "good fortune that can attend poor Atkinson" weighs much with Amelia against a passing shadow on her own reputation, and Mrs. Atkinson, stung into a near-rage by her virtuous reproaches, pronounces a dangerous word:

[41] Vol. I, p. 3.
[42] See n. 22 above.
[43] X, viii, Vol. II, p. 206.

"Indeed, my dear friend, . . . you are terrified at nothing—indeed, indeed, you are too great a prude."

The charge is not easy to dismiss. Coming from Mrs. Atkinson, and in this particular juncture, it is both better defined and more telling than it could be from a Miss Matthews in the process of seducing Amelia's husband. It amounts to a denial of the validity of Amelia's hermetic kind of goodness. For the first and only time in the book Amelia goes into a real pet, and a highly credible, ordinary female spat ensues between the two.

The men soon appear and immediately take Amelia's side without inquiry. Amelia casts herself upon her knees to her husband and cries, "For Heaven's sake do not throw yourself into a passion—some few words have passed—perhaps I may be in the wrong." The gesture is hardly well calculated to have the effect at which it supposedly aims:

> "Damnation seize me if I think so!" cries Booth. "And I wish whoever hath drawn these tears from your eyes may pay it with as many drops of their heart's blood."
> "You see, madam," cries Mrs. Atkinson, "you have your bully to take your part; so I suppose you will use your triumph."
> Amelia made no answer, but still kept hold of Booth. . . .[44]

All this is just what Amelia would do, but how we assess it depends on our attitude both toward her and toward Mrs. Atkinson at this moment. At least we can understand how it all looks to Mrs. Atkinson, and, even though we are told now that "she had, as the phrase is, taken a sip too much that evening," she probably does not leave the field entirely disgraced in the reader's opinion.

The scene is extraordinarily vivid. It develops interactions of motive and character with a subtle and, so to speak, spontaneous rightness to which the splendid simplicity of Fielding's comic art in *Tom Jones* is not to be compared; and, in following the reactions of these characters whom he has imagined so truly, Fielding appears to be led toward a conclusion from which he himself draws back. Perhaps, indeed, Amelia may be in the wrong, as in a distressing moment it occurs to her to say. Perhaps it is possible to see in this scene a kind of premonition of that disenchantment which Thackeray was ultimately to experience with his Amelia. However, Fielding, like Booth, abruptly rejects any such thought.

The novel approaches its close, and Mrs. Atkinson does not again become the center of attention. The morning after the quarrel she goes to see his lordship and reveals the whole maneuver to him.[45] Later on,

---

[44] X, viii, Vol. II, pp. 210-211.

[45] Why did she propose to Amelia that she should make an appointment in Amelia's name, seeing that it was apparently just as easy to gain admittance under her own name? Perhaps this is a flaw in the plot, but in the place where it occurs it does not seem psychologically unlikely that she should more or less deliberately provoke Amelia in this way.

Amelia is reconciled to her, though Booth seems to remain more or less set against her. In the final passing-in-review of the persons of the story we take our leave of her in much the same manner as we did the characters of *Tom Jones*: but if we think back now to the quiet, grief-wasted young lady who aroused Amelia's compassion and interest—the woman who matched Latin with Dr. Harrison to their mutual provocation, who said, "guilt, I hope, it cannot be called," or who called Amelia a prude—we realize the difference between her character and any to be found in *Tom Jones*. The characters of the people who inhabit the world of *Tom Jones* are entire and the same at any moment in the story; that of Mrs. Atkinson is the compound sum of her words and actions to date.

That such a character holds together, producing a recognizable, unified, personal image, is an achievement of a different kind from the conservation of character in *Tom Jones*. The character of Mrs. Atkinson seems the product of a more thoroughgoing, in a sense a less controlled, process of imagination than Fielding had hitherto ventured upon. In that process he develops a conception of the relation between good and evil in human life which challenges that represented by his Amelia. He shows good will—the will to good—painfully struggling not so much to exclude evil as to get the better of it. Amelia's and Mrs. Atkinson's attitudes toward Mrs. Ellison, once that lady's activity has been made clear to both of them, are revelatory. For Amelia she is now simply a figure of evil; Mrs. Atkinson is willing both to find good in her and to put her to good use.[46]

It hardly seems too much to say that Mrs. Atkinson saves the novel. Booth's conversion by reading some sermons is as arbitrary as any of those fifth-act reversals of character which Fielding so effectively mocks in his "chapter concerning the marvellous" in *Tom Jones*. The fortunate coincidence that brings Robinson—dying, supposedly, and eager to confess—into the same house with Booth can hardly be ascribed to Booth's or anyone else's mastery of "the ART of LIFE"; and the restoration of the legacy, by which merit and virtue are finally rewarded, could provide an encouraging example to real-life couples in Booth's and Amelia's circumstances only if it convinced them that a benevolent deity would certainly intervene for them sooner or later. Failing such a faith, the best comfort the example of Booth and Amelia can offer is the stoic assurance that "however few of the other good things of life are thy lot, the best of all things, which is innocence, is always within thy own power; and, though Fortune may make thee often unhappy, she can never make thee completely and irreparably miserable without thy own consent." [47] Fielding surely wished to offer more than that. In the purposes which he set himself in *Amelia* he could not succeed, and his

[46] VII, viii, Vol. II, p. 41; chap. ix, Vol. II, p. 46; chap. x, Vol. II, p. 52.
[47] VIII, iii, Vol. II, p. 69.

achievement in the character of Mrs. Atkinson is one which, to all appearances, he neither desired at the outset nor welcomed when it came.

But to suggest that *Amelia* ends dishearteningly would belie its tone and the character of its author. There is a new hope at the end of the book; it is of an extraliterary nature, to be sure, but that would not bother Fielding. The relationship between *Amelia* and Fielding's work as a magistrate is aptly indicated by Wilbur Cross when he suggests that the book might almost be called "a criminal pamphlet expanded into a novel." [48] Its purpose is not merely the general reformation of manners which defenders of comedy had traditionally asserted to be its aim; like the "muckraker" of a later day, Fielding now has the more immediate and practical intention "to expose some of the most glaring evils, as well public as private, which at present infest the country." [49] As Sherburn says, Fielding "never allows society to become the scapegoat for the individual," [50] and if Booth, in the end, can still not be trusted to survive in London,[51] the fault is his own. Nonetheless, London is not a just society, and the best hope for the Booths and Amelias who must live in it is that able individuals will dedicate their efforts to the immense task of making it more just. *Amelia* is itself a part of the work of social reform which Fielding was soon to concede that he had "thought of too late" to accomplish before his own death[52] but which he was confident could be carried out. Where the beginning of the novel is presided over by the capricious incompetence of Justice Thrasher, a different kind of man administers a different kind of justice at the end and, having treated the good people of the book according to their merit at last, invites them to a feast.

[48] Cross, II, 312.
[49] "Dedication to Ralph Allen," Vol. I, p. xv.
[50] "Fielding's Social Outlook," *PQ*, XXXV (January, 1956), 16.
[51] ". . . for if you are wise, you will not trust your husband a day longer in this town—therefore to packing" (XII, iii, Vol. II, p. 279).
[52] *Journal of a Voyage to Lisbon*, Introduction.

# Chronology of Important Dates

| | |
|---|---|
| 1707, April 22 | Born at Sharpham Park, Glastonbury, Somersetshire. |
| 1719-24 | Attends Eton. |
| 1724-28 | Man-about-London. |
| 1728, February 16 | *Love in Several Masques* produced. |
| March 16 | Commences study of law at the University of Leyden. |
| 1729, autumn | Returns to London. |
| 1730-37 | Career as dramatist: e.g., *The Author's Farce* (1730), *The Tragedy of Tragedies, The Grub-Street Opera* (1731), *The Modern Husband, The Covent-Garden Tragedy* (1732), *The Miser* (1733), *Don Quixote in England* (1734), *Pasquin* (1736), *Eurydice, The Historical Register* (1737). |
| 1734, November 28 | Marries Charlotte Cradock. |
| 1737, June 21 | The Licensing Act ends his career as dramatist. |
| November 1 | Admitted as a law student at the Middle Temple. |
| 1739, November 15-June, 1741 | Edits *The Champion.* |
| 1740, June 20 | Called to the Bar at the Middle Temple. |
| November 8 | Richardson's *Pamela* published. |
| 1741, April 4 | *Shamela* published. |
| 1742, February 2 | Fall of Sir Robert Walpole. |
| February 22 | *Joseph Andrews.* |
| 1743, April 12 | *Miscellanies* (containing, besides essays and poems, *A Journey from this World to the Next* and *Jonathan Wild*). |
| 1744, autumn | Contributes a preface to his sister Sarah's *David Simple* (second edition). |
| November | Death of Charlotte Cradock Fielding. |
| 1745, July 23-April 16, 1746 | Invasion attempt by the Young Pretender. |

| | |
|---|---|
| 1745, November 5-<br>June 17, 1746 | Edits *The True Patriot.* |
| 1747, April 10 | Second marriage, to Mary Daniel. |
| 1747, December 5-<br>November 5, 1748 | Edits *The Jacobite's Journal.* |
| 1748, October 15 | Letter of congratulation to Richardson on *Clarissa.* |
| October 25 | Commissioned as justice of the peace for Westminster. |
| 1749, February 19 | Founds the Universal Register Office. |
| February 28 | *Tom Jones.* |
| June 29 | *A Charge to the Grand Jury.* |
| November 18 | *The Case of Bosavern Penlez.* |
| 1751, January | *Enquiry into the Causes of the Late Increase of Robbers.* |
| December 18 | *Amelia.* |
| 1752, January 4-<br>November 25 | Edits *The Covent-Garden Journal.* |
| 1753, January | *A Proposal for Making an Effectual Provision for the Poor.* |
| March | *A Clear State of the Case of Elizabeth Canning.* |
| 1754, March 19 | Revised edition of *Jonathan Wild.* |
| June 26-<br>August 7 | Sails to Lisbon. |
| October 8 | Death; burial in Lisbon. |
| 1755, February 25 | *Voyage to Lisbon,* edited edition (unedited edition, December 1). |

# Notes on the Editor and Contributors

RONALD PAULSON (b. 1930), editor of the anthology, is Assistant professor of English at the University of Illinois. He is the author of *Theme and Structure in Swift's "Tale of a Tub"* (1960).

JOHN S. COOLIDGE (b. 1926) is Assistant Professor of English at the University of California (Berkeley).

AURÉLIEN DIGEON (1884-1960) taught at the Lycée Condorcet and the universities of Lille, Caen, and Paris (Sorbonne). He was author of *Les Romans de Fielding* (1923) and *The English School of Painting* (1955), and translator of the works of Sterne, Congreve, Shakespeare, and Scott.

WILLIAM EMPSON (b. 1906), Professor of English at Sheffield University, is a pioneer of modern literary criticism. He is the author of *Seven Types of Ambiguity* (1930), *Some Versions of Pastoral* (1935), *The Structure of Complex Words* (1951), *Milton's God* (1961), and two volumes of poetry (1935, 1955).

ANDRÉ GIDE (1869-1951), French novelist and man of letters, was author of such well-known works as *L'Immoraliste* (1902), *La Porte étroite* (1909), *Les Caves du Vatican* (1914), *Les Faux-monnayeurs*, and *Si le grain ne meurt* (both 1926).

A. R. HUMPHREYS (b. 1911), Professor of English at the University of Leicester, is the author of *William Shenstone* (1937), *The Augustan World* (1954), and *Steele, Addison, and their Periodical Essays* (1959).

ARNOLD KETTLE (b. 1916) is Senior Lecturer in English at the University of Leeds and is a member of the editorial board of *Marxism Today;* besides numerous articles and reviews, he has written *An Introduction to the English Novel* (1951).

MAYNARD MACK (b. 1909), Professor of English at Yale University, is author of essays on eighteenth-century and Shakespearean subjects; editor, Fielding's *Joseph Andrews* (1948), Pope's *Essay on Man, The Augustans,* and *Milton* (1950), Shakespeare's *Antony and Cleopatra* (1960), and *The Manuscripts of the Essay on Man* (1962).

JOHN MIDDLETON MURRY (1889-1957), British man of letters, was author of a variety of works of criticism: e.g., *Aspects of Literature* (1920), *The Problem of Style and Countries of the Mind* (1922), *Unprofessional Essays* (1956), and studies of Shakespeare, Keats, Swift, Dostoyevsky, D. H. Lawrence, Blake, Clare, etc.

WINFIELD H. ROGERS (1902-1945) was Professor of English at Women's College of North Carolina; editor, *American Sketchbook* (1939, with J. T. Flanagan, H. H. Blain), *Explorations in Living, A Record of the Democratic Spirit* (1941, with R. V. Redinger, H. C. Haydn).

GEORGE SHERBURN (b. 1884) is Professor Emeritus of English, Harvard University; author of *The Early Career of Alexander Pope* (1934), *The Restoration and Eighteenth Century* (1948); editor, *The Best of Pope* (1929), *The Correspondence of Alexander Pope* (1956).

MARK SPILKA (b. 1925), Assistant Professor of English, Universtiy of Michigan, is author of *The Love Ethic of D. H. Lawrence* (1955).

IAN P. WATT (b. 1917) is Professor of English, University of California at Berkeley, and author of *The Rise of the Novel* (1957) and editor of Fielding's *Shamela* (1956).

# Bibliography

The largest collection of Fielding's works is in *The Complete Works of Henry Fielding, Esq.,* ed. W. E. Henley and others (16 vols.; London: William Heinemann, Ltd., 1903). For works not included in Henley, see *The Covent-Garden Journal,* ed. G. E. Jensen (2 vols.; New Haven: Yale University Press, 1915); *Shamela,* ed. Ian Watt ("Augustan Reprint Society," No. 57 [Los Angeles: William Andrews Clark Memorial Library, 1956]), a facsimile of the second edition; *The Voyages of Mr. Job Vinegar* (from *The Champion*), ed. S. J. Sackett ("Augustan Reprint Society," No. 67, 1958). The standard biography (with a bibliography of Fielding's works) is Wilbur Cross's *The History of Henry Fielding* (3 vols.; New Haven: Yale University Press, 1918). F. Homes Duddon's *Henry Fielding, His Life, Works, and Times* (2 vols.; New York: Oxford: Clarendon Press, 1952) collects much useful data on sociohistorical background and on individual works, but does not challenge Cross.

## GENERAL STUDIES

Blanchard, Frederic T. *Fielding the Novelist: A Study of the Novelist's Fame and Influence.* New Haven: Yale University Press, 1926. A valuable study of Fielding's changing reputation in relation to Richardson's.

Butt, John. *Fielding* ("Writers and Their Works," No. 57.) London: Longmans, Green and Co., Ltd., 1954. A brilliantly concise picture of Fielding's career, with a particularly useful account of *Joseph Andrews.*

Digeon, Aurélien. *The Novels of Fielding.* London: Routledge & Kegan Paul Ltd., 1925; tr. of *Les Romans de Fielding* (Paris, 1923). Still the best book-length general introduction to Fielding's novels.

Greene, Graham. "Fielding and Sterne," in *From Anne to Victoria.* Edited by Bonamy Dobrée (London: Cassell & Company, Ltd., 1937), pp. 279-289; reprinted in *The Lost Childhood* (London: Eyre & Spottiswoode, Ltd., 1951), pp. 58-65. Greene contrasts Fielding ("the work that Fielding put into his books, the importance

of his technical innovations") with "Sterne, who contributed nothing, [but] can give us more pleasure because of what we call his
genius."

McKillop, A. D. "Henry Fielding," in *The Early Masters of English
Fiction* (Lawrence, Kansas: University of Kansas Press, 1956), pp.
98-146. Sound and perceptive discussions of the novels.


## FIELDING'S "INTENSE MORAL PREOCCUPATION"

Coley, William B. "The Background of Fielding's Laughter," *Journal
of English Literary History* (hereafter *ELH*), XXVI (1959), 229-
252. A defense of Fielding's "low" qualities, in reaction to Cross,
Work, etc., with a revaluation of the influences of South, Shaftesbury, and Swift on Fielding.

Kermode, Frank. "Richardson and Fielding," *Cambridge Journal*, IV
(1950), 106-114. A penetrating criticism of Fielding's dualistic ethic
(the split of "character" from "conduct" in his ideal characters like
Tom Jones) and a defense of Richardson.

Sherburn, George. "Fielding's Social Outlook," *Philological Quarterly*
(hereafter *PQ*), XXXV (1956), 1-23; reprinted in *Eighteenth Century English Literature*, ed. J. Clifford (New York: Oxford University Press, 1959), pp. 251-273. An analysis of those aspects of
Fielding's moral philosophy that made him a social reformer.

Swann, George R. "Fielding and Empirical Realism," in *Philosophical
Parallelism in Six English Novelists: The Conception of Good,
Evil and Human Nature* (Philadelphia: University of Pennsylvania
Press, 1929), pp. 46-64. A persuasive statement of the influence of
Shaftesbury on Fielding's moral thought; a less persuasive one of
the influence of Hume.

Work, James A. "Henry Fielding, Christian Censor," in *The Age of
Johnson: Essays Presented to Chauncey Brewster Tinker* (New
Haven: Yale University Press, 1949), pp. 139-148. An influential
essay arguing for an orthodox Christian morality at the base of
Fielding's work.


## FIELDING'S FORM: "COMIC EPIC IN PROSE"

Baker, Sheridan. "Henry Fielding's Comic Romances," *Papers of the
Michigan Academy of Sciences, Arts, and Letters*, XLV (1960),

411-419. "Romance" is the key word in the preface to *Joseph Andrews*; Fielding's debt to Scarron's *Comical Romance* is greater than has been noticed; and, in Fielding's later works, the tone of real romance emerges.

Booth, Wayne C. "The Self-Conscious Narrator in Comic Fiction before *Tristram Shandy,*" *Publications of the Modern Language Association* (hereafter *PMLA*), LXVII (1952), 163-185. Pp. 175-180 deal with Fielding's use of his first-person narrator.

Cooke, Arthur L. "Henry Fielding and the Writers of Heroic Romance," *PMLA,* LXII (1947), 984-994. Though his practice was very different, Fielding's theory of the comic prose epic bore marked similarities to that of Mlle. de Scudéry.

Dyson A. E. "Satiric and Comic Theory in Relation to Fielding," *Modern Language Quarterly*, XVIII (1957), 225-237. This study defines satire as judging man against an ideal and comedy as judging him against a norm, and places Fielding's work in the second category.

Irwin, W. R. "Satire and Comedy in the Works of Henry Fielding," *ELH,* XIII (1946), 168-188. Lists Fielding's particular objects of satiric attack—pedantic critics, bad plays, meddling producers, etc.; then shows that in "his theory of the comic prose epic Fielding achieved a principle to which the various satirical motifs could be subordinated and related."

Lutwack, Leonard. "Mixed and Uniform Prose Styles in the Novel," *Journal of Aesthetics and Art Criticism*, XVIII (1960), 350-357. Contrasts Fielding's and Richardson's styles, the former being characterized by shifts from narrative to essay to drama.

Thornbury, Ethel M. *Henry Fielding's Theory of the Comic Prose Epic* ("Studies in Language and Literature," No. 30.) Madison: University of Wisconsin Press, 1931. Background on the epic tradition and epic criticism, and an attempt to connect *Joseph Andrews* and *Tom Jones* with the epic.

Tillyard, E. M. W. *The Epic Strain in the English Novel* (New York: Oxford University Press, 1958), pp. 51-58. Beginning with Cooke, Tillyard believes that "romance" describes *Tom Jones* better than epic: Tom is a knight errant rather than an epic hero; the narrative is too leisurely and lacks intensity; and Fielding does not speak for a broad society, as the epic poet must.

Watt, Ian. "Fielding and the Epic Theory of the Novel," in *The Rise of the Novel: Studies in Defoe, Richardson and Fielding* (Berkeley and Los Angeles: University of California Press, 1957), pp. 239-259. Argues that *Joseph Andrews* is not an epic, although Fielding wanted to connect it with the epic tradition in order to give the novel the respectability of a classical genre.

## THE PLAYS

Bateson, F. W. "Henry Fielding," in *English Comic Drama, 1700-1750* (New York: Oxford: Clarendon Press, 1929), pp. 115-143. A general survey of the plays, divided into comedy, farce, and burlesque; only the burlesques are successful, the masterpiece being *The Historical Register*. The conclusion is that Fielding is good to the extent that he is realistic and depicts contemporary life.

Goggin, L. P. "Development of Techniques in Fielding's Comedies," *PMLA*, LXVII (1952), 769-781. Takes the opposite view to Bateson and Winfield Rogers: that Fielding's novels derive from his comedy of manners, that these plays are his major work as a dramatist.

Loftis, John. *Comedy and Society from Congreve to Fielding* (Stanford: Stanford University Press, 1959), pp. 114-121. Social history and background to Fielding's plays.

Rogers, Winfield H. "The Significance of Fielding's Temple Beau," *PMLA*, LV (1940), 440-444. Discusses Fielding's symbolic use of humor characters.

### SHAMELA

Kreissman, Bernard. *Pamela-Shamela: A Study of the Criticisms, Burlesques, Parodies, and Adaptations of Richardson's "Pamela"* (Lincoln: University of Nebraska Press, 1960), pp. 7-22. A brief review of *Shamela* and *Joseph Andrews;* fills in the context of the reaction against *Pamela.*

Woods, Charles B. "Fielding and the Authorship of *Shamela*," *PQ*, XXV (1946), 248-272. A thorough case for Fielding's authorship, with notes on the parody, satire, and general intention of the work. It also argues that *Joseph Andrews* offers an alternative to, rather than a further parody of, *Pamela.*

### JOSEPH ANDREWS

Battestin, Martin C. *The Moral Basis of Fielding's Art: A Study of "Joseph Andrews."* Middletown, Connecticut: Wesleyan University

Press, 1959. An important study of the religious (Latitudinarian) background and content of *Joseph Andrews*. It argues that *Joseph Andrews* is a Christian epic, and brings forward sources in Barrow's sermons (one of many possible sources) where we find (1) the good man depicted as hero, (2) life referred to as "pilgrimage," (3) the embodiment of the two great virtues of chastity and charity (the one private, the other public) in the Old Testament figures of Joseph (with Potiphar's wife) and Abraham, respectively.

Cauthen, I. B. "Fielding's Digressions in *Joseph Andrews*," *College English*, XVII (1956), 379-382. An attempt to show the relevance of the digressions.

Ehrenpreis, Irvin. "Fielding's Use of Fiction: The Autonomy of *Joseph Andrews*," in *Twelve Original Essays on Great English Novels*. Edited by Charles Shapiro (Detroit: Wayne State University Press, 1960), pp. 23-41. A series of insights into the structure of *Joseph Andrews*, its relation to Fielding's plays, and to his own childhood experiences.

Taylor, Dick, Jr. "Joseph as Hero in *Joseph Andrews*," *Tulane Studies in English*, VII (1957), 91-109. An interesting case for Joseph's development in character and maturity in the manner of Tom Jones.

## JONATHAN WILD, THE MISCELLANIES, AND MINOR WRITINGS

Goggin, L. P. "Fielding's *The Masquerade*," *PQ*, XXXVI (1957), 475-487. An historical and critical study of Fielding's earliest published work.

Irwin, W. R. *The Making of "Jonathan Wild": A Study in the Literary Method of Henry Fielding* ("Columbia University Studies in English and Comparative Literature," No. 153.) New York: Columbia University Press, 1941. A study of the sources and backgrounds of *Jonathan Wild*, with some attention to its use of epic analogy; argues that Fielding's form is the mock-epic.

Miller, Henry K. *Essays on Fielding's "Miscellanies": Commentary on Volume One*. Princeton: Princeton University Press, 1961. A critical and philosophical study of the works in the *Miscellanies*, Vol. I.

Wendt, Alan. "The Moral Allegory of *Jonathan Wild*," *ELH*, XXIV (1957), 306-320. An argument (stemming from Fielding's preface to the *Miscellanies*) that Wild and Heartfree are thesis and antithesis, greatness without goodness and goodness without greatness, and that the implied synthesis is an ideal of greatness *and* goodness.

## TOM JONES

Crane, R. S. "The Plot of Tom Jones," *Journal of General Education,*
IV (1950), 112-130; reprinted as "The Concept of Plot and the
Plot of *Tom Jones*" in *Critics and Criticism: Ancient and Modern.*
Edited by Crane (Chicago: University of Chicago Press, 1952), pp.
616-647. An elaborate analysis of *Tom Jones'* plot, using "plot" in
the Aristotelian sense of an action-character-thought synthesis.

Hutchens, Eleanor N. " 'Prudence' in *Tom Jones:* A Study of Connotative
Irony," *PQ,* XXXIX (1960), 496-507. Fielding takes the word "prudence," with its normally positive connotations, and puts it in a
context in which its literal meaning pertains, but its positive
connotations do not (as calling Blifil's calculation "prudence").

McKillop, A. D. "Some Recent Views of *Tom Jones,*" *College English,*
XXI (1959), 17-22. A survey of the interpretations of Crane, Van
Ghent, Watt, and others.

Van Ghent, Dorothy. "On *Tom Jones,*" in *The English Novel, Form and
Function* (New York: Holt, Rinehart & Winston, Inc., 1953), pp.
65-81. An excellent discussion of the theme of form and feeling;
"Problems for Study and Discussion" (pp. 322-336) are also sug-
gestive.

## AMELIA

Powers, Lyall H. "The Influence of the *Aeneid* on Fielding's *Amelia,*"
*Modern Language Notes,* LXXI (1956), 330-336. Lists parallels
with the *Aeneid.*

Towers, A. R. "*Amelia* and the State of Matrimony," *Review of English
Studies,* new series, V (1954), 144-157. A study of the marriage
theme.

Wendt, Allan. "The Naked Virtue of Amelia," *ELH,* XXVII (1960), 131-
148. An examination of Amelia as woman, symbol, and Job-like
sufferer.